Fron
the
coll
tura
ahist
his t
fessi
are l
a pa
ecor
T
Wooo
the
seek
Mo:
Mo:
teen
cano
has

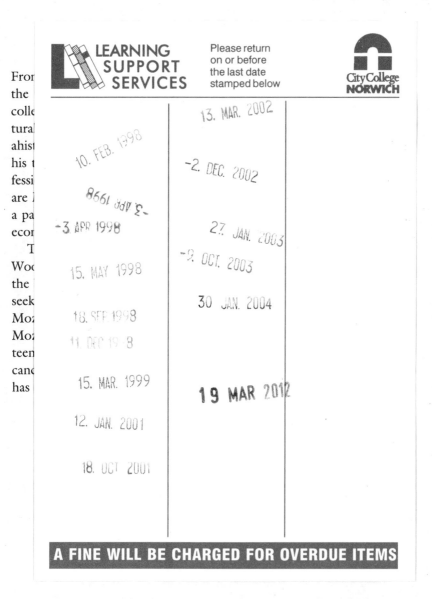

WOODROW WILSON CENTER SERIES

On Mozart

Michael J. Lacey, editor, *Religion and Twentieth-Century American Intellectual Life*

Michael J. Lacey, editor, *The Truman Presidency*

Joseph Kruzel and Michael H. Haltzel, editors, *Between the Blocs: Problems and Prospects for Europe's Neutral and Nonaligned States*

William C. Brumfield, editor, *Reshaping Russian Architecture: Western Technology, Utopian Dreams*

Mark N. Katz, editor, *The USSR and Marxist Revolutions in the Third World*

Walter Reich, editor, *Origins of Terrorism: Psychologies, Ideologies, Theologies, States of Mind*

Mary O. Furner and Barry Supple, editors, *The State and Economic Knowledge: The American and British Experiences*

Michael J. Lacey and Knud Haakonssen, editors, *A Culture of Rights: The Bill of Rights in Philosophy, Politics, and Law—1791 and 1991*

Robert J. Donovan and Ray Scherer, *Unsilent Revolution: Television News and American Public Life, 1948–1991*

Nelson Lichtenstein and Howell John Harris, editors, *Industrial Democracy in America: The Ambiguous Promise*

William Craft Brumfield and Blair A. Ruble, editors, *Russian Housing in the Modern Age: Design and Social History*

Michael J. Lacey and Mary O. Furner, editors, *The State and Social Investigation in Britain and the United States*

Hugh Ragsdale, editor and translator, *Imperial Russian Foreign Policy*

Dermot Keogh and Michael H. Haltzel, editors, *Northern Ireland and the Politics of Reconciliation*

Joseph Klaits and Michael H. Haltzel, editors, *The Global Ramifications of the French Revolution*

René Lemarchand, *Burundi: Ethnocide as Discourse and Practice*

James R. Millar and Sharon L. Wolchik, editors, *The Social Legacy of Communism*

On Mozart

EDITED BY JAMES M. MORRIS

WOODROW WILSON CENTER PRESS

AND

CAMBRIDGE
UNIVERSITY PRESS

Published by the Woodrow Wilson Center Press and
the Press Syndicate of the University of Cambridge
The Pitt Building, Trumpington Street, Cambridge CB2 1RP
40 West 20th Street, New York, NY 10011-4211, USA
10 Stamford Road, Oakleigh, Melbourne 3166, Australia

© Woodrow Wilson International Center for Scholars 1994

First published 1994
Reprinted 1995

Printed in the United States of America

Library of Congress Cataloging-in-Publication Data
On Mozart / edited by James M. Morris.
p.   cm.—(Woodrow Wilson Center series)
Papers presented at a symposium organized by the Woodrow Wilson
International Center for Scholars in 1991.
Includes index.
ISBN 0-521-47065-X (hbk.).—ISBN 0-521-47661-5 (pbk.)
1. Mozart, Wolfgang Amadeus, 1756–1791—Criticism and
interpretation—Congresses.   I. Morris, James M. (James Malachy),
1940–   II. Series.
ML410.M9032   1994
780'.92—dc20   94–20281
                                                   CIP
                                                   MN

A catalog record for this book is available from the British Library.

Calligraphy and autography by Christina T. Davidson

Cover illustration: Quartet Movement in E Minor, K. 417d
(Internationale Stiftung Mozarteum, Salzburg)

ISBN 0-521-47065-X hardback
ISBN 0-521-47661-5 paperback

In Memory of

JOHN L. CLIVE

1924–1990

Historian, Raconteur, Mozartian

"Soave sia il vento . . ."

Contents

Introduction

JAMES M. MORRIS

NOW COMES THE TEST. It is 1994 as I write, and the fever that marked the celebration, in the United States at least, throughout 1991 of the two hundredth anniversary of Mozart's death has long since broken. The recordings of his music claim less space, though not much less space, in record shops, and concert programming has become attentive once again to the riches of the non-Mozartean repertoire. But the public's love for Mozart holds. It's true that the Mostly Mozart Festival in New York City suffered a drop in attendance during the summer of 1992, a consequence perhaps of the need for some concertgoers to clear their heads and recover their footing after over-dosing on *Nachtmusik* in 1991. Yet they were surely not inclined to kick the habit, and attendance rebounded last year. So far, the composer's popularity has survived the adulation.

Now that we are some distance from the Mozart bicentennial, the occasion invites further comment, as a striking instance of what can happen when the culture decides to bearhug an icon. Gioacchino Rossini had a birthday party in 1992, and it was a modest business indeed by comparison with the preceding year's exuberance. Bruckner and Brahms will soon claim centennial years of their own (1996 and 1997, respectively), and each observance will no doubt engage the intellect but probably not stir the heart. No other composer, with the exception perhaps of Beethoven, has so strong a claim on universal affection

1

as Mozart. That the enthusiasm of the bicentennial year should sub-
side a bit and that the commercial clutter—the sweatshirts and ashtrays
and coffee mugs bearing likenesses of the composer—should be swept
from the shelves are both natural and healthy. The esteem had grown
to idolatry and brought the concomitant abdication of critical sense
that characterizes most worship.

What was sometimes dismaying about the bicentennial was neither
its bountiful celebration of Mozart nor the enjoyment that so many
people took in his music. It was rather the sense of lost opportunity,
the failure to educate people to hear the differences in the music and
to make confident judgments about its quality. Many listeners went
on the equivalent of aesthetic automatic pilot. "If it's Mozart, it must
be good," they believed, because that is the signal the culture sent
through its secular canonization of the man.

Of course, "it" was always at least interesting. We are speaking,
after all, of the work of a prodigy and a genius. But "it" was not
always riveting or transcendent, despite what the evenness of the public's enthusiasm might have tempted one to believe. Indeed, what was
missing too often from the year's festivities was a finer measure of
discrimination. Too little was done to alert the engaged public—
not the musicologists, who already know—to what is good, better,
best in Mozart's music and what is really rather ordinary by late-
eighteenth-century standards. The opportunity to popularize a realistic
Mozart, a figure from life and history, was seized only halfheartedly.
It was as if the composer had emerged without a context and a progress through time, or had risen so far above his natural landscape
that its contours were no longer visible beneath him.

Consider Lincoln Center's determination to program over a period
of some eighteen months just about every finished bit of music left by
Mozart. He came through the exposure with reputation intact, and
that confirmed his greatness. At the same time, the rationale that all
of this music is worth hearing, if only because it is by Mozart, flattened
his achievement. Better perhaps to have played fewer pieces over and
over again than to have made room for everything by invoking the
criterion of completeness.

In the same vein, one wonders what people will do with those
compact-disc sets of "the complete Mozart" issued by Philips in
1990. Virtually every work is there, the slight along with the sublime,

sitting on a countertop in my local music store even as I write—145 compact discs for $1,699.99, in forty-five volumes available separately or packaged together in two large boxes, with plastic handles, like super economy sizes of laundry detergent. According to a special supplement to the April 1993 issue of *The Gramophone,* world sales of performances in these sets had reached the extraordinary figure of nine million discs by the end of 1992. But what part of the vast corpus will actually command the attention of nonspecialist buyers? The portion already well known and well loved, I would wager, after some selective satisfaction of curiosity about the rest. We are less patient with the tunes of Mozart at sixteen because we know the melodies of Mozart at thirty. Best to regard these sets as one would an encyclopedia in which one invests with no intention of reading through each volume. The many pages on the many topics are there to be consulted should circumstances one day require, but to be left otherwise without thumbprint.

For the past several years in the United States, professing to love Mozart has become a kind of password that admits one to the high-culture club for a modest initiation fee. Individuals who might face with dismay the prospect of hearing Haydn or Schubert go placidly to Mozart concerts, happy to be in the presence of genius—because they have been told that's where they are. Were they then to hear a couple of Haydn symphonies under the impression that they were hearing Mozart, they would not know the difference.

The Mozart mania has been the equivalent of a pop-culture binge in the high-culture playground—like one of those blockbuster museum shows of recent decades that invite crowds to contemplate room after room of Picasso or Matisse while they are being funneled toward a merchandising operation, where they can buy genuine replicas of what they have just seen. The souvenirs confirm the experience, the way a small photograph of the Grand Canyon guarantees, when the recollection has clouded, that one actually stood on the brink.

What were the enduring consequences of the celebration? There were opportunities to hear works by the young Mozart (young being a relative term when the dead Mozart was, after all, still a young Mozart), and they proved by and large inferior to what he would compose when older. No surprises there. They reveal that he had mastered classical forms early on—he was of his time, and more quickly than his competition—but that he could not yet breathe his peculiar genius into them. We knew all along that this was so and needed no bicentennial display to instruct us.

The Belgian Théâtre Royale de la Monnaie, for example, toured the world with a highly praised production of *La finta giardiniera,* an opera composed by Mozart when he was eighteen years old. This is remarkable for an eighteen-year-old, I recall thinking, and yet not remarkable for Mozart. In fact, the opera proved difficult to hear— not because one had any aural difficulty apprehending the music and the text, but because one kept hearing through them to the operas that would come afterward: the musical ideas presented by the composer in *Giardiniera* in scrupulous classical form would blossom gloriously one day into the transformed and, indeed, transforming musical landscapes of *Le nozze di Figaro* and *Così fan tutte.* In *Giardiniera* one senses Mozart's confidence in his mastery of form. The piece goes on at great length, as if to demonstrate the extravagance of the composer's talent. But that is the problem. The opera demonstrates talent, not genius, and familiarity with the eventual passionate manifestations of that genius engenders impatience with its expert but merely ordinary antecedents.

There is a risk of trivialization. Mozart is on his way to becoming background music for the age, safe because never really attended to except as a kind of cushion against the petty hurts of the day: white noise as civilized and elegant as any ever devised. Uncritical acceptance of the entire canon, as if it were all of a piece because all Mozart, does not serve the composer well.

Of course, no music is easier to listen to. It rewards even modest effort with great delight. It does not shake or disturb, not really, even when a stone spirit is dragging a man to his doom. It is kept in bounds by its conventions. If *Le nozze di Figaro* is subversive of established social order, as some wish to believe, the threat barely registers on grateful modern audiences. The larger threat is that Mozart will spoil us for other music, particularly music that demands work on the part of an audience if it is to be understood, respected, and, in time perhaps, with enough effort and familiarity, loved. But why make the effort when we already have this great body of work that is at once accessible and capable of imparting such life-enhancing pleasure?

It is not Mozart's fault that he claims so much of the programming time of the contemporary orchestra or chamber group or opera company or soloist out to fill the seats of an auditorium. To decry the absence of newer work is to pit the untried and surely unliked against genius long embraced and lovingly guarded. The compromise solution is to sneak the newer music ("new" in this setting being a term that bears little relation to the common understanding of the chronological schemes by which the world orders its affairs) onto a program that prominently features Mozart, and to serve the rare stuff first—as if it were a disagreeable course at dinner, some strange crustacean or mutated vegetable that one ingests only because promised a creamy dessert. Of course, too much creamy dessert will slow the blood.

What did Mozart's contemporaries hear when they heard his music? How different for them was he from Haydn or Salieri or Dittersdorf or Süssmayr? Why has it been left to our age to enact the final stages of an elaborate ritual of divinization? Why is it well-nigh blasphemous to be critical of the man or confess that, on the whole, one prefers Beethoven or Schubert or Brahms or even Verdi? How can one take exception to perfection? These are mysteries beyond the deciphering capacity of reason. We may speculate and bring to bear the conclusions of methodical research, but in the end we scratch our heads or, more operatically, throw up our hands. In the realm of taste, some regions will be marked forever with stakes that warn "Here be dragons."

So perhaps we should not judge the bicentennial salute too harshly. Mozart himself would have been pleased with the notoriety—and the royalties. Imagine him in a well-stocked contemporary music and video store, searching the shelf after shelf of recordings under his name, calculating with satisfaction how much more space he has been given than even Papa Haydn, and noting with greater pleasure still, while leafing through the "S" bin, the likely absence of anything by Salieri. Surely he would be curious about these last two centuries of competition against which he has held his own—and, by linear measure at least, prevailed. So many unfamiliar names! What sounds did they propose, he wonders, for their publics' pleasure?

The imagined happiness of this fantastic shopping Mozart may be reason enough to justify the bicentennial, which was not all missed opportunity. Some institutions did take the occasion to educate (that was an implicit purpose of even the Lincoln Center marathon), and this volume commemorates one conspicuously public attempt to do so. Late in 1991, a group of the most important cultural organizations in Washington, D.C., joined forces to observe the two hundredth anniversary of Mozart's death. The John F. Kennedy Center for the Performing Arts, the Library of Congress, the National Gallery of Art, the Smithsonian Institution's National Museum of American History, and the Woodrow Wilson International Center for Scholars sponsored a series of performances, exhibitions, and symposia to honor the composer. The Woodrow Wilson Center organized the most significant of these symposia, "Mozart and the Riddle of Creativity." It took place over four days in the first week of December and concluded on the afternoon of December 5, the date of Mozart's death, in time for participants to attend the performance of the *Requiem* given that evening by the National Symphony Orchestra at the Kennedy Center.

The symposium began as an idea in the mind of the late historian John Clive, loving reader of the great historians of the past, biographer of Thomas Macaulay, and Mozart enthusiast. He conceived of a bicentennial event that would instruct intelligent lay audiences about Mozart, and entertain them as well, by presenting the composer in a context that had the density of real life and was, by turns, personal, psychological, historical, cultural, and aesthetic. Clive died early in 1990, and it fell to his friend Charles Blitzer, director of the Woodrow Wilson Center, to shape the agenda of the symposium, to choose its participants, and to raise support for it. Three foundations—the Morris and Gwendolyn Cafritz Foundation, the John D. and Catherine T. MacArthur Foundation, and the Andrew W. Mellon Foundation—contributed generously, and the National Gallery of Art and the National Museum of American History provided space for the sessions.

A group of scholars—some expert on Mozart and some not, but all knowledgeable appreciators—met for three mornings in the East Building Auditorium of the National Gallery of Art to deliver papers, debate with one another, and field questions from the audience. The symposium took for its point of departure an inquiry into the nature of creativity generally, as background to situating the particular genius of Mozart. It set him first in the timeless ahistorical space reserved for individuals of spectacular creativity, then in his time, and finally in our time. Each afternoon, for example, the audience watched a filmed version of a Mozart opera, introduced by critic Stanley Kauffmann, who reflected not just on the success or failure of the film but on the larger issue of how a work of art created for one medium can be transposed into another medium that has quite different rules. Kauffmann's generously expansive approach was typical of the entire event.

For this volume the original lectures have been expanded and revised, and their order has been shifted. Two papers that were not part of the original mix—those by Christoph Wolff and Denis Donoghue—have been added. In the opening chapters, Donoghue offers philosophic and aesthetic reflections on music and genius and on how we might approach the two in the conspicuous case of Mozart, while psychologists Howard Gardner and David Henry Feldman write of prodigies in general and of the prodigious Mozart in particular. William and Hilda Baumol then set the composer within the social and economic context of his time, and Neal Zaslaw and Christoph Wolff observe him among the workaday circumstances of his craft. Subsequent chapters enlarge our understanding of a Mozart who is at once all too human and consummately professional. Maynard Solomon uses textual evidence to explore the troubled relationship between Mozart and members of his family, and Joseph Kerman uses musical evidence to suggest the collapse of a relationship between Mozart and his Viennese audience in the 1780s. Like Kerman, Wye Allanbrook works from the music, but she hears in it a different aspect of the composer's personality—a "comic" Mozart, whom she urges us to take seriously. Michael Steinberg pits the composer against the dominant culture of his age, and Leon Botstein traces his fate through the next century (and more) of musical and cultural development. Finally, Stanley Kauffmann explains how directors harnessing the technologies of film and television have presented certain of the composer's works to contemporary audiences.

Denis Donoghue begins the volume with a discussion of the many contexts, "spiritual" and "sensual," against which Mozart's music has been heard over the years and asks how well any of them will serve us today. How are we to speak of the manifestations of genius, even if we cannot account for them? Schumann, for example, believed Mozart to be a composer of lightness, grace, and charm, though others have heard, in the same measures, the demonic, the sinful, and the terrifying. How can this be? Is a political, economic, civil, and essentially secular context sufficient for our appreciation of Mozart, or must we have recourse to categories that invoke metaphysical realms and religious experience? Using as his text *Die Zauberflöte*, which might seem the hardest case, Donoghue opts for a secular Mozart. *Die Zauberflöte*, he says, "is entirely secular, despite its invocations of Isis and Osiris. . . . [W]hen there is an allusion to a religious theme, Mozart quickly disperses it into sociality." And yet, for Donoghue, as for Gardner and Feldman in the essays that immediately follow his, there remains within the achievement of the individual genius, at the core of any appreciation, a degree of mystery that resists solution.

The psychologists Howard Gardner and David Feldman bring to their study of Mozart the experience of having worked for many years with gifted and creative people. Their research is closely linked. Gardner has been investigating whether there are characteristics of the creative process that are common across various realms of endeavor. He discerns in all the individuals he has studied a pattern whereby each achieves mastery over some area of creativity after a period of about ten years, and then makes a second breakthrough some ten years later. "One can find other individuals of Mozart's era, or of our own era," writes Gardner, "with whom he shared salient characteristics: individuals as prodigious as Mozart, individuals as productive, individuals as personally pugnacious and troubled." It is the combination of prodigality, productivity, and pugnaciousness that marks Mozart as extraordinary. Gardner identifies several factors that argue for Mozart's uniqueness: the evenness of his growth and productivity; the combination of immature and adult traits in his personality; the sharpness of his insight into human personalities (as manifested in the operas but not in his own life). Yet he is forced to acknowledge finally the mystery against which our passion to lay bare the sources of genius proves ineffectual: "All that we know of Mozart's brief life provides scant insights into his music. . . . Mozart remains among the most compelling arguments for respecting the distance between the personal life and the life of the creative mind."

Feldman has spent more than a decade studying child prodigies and constructing a framework for the study of creativity. He finds that Mozart exhibits characteristics of both the typical and the untypical prodigy; unlike most prodigies, for example, Mozart had a successful adult career. Feldman reflects on the mind and emotions of the composer at "a level of interpretation above the flow of events themselves" that is nonetheless "respectful of the facts as we know them." To the study of two aspects of Mozart's behavior—his love of verbal play, as manifested especially in his letters, and his exceptional sociability— Feldman applies his concept of "the transformational imperative." By this he means the tendency human beings exhibit, in markedly different degrees, "to take intentional liberties with the world, and thereby to change it." Mozart's transformative impulses were incessant, according to Feldman, and he can document their occurrence. Yet, for all the evidence, he concedes that the scale and the individual character of Mozart's achievement remain unexplained, and perhaps inexplicable.

If the interior workings of genius remain closed to our inspection, the trappings of the world in which it flourished are another matter. In their exceptionally interesting chapter, William and Hilda Baumol consider the political, social, and economic circumstances of the late eighteenth century that favored the emergence of so many talented composers—not just Mozart, of course, but Gluck, Haydn, Dittersdorf, Salieri, Beethoven, Schubert, and more. Unlike Feldman and Gardner, the Baumols do not attempt to account for the sources of creativity. They are concerned rather with the circumstances that encourage its manifestation and growth. These they trace in part to the rising prosperity of the age and to the sheer number of petty states that existed at the time in the Holy Roman Empire, each with its own petty prince and each a potential home for court orchestra and court composer. Thus, musical talent was a marketable commodity (the authors draw an analogy with the situation of playwrights in Elizabethan England). Romantic notions of Mozart's impoverished circumstances die hard, but the Baumols' careful economic analysis edges such notions somewhat closer to the grave.

Neal Zaslaw continues in this practical vein. After Gardner's and Feldman's speculations, it is startling to have him suggest that Mozart went about his business not for the high-minded motives we might like to hear in the music—"inner necessity" or "pure inspiration" or "for posterity"—but simply to make money and to live well, to buy furniture and clothes and carriages. Here is a counterweight to the received tradition of the beatific composer in direct communication with heaven, and to comments such as George Bernard Shaw's that "if God had a voice it would be Mozart's." Some part of us might still prefer the myth to the reality that the composer increased his output to remedy a cash-flow problem. Though we live in an age when art and the marketplace regularly bed down together, we would prefer to avert our eyes from their lusty union when certain hallowed figures are involved. Zaslaw's cold water on the flame of piety is a bracing corrective. The alternative he proposes has in its favor the texture of real life.

So too does the chapter by Christoph Wolff, which invites us to reflect on Mozart's work habits. There was, after all, for each piece a moment when the composer had to mark the first note on a blank page. Wolff does not speculate about the nature of creativity, which he believes nebulous and probably unfathomable. He builds his case instead on "historically trustworthy and informative sources"—the large repertoire of works-in-progress that Mozart composed in his head but left in skeletal form on his notebook pages. The evidence is persuasive that musical ideas came easily to Mozart but that filling them out could be hard work, though we seldom associate the composer with hard work because the myth of his divine inspiration has been so seductive. He may be contrasted with Beethoven, who found it difficult to invent tunes and themes and motifs, of the kind that Mozart carried in abundance, but easy to manage their elaboration. Wolff reads the fragmentary evidence to suggest that Mozart had reached a point in his life when, had death not intervened, he was ready to explore entirely new musical directions.

Maynard Solomon finds tangled and troubled relationships within the circle of Mozart's family: His father, Leopold, sets the composer against his sister, Marianne, and brother and sister forsake their childhood closeness for adult estrangement and mutual bitterness. Solomon traces in the textual evidence a disjunction between the lofty aspirations of art and the heavy pull of the mundane, and an inexorable downward spiral into conflict and resentment. The composer, who communicates so successfully with his public, suffers a private rupture of communication. The saddest figure in the drama is Marianne, desperate for her father's love yet aware always of the strength of his attachment to Wolfgang—and of the impossibility of her ever having a like hold on his affections. What is extraordinary about all this, in Solomon's account, is the extent to which money and property and the pull of material things are at the heart of the conflict, which grows more ruinous with time, even as Mozart's music grows more perfect.

Joseph Kerman gives us a public Mozart, in Vienna in the years 1782–86, whose concern was to communicate effectively with his audiences through his work. He composed for them fourteen piano concertos, performed at his academies, the public concerts through which Mozart attempted to make his mark on what was then music's capital city. Kerman describes how the concertos follow a standard three-movement plan—a sequence from interaction to some sort of respite to complicity, from collaborative and creative exchange to accommodation. He then hypothesizes, ingeniously, that in the drama of the relationship between the movements of these piano concertos over the four-year period, in the interaction between soloist and orchestra, there can be traced the course of the social dynamic between Mozart and his audiences. He discerns in the C Minor Concerto, K. 491, composed in March 1786, a change in the relationship: the soloist challenges the orchestra's authority, and the power relations are in doubt. Did Mozart grow tired of his Viennese audiences and of the ritual they had enacted together for five years—or did they tire of him? And do the last piano concertos signal the change? Kerman's examples conclude with the austere C Major Concerto, K. 503, composed late in 1786, which seems to him to register a clear alteration in mood in the sequence of the concertos. Might it also be said to register a loss of heart? Was there a severance of ties analogous in its way to the private rupture within the Mozart family described by Maynard Solomon? At any rate, after 1786, Kerman observes, opera replaced the piano concerto as Mozart's most important public genre.

Wye Allanbrook challenges the notion that taking Mozart seriously means having to take him tragically. She argues that many of his compositional choices, such as his being drawn repeatedly toward ending works in major keys (although many critics make a great deal of the relatively few works that conclude in minor), suggest the model of the *commedia*. She urges that we give proper value to the brilliant surface variety of the instrumental works—"the foreground play of musical style and topic across the background of harmonic process." It is the comic, the various, that Allanbrook would have us celebrate in Mozart, against the ingrained assumption that profundity and melancholia always go hand in hand. By exploring one particular topos, which she calls playfully "the tune that sprouts from the top," used by Mozart from time to time at moments of closure to give a sense of comic superfluity, she reminds us of the vigor and significance of habits that may be dismissed too easily as mere convention. She portrays an essentially comic vision in Mozart, but a vision no less profound for being so.

Kerman and Allanbrook bring to their appreciation of Mozart the skill of professional musicologists. Michael Steinberg hears the music as a historian, and in so doing he hears yet another Mozart. He takes for his text *Don Giovanni* and argues that its greatness lies not only at the level of the universal and the existential, but also at the level of the specific, the historical, and the political. For Steinberg, baroque culture is not merely a periodizing label or an artistic style but "a cosmological claim representing theological, cultural, and political principles of the Counterreformation." It wants to "hold still the world against the modernizing and dissipating momentum of the Reformation." Don Giovanni stands against the traditional worldview, and for his aggressive punishment of the culture the culture punishes him back. The opera is a work of "concentrated political power and critique, wrestling in contestatory fury with the politics and the political culture of the Habsburg Empire." Steinberg punctuates his essay with provocative comment: "Time, temporality, movement, and sensuality inform the musical side of *Don Giovanni* that carries the Mozartean energy of modernity. . . . The modernist spirit moves; the baroque spirit holds still. . . . The grasp of the baroque is the staying hand of death."

Steinberg's sense of the opera leads him to admire the Joseph Losey film version, which was one of the three filmed operas shown at the symposium: "More than any other reading of the work, Losey's has restored the dialogue between *Don Giovanni* and history." In this, Steinberg the cultural historian is at odds with Stanley Kauffmann the film critic, whose opinion of the Losey film, as the reader will see, is largely dismissive. The two watch it with different sensibilities.

What happens to an artist and his legacy when they become the property of history, to be tugged this way and that by critics and idolaters who disfigure them in the process? Leon Botstein traces the posthumous life of Mozart through the nineteenth century, which culminated in a fin de siècle "back to Mozart" movement on the part of individuals profoundly dissatisfied with the state of contemporary musical culture. Indeed, Mozart was invoked aggressively throughout the century, but to sometimes contradictory aesthetic ends. By the century's close, his music had acquired the status of an idealized alternative to the music of the present day, which for many had become only a mirror of modernity rather than a universal language of art. "A new model and source of inspiration was needed as an antidote to the musical aesthetics associated with Wagner and his followers," writes Botstein. The "return to Mozart" was the musical analogue of a larger fin de siècle stylistic movement favoring visual simplicity, directness, and a respect for function over the prevailing love of decoration and aesthetic camouflage, which might be construed as the visual analogue of Wagner's music. So a canon of classicism, music's past, would be employed as a weapon against new music, music's future. Botstein believes that the nineteenth-century revival of interest in Mozart and his music was the beginning of a process that has continued, to sad effect, throughout the twentieth century—the "domination of the concert repertoire by the past to the exclusion of contemporary music."

However one may judge the principal argument of his essay, much of the detail is fascinating. For example: "The demand for Mozart on the part of the audience in the mid and late nineteenth century had been weak indeed. . . . Between 1848 and 1910, only seven symphonies were in the repertoire of the Vienna Philharmonic, which also included three serenades, two overtures, five piano concertos, two violin concertos, and a host of operatic excerpts." And: "The accepted notion during the second half of the nineteenth century was that Mozart had been brilliant, elegant, and divine. But his music appeared mannered and dated." To us, of course, that state of affairs is incomprehensible. But who is to say that in another hundred years, in time for the tricentennial, it may not once again become the ruling view?

Botstein concludes on a distinctly somber note, decrying the way our contemporary glorification of Mozart uses him in effect to celebrate music's past and stifle its future. We are lulled and enchanted by Mozart, but not inspired as we should be. We miss his true significance: "The range and depth of Mozart's music should give us the courage to believe that, in contemporary life, new music can be written, played, and heard that possesses the same unforgettable power of communication and transfiguration."

Stanley Kauffmann analyzes how three of Mozart's operas have weathered the transition from the stage, for which they were originally conceived, to film, which operates under quite different conventions and unpredictable rules for success. Few filmed operas can succeed aesthetically, says Kauffmann, because "the union is too strange." Film directors make a contract with their audiences to persuade them to accept this risky mix of conventions. None of the contracts is ironclad or fits every case. "The only occasions when the combination [of operatic conventions and film conventions] succeeds are, to be tautological about it, when it succeeds." Of the three instances of transformation he describes—Ingmar Bergman's *The Magic Flute,* Joseph Losey's *Don Giovanni,* and Peter Sellars's *The Marriage of Figaro*—

only the first strikes him as unequivocally successful. At the Mozart symposium, Kauffmann's comments preceded the showing of the films. But the range and intelligence of his remarks, and the easy grace of their expression, give them a life apart from the occasion, and even from a screen.

I hope that the essays as herein disposed speak with reasonable coherence to the intelligent lay audience for which they were intended. There are disagreements among them, some subtle, some open, and no attempt has been made to reconcile the differences. The protean character of the man they celebrate invites the disparate readings. Genius slips finally from the confines of categorization as nimbly as old Proteus in the myth changed shape and identity to slip from one's grasp. The difference is that, if one held on to Proteus long enough and was not shaken by the transformations, he returned to his true shape and was amenable to interrogation. However long one grapples with genius and endures its vexing permutations, it will elude to the end the domesticating hold of the critic.

Acknowledgments

This book and the Woodrow Wilson Center's Mozart bicentennial symposium were made possible through the support of the Morris and Gwendolyn Cafritz Foundation, the John D. and Catherine T. Mac-Arthur Foundation, and the Andrew W. Mellon Foundation.

1

Approaching Mozart

DENIS DONOGHUE

HOW TO BEGIN? How to describe a piece of music, a piece by Mozart as a case in point? To be any good, the description should let the music elude whatever may be said about it and stay elusive to the end. It is better to fail in the description, failing in advance and as if on principle, than to think the description adequate. To describe is not to encompass. Tact suggests that one should not consider the music well served merely by having a multitude of nouns and adjectives attend upon it. It may be appropriate to settle for approximations and take as much care to undermine them in the end as to put them forward at first. So I proceed circuitously in the hope of making whatever I say tentative, every assertion shadowed by doubt. I shall give variations on a theme and let the theme move irregularly among them. Meanwhile, I have been persuaded by Susanne Langer's *Feeling and Form* that music presents a semblance of time, virtual rather than real, time perceived but not otherwise lived. A work of art is offered only for perception.

In the first volume of *Either/Or*, Kierkegaard asserts that music is a Christian art. There was music before Christianity—let David and Saul indicate as much—but music is revealed in its full validity only under the Christian dispensation. Mostly under its suspicion. Church music was composed under strict conditions of form and observance. Think of the Catholic Church's objection to stringed instruments and to music that displayed its adornments while pretending to serve a ritual or sacramental occasion. But secular music developed under a more fundamental censure. Kierkegaard argues that Christianity posits secular music by excluding it: Music is the medium for what Christianity excludes from itself, the demonic, the erotic-sensuous.[1] Christianity is a vision of human life as spirit. Everything that falls outside spirit or beneath it is a scandal. Music is the expressive form of scandal because it has its absolute object in the erotic-sensuous genius. It can express other things, but it exists to express the sensuous immediacy that falls outside spirit. The difference between music and language arises from their different relations to immediacy. Language is never in a direct or immediate relation to experience; it necessarily involves reflection and is therefore congenitally belated. Music expresses immediacy, has no interest in reflection, and commits itself to the sound of sense. In language, the acoustic character of the words is more or less incidental. That is why translation is possible, however imperfect. Music exists in movement, force, succession, and repetition of sounds. But repetition is not reflection; it is recovered immediacy.

Kierkegaard does his best with the idea of immediacy, but he soon moves on to a vocabulary of desire and identifies three stages of it. The first two are the dreaming stage and the seeking stage. Only in the third stage is desire satisfied. The distinctions between the three are not my concern. Nor is it crucial to report that the first stage, according to Kierkegaard, is exemplified by *Le nozze di Figaro*, the second by *Die Zauberflöte*, the third by *Don Giovanni*. So far as I know, readers of Kierkegaard take these distinctions seriously because he made them, not because they are persuasive. The whole argument of *Either/Or*, culminating in a long meditation on *Don Giovanni*, has been mocked. It has been deemed wild, bizarre, a conceit of the saddest Dane since Hamlet. No matter. Let us stay with the essay as if it survived mockery, since it has; especially with the idea of secular music as expressive of the demonic, the erotic-sensuous. But we may put aside the demonic for the moment and stay with the erotic-sensuous, as Kierkegaard does.

A preamble: In *Millions of Strange Shadows*, Anthony Hecht has a poem called 'Dichtung und Wahrheit,' a meditation on images and

---

1. Soren Kierkegaard, *Either/Or*, trans. David F. Swenson and Lillian Marvin Swenson, rev. Howard A. Johnson (Princeton: Princeton University Press, 1959), vol. 1, 63.

how one construes them. He begins with a famous image, the Discus Thrower, presumably the *discobolus* of Myron: Many of us have seen photographs of it; few, the original. Hecht then moves to an image that cannot be known to many, a photograph of the infantry platoon in which he served during World War II. From these he comes to a more diffuse image that attends his sense of Mozart, presumably after listening to many performances of his music:

> Easy enough to claim, in the dawn of hindsight,
> That Mozart's music perfectly enacts
> Pastries and powdered wigs, an architecture
> Of white and gold rosettes, balanced parterres.
> More difficult to know how the spirit learns
> Its scales, or the exact dimensions of fear:
> The nameless man dressed head-to-foot in black,
> Come to commission a requiem in a hurry.
> In the diatonic house there are many mansions:
> A hunting lodge in the mountains, a peaceable cloister,
> A first-class restaurant near the railroad-yards,
> But also a seedy alms-house, the granite prisons
> And oubliettes of the soul. Just how such truth
> Gets itself stated in pralltrillers and mordents
> Not everyone can say. But the 'cellist,
> Leaning over his labors, his eyes closed,
> Is engaged in that study, blocking out, for the moment,
> Audience, hall, and a great part of himself
> In what, not wrongly, might be called research,
> Or the most private part of honesty.[2]

Not everyone can say. I doubt that anyone can say. Hecht's poem is not an essay in musicology. It asks to be read as a poem, the words someone would say in a certain context and subject to many observances of measure and decorum. But I intend to read it badly because opportunistically, as if it existed not as poetry but in a conversation about ways of listening to Mozart—a conversation with Kierkegaard, let us suppose.

Kierkegaard complains that Hecht's poem moves too quickly from

---

2. Anthony Hecht, *Collected Earlier Poems* (New York: Alfred A. Knopf, 1990), 114.

considerations of immediacy, desire, and the erotic-sensuous to the
mere occasions and places in which these are found. Pastries and pow-
dered wigs are well enough, and sufficiently distant from our mundane
preoccupations to make their consortings with the erotic-sensuous
clear. Similarly the balanced parterres, the architecture of white and
gold rosettes. The spirit is well described, Kierkegaard allows. It is
according to Christianity that the spirit is found in discipline, ascesis,
meditation, and practice, including the practice of scales, a routine not
done routinely, an action safe from nearly every form of vanity. A
musician who practices scales is engaged in the secular correlative of
prayer. The discipline of the work may hold him or her in something
akin to a state of grace. But Kierkegaard claims that Hecht has been
misled, drawn away from music and the erotic-sensuous, by listening
to a divine voice saying that in His Father's house there are many
mansions. So, too, in the diatonic scale, according to Hecht's poem.
But the word "mansions" leads the poet astray; he lists the mansions
he sees in the diatonic house, a hunting lodge, cloister, restaurant,
alms-house, prisons, and oubliettes. Before he is well started, Hecht
has talked himself into assigning truth to these things and wondering
how this truth gets itself stated in pralltrillers and mordents.

Kierkegaard protests that it does not get itself stated: Truth has
nothing to do with the case; it is a question of desire. There are no
hunting lodges in Mozart any more than there are bullfights in Hem-
ingway. Hecht's verses imply that a work of art stands for something
else, that the purpose of art is vicarious. We cannot have everything
at once, so we have one thing that stands for another. Kierkegaard,
still protesting, claims that a work of art expresses real or imagined
desire, the erotic-sensuous, and may develop further riches of desire
by formal discovery as it goes along. But it has no interest in hunting
lodges. In a study of Renaissance history, Walter Pater asserts in similar
vein that all art constantly aspires toward the condition of music, because in music there is no distinction between matter and form. It
follows that art "is always striving to be independent of the mere
intelligence, to become a matter of pure perception, to get rid of its
responsibilities to its subject or material."[3] So the cellist, leaning over
his instrument, should ignore the hunting lodge and other mansions,

3. Walter Pater, *The Renaissance: Studies in Art and Poetry,* ed. Donald L. Hill (Berkeley: University of California Press, 1980), 108.

block them out as sternly as he blocks out the audience, the hall, and a great part of himself. He should play the notes and think only of desire, force, life, movement, the privilege of being alive, the voluptuousness of having a body, hands, eyes, ears, mind, and spirit.

At this point I hear the poet protesting: My cellist, bent over his labors, is studying, researching, gathering up for the occasion his years of practice, all those terrible scales, the blistered fingers. Hecht maintains that the sensuous thrill, the immediacy, is Mozart's, not the cellist's. Kierkegaard concedes the point. The cellist should resign his life for the composer's life, and assume that the composer and he meet at the only moment that matters, here and now, the performance, the sounding of desire.

Another poet enters the conversation. He wrote a poem called "Mozart, 1935" smack in the middle of the decade that W. H. Auden denounced as low, dishonest. Some thought the decade Marx's providential time and worked to make it come true. In the poem, Wallace Stevens made up words for things that lacked them or for events that had received their words prematurely. He thought that poets should use common speech for the most part but hold themselves free to devise their own gibberish, responsive to life's sundry unnamed nonsenses, probable sources incidentally of the erotic-sensuous. Here is "Mozart, 1935":

> Poet, be seated at the piano.
> Play the present, its hoo-hoo-hoo,
> Its shoo-shoo-shoo, its ric-a-nic,
> Its envious cachinnation.
>
> If they throw stones upon the roof
> While you practice arpeggios,
> It is because they carry down the stairs
> A body in rags.
> Be seated at the piano.
>
> That lucid souvenir of the past,
> The divertimento;
> That airy dream of the future,
> The unclouded concerto . . .
> The snow is falling.
> Strike the piercing chord.

Be thou the voice,
Not you. Be thou, be thou
The voice of angry fear,
The voice of this besieging pain.

Be thou that wintry sound
As of the great wind howling,
By which sorrow is released,
Dismissed, absolved
In a starry placating.

We may return to Mozart.
He was young, and we, we are old.
The snow is falling
And the streets are full of cries.
Be seated, thou.[4]

The poem is a defense of poetry, written at a time when poets were regularly accused of being frivolous, morally obtuse. Stevens's poem says that even in a grim time, one should not be deterred from arpeggios, divertimentos, and concertos by people throwing stones upon one's roof. These people have cause, though it is not enough. Music has cause. The merit of music, according to this Shelleyan and Kierkegaardian poem, is that it is the voice of such immediacies as angry fear and besieging pain. It speaks of winter nearly as quickly as the great wind howling. "Howling" refers, at the inevitable distance of reflection, to sorrow and the wind. "Be thou the voice,/Not you." Not your psychological or biographic self. You should be your demon or pneuma, if we need a word for it. So we may return to Mozart, the poem assures us, after considering the many reasons proposed for leaving him. A poet should play the present, practicing inherited forms that speak of times gone or still to come, as the concerto may invoke the past or summon a future without cloud. Playing the present is difficult because there are no agreed words for it. The poet makes up nonce words and hopes that with all their semantic penury they will come closer to immediacy than the conventional words, which are already belated.

4. Wallace Stevens, *The Palm at the End of the Mind,* ed. Holly Stevens (New York: Vintage Books, 1990 reprint), 115.

Kierkegaard does not complain of Stevens's poem. He congratu-
lates the poet on the gibberish of hoo-hoo-hoo, shoo-shoo-shoo, and
ric-a-nic, because these speak of the demonic, the erotic-sensuous,
with the freedom of debonair vowels and repetitions. These syllables
have come into expressiveness without yet being caught for the
dictionary. Kierkegaard is pleased, too, that Stevens allows for the sequence by which sorrow is first released, then dismissed, and finally
absolved in a starry placating. The syntax is liberal, as if the sorrow
were released from its word, its domesticating name.

The conversation is over. Kierkegaard and Stevens have agreed that
music acts before language and resists every attempt to assimilate it
into the stability of grammar and syntax. Hecht is not persuaded, so
he challenges his companions to say whether genius, too, eludes grammar and syntax.

In *Either/Or* genius means the form of energy that sets itself against
spirit, considers itself equal and opposite to spirit. It is unfashionable
to speak of genius, especially when one ascribes it to a mere person
rather than to such an abstraction as "the genius of the age" or the
genius loci. I can think of two reasons for this reluctance to use the
word, and there may be several I have missed. The first is that the
word is tainted with the grandiloquence of Romanticism; it is associated with Romantic afflatus, recourse to the Muses, and ultimately
with Plato's notion of divine frenzy. These are out of fashion as causes
and are widely denounced as instances of obscurantism and self-
bewilderment. The second reason is that we are still sufficiently intim-
idated by structuralism to look for explanations in codes and systems
rather than in the apparent ability of a few people to float free of these.
But the case is not settled. I was surprised recently to find James Gleick
calling his new book *Genius: The Life and Science of Richard Feynman.*
Alan Lightman began his review of it in the *New York Review of Books*
by saying that "Richard Feynman was the Michael Jordan of physics."
Presumably Michael Jordan is the Richard Feynman of basketball, so
where does that leave us? In the same review Lightman quoted mathematician Mark Kac's distinction between two kinds of genius, the
ordinary and the magical. "An ordinary genius is a fellow that you
and I would be just as good as, if we were only many times better."
But with magicians, we feel that "even after we understand what they

have done, the process by which they have done it is completely dark."[5] That does not help.

It does not make much sense to speculate whether Gluck could have written the finale of the *Jupiter* Symphony or Haydn the overture to *Die Zauberflöte* if they had been more gifted than they happened to be, or whether the creative difference between Mozart and these ruled out the possibility. But there is some point in remarking that generally we listen to a piece of music knowing the composer's name and reputation, and that this knowledge colors the listening. We accommodate the music to the knowledge and the lore. Why, in visiting an art gallery, do we look at the name at the bottom of each painting before we look at the painting? Is it to avoid the uncertainty of facing the painting without the painter's name as guarantee of safe passage? We want to take the painting into a context we have already formed under the governance of the name. Looking at a painting by an artist I never heard of is not the same as looking at a Klee. I am not the same. Hearing a work by Mozart, I have already prepared myself to hear a work by Mozart, participating in his name. The name holds in place an intimation of genius, a particular tone of creative power different from Beethoven's or Schubert's. It would be a different experience if I did not catch the name and mistook the music for Gluck's. The name alludes to genius but otherwise tries to protect us from the blow of immediacy, the erotic-sensuous; it draws our reception of the work toward discourse and reflection. Since the eighteenth century it has been impossible to separate genius from its name. We cannot believe that the world contains mute, inglorious Miltons. But these notions are probably useless. There is no alternative to the common notion of a genius, a person who possesses to an extraordinary degree the creative power we diversely call imagination or vision. William Blake nearly settled for calling it "energy." Each of us has a little of it.

About genius there is little to be said, apart from recognizing its manifestations. But something may be said about the conditions in which it has flourished or been thwarted. In *Noise: The Political Economy of Music*, Jacques Attali went some way toward explaining these. His basic idea is that music is prophetic; it anticipates forms of social and political

5. Alan Lightman, "The One and Only," *New York Review of Books* 39, no. 21 (December 17, 1992): 34.

organization because it is the first art to respond to change. Attali does not say, as Kierkegaard implies, that music knows change immediately because it does not pause to reflect upon it. Music precedes the politics that hopes to fulfill it. Mozart and Bach prophesy "the bourgeoisie's dream of harmony," Attali says, "better than and prior to the whole of nineteenth-century political theory." How, then, is music to be understood in relation to representation, exchange, the determination of value? That is Attali's main theme. The value ascribed to music was not that of the labor expended in producing or performing it: Music could not be organized by that measure. It is true that composers were for hire, attached to emperor or bishop, Lully to Louis XIV, Haydn to Prince Esterhazy. I suppose a man in black did indeed come to Mozart to commission a made-to-measure requiem in a hurry. But by the end of the century the bourgeoisie was beginning to assume the privilege of renting a musician for the evening. Tickets for the concert were sold and bought, but the bourgeoisie assessed the musician's value by declaring him a genius. An aura suffused his name. As a genius, he was to be seen and heard; witnessed, rather. As a spectacle, he was a force of nature become a force of culture, like—in the twentieth century—Ferlinghetti and Ginsberg giving a reading of their poems. There was also use-value, socially a more feasible consideration because it consisted in recognizing the public character of music. Concerts stimulated a sense of community and reconciliation. Attali maintains that in the insignia of social order the orchestra, the conductor, and (in a concerto) the soloist made a socially fulfilling image. The conductor embodied the order the ruling class wished to see and hear. The orchestra represented, in a sense, the people. In a concerto, the soloist is a musician who has risen above the group. He can deal with the conductor as an equal, but without challenging his authority. So he saves concertgoers the necessity of choosing between identifying themselves with the community of the players or the glory of the leader.

Attali makes a point that bears upon our experience of Mozart's music. There was a shift, at the end of the eighteenth century, from one conception of harmony to another:

> The conception of natural harmony, an inevitable order in the world, is found as late as Rousseau, who argued in favor of natural, Italian music, against the artificial, contrived music of the French; music, according to Rousseau, should be a language, it should evoke conversation and thus preserve political order. For Gretry and

Villeteau, the model for music is declamation. The link between harmony and representation is here clearly evident: harmony presupposes represented dialogue; it leads to the opera, the supreme form of the representation by the bourgeoisie of its own order and enactment of the political.

But it was at this same time that modern theorizing about the foundations of harmony was born. The idea was no longer to conceptualize music as a naturally ordered whole, but to impose upon it the reign of reason and the scientific representation of the world: harmonic order is not naturally assured by the existence of God. It has to be constructed by science, willed by man.[6]

Rousseau is a fairly late rhetorician of natural harmony, the axiom of *Stimmung* that we find in Pythagoras and virtually everywhere until the eighteenth century. But the dates are not binding. It was always possible, even as late as Wordsworth, to feel that there was natural harmony between the world and man; one had only to take one's moods genially and assume that there was some reason, however occult, for their buoyancy. Such moods are still possible, though the natural world is harder to find and an act of faith is required before we can feel concord between that world and ourselves. There are also works, like *Die Zauberflöte*, in which the harmony constructed by science and willed by man turns out to be nature articulated and produced but not imposed upon. That is an especially pleasant discovery to those who want reason and science to take charge of the world.

It is a commonplace that *Die Zauberflöte* is in the service of enlightenment. Scholars have drawn attention to the elements of Masonry in the opera, to certain features of the harmony that are correlated with Masonic rituals. Masonry and the Enlightenment go hand in hand, prescribing the terms of the drama. The conflict the opera exhibits is not between good and evil. Evil, embodied in the Queen of the Night, is merely the folly of thinking that any force could prevail against reason. The conflict is presented as one between superstition and light, and it ends when the Queen, the Three Ladies, and Monostatos sink into the earth, confessing themselves "plunging into destruction and infinite night." Sarastro announces that the sun's glory has vanquished night, the powers of darkness have yielded:

6. Jacques Attali, *Noise: The Political Economy of Music,* trans. Brian Massumi (Minneapolis: University of Minnesota Press, 1985), 60.

Die Strahlen der Sonne vertreiben die Nacht,
Vernichten der Heuchler erschlichene Macht.

Every scene in the opera points to this conclusion. Tamino anticipates it when he asks the priests of the Temple of Wisdom how long he must remain in darkness: "Wann also wird die Decke schwinden?" The melody that Mozart writes for those words is virtually unaccompanied, as if in miming the translucence of Tamino's desire he allowed nothing to come between Tamino and the light. A moment later, Tamino makes his apostrophe even more specific:

O ew'ge Nacht! Wann wirst du Schwinden?
Wann wird das Licht mein Auge finden?

Even Sarastro's "In diesen heil'gen Hallen" makes sense only because vengeance is unnecessary; enlightenment is sure to prevail. When the Three Boys lead Tamino to the temples, they merely tell him (twice) to be silent, steadfast, and tolerant. He divines at once that the temples embody Nature, Reason, and (in the center) Wisdom. These values emerge not from a religious sense of life but from reiterated confidence in the powers of reason and its metaphorical kinship with light and the sun. When the Spokesman is concerned that Tamino, being a prince, may not take well to the initiation, Sarastro assures him that he need not worry: "Noch mehr—Er ist Mensch!" Similarly, Sarastro explains at the beginning of the second act why he tore Pamina from her mother's side: because her mother, the Queen of the Night, planned "by guile and superstition" to deceive the people and to "destroy the firm foundations of our temples." The axioms of the opera are humanist and rationalist; they take for granted the veridical power of enlightenment.

The first premise of enlightenment is that knowledge is the great means of wisdom, happiness, and power. The purpose of the initiation trials in *Die Zauberflöte* is to ensure this access. Intelligent love of a man and a woman is the symbol of happiness. Jean Starobinski has noted that in Mozart's opera "the purified hero takes as his bride one who is heiress both to the world of day and to the frenzy of night, for Pamina is daughter at once of a beneficent magician and of the dark queen."[7] In the happiness of Tamino and Pamina we see the

---

7. Jean Starobinski, *1789: The Emblems of Reason*, trans. Barbara Bray (Charlottesville: University Press of Virginia, 1982), 39–40.

virtue of reason rewarded. Pamina is Tamino's reward for the achievement of discipline, knowledge, and order. They endorse a myth of knowledge and power, a man's world of reason. The public consequence of knowledge is power, supremely represented in *Die Zauberflöte* by Sarastro, high priest of enlightenment. This power is exercised magnanimously because it knows in advance, as Sarastro does, that it will triumph. Papageno is a device to show power in action. He fails the initiation trials, but enlightenment gives him a place in its society nonetheless. Papageno is the crude energy that is refined in others, so he must be acknowledged.

I emphasize the rhetoric of enlightenment in *Die Zauberflöte* to make the point that the opera is entirely secular, despite its invocations of Isis and Osiris. It is true, as Starobinski remarks, that Masonry borrowed its ordeal ritual from the mystery cults of antiquity and from certain practices of medieval chivalry. But this does not justify Starobinski's reference to "the Masonic religion." In Mozart's day, Masonry was not a religion; it was a system of social, economic, and political kinship directed toward worldly power. In *Die Zauberflöte*, as in Masonry, the God of Christianity is dispersed into Isis and Osiris, and the power of these gods is taken into human hands, the rhetoric of the Enlightenment silencing the claim of Christian theology. By a potent irony, the promise of a redeemed because enlightened humanity is made at the end of the first act by the priests, who sing that, when virtue and justice shed glory upon this noble path, "the earth is a kingdom of heaven and mortals are like gods":

> Dann ist die Erd' ein Himmelreich
> Und Sterbliche den Gottern gleich.

Similarly, when there is an allusion to a religious theme, Mozart quickly disperses it into sociality. Take for instance the extraordinary scene of the Men in Armor. They recite to Tamino the legend they see on the pyramid at center stage. Man must bear the tribulations of fire, water, earth, and air—"Der, welcher wandert diese Strasse." If he succeeds, he will be enlightened (*Erleuchtet*) and enabled to devote himself to the Mysteries of Isis. The melody sung by the Men in Armor is a Lutheran chorale, "Ach Gott, vom Himmel sieh darein" ("Oh God, look down from Heaven"). It is cantus firmus, sung in octaves, accompanied by a four-part fugato in the strings. Ernst Bloch chose it to illustrate the effect Mozart achieved by introducing fugal form into music dominated by the sonata:

> The fugato, which is only an approximation to fugal form, will or can produce something uneasily rigid, most eerily so in the fugued chorale of the Men in Armor in *The Magic Flute*. Mozart was forging a new expression. It had its sequel in the fugato of the *Eroica* funeral march, which would scarcely have been conceived without Mozart's precedent and is an altogether dynamic cortege, no longer a *quietas* in fuga.[8]

So we have the Lutheran chorale and a verbal allusion to it in the libretto—"Schwingt er sich aus der Erde himmel an"—but the only God that looks down from this heaven is the spirit of Enlightenment Rationalism. We are removed from God and Luther at once. Tamino accepts the challenge of initiation. Pamina, offstage, calls out to him: "Tamino, halt! Ich muss dich sehn!" Tamino answers, "Was hor ich? Paminens Stimme?" "Ja, ja, das ist Paminens Stimme," the Men in Armor helpfully explain, and they are all socially at one, hierarchic distinctions dissolved.

The claim of enlightenment is enforced still further. Nature and mind are in harmony, as in the gentle music of the flute, but only if the mind is in charge. Natural processes are understood as perennial music, the sound of the sea, waves rising and falling, rivers, mountain torrents, the wind, but these are to be controlled by being understood. Categories and genres are constructed for this purpose: the beautiful, the picturesque, the sublime, the ode, the sonata. The sublime is dangerous because it recognizes the natural processes that cannot quite be controlled—mountain gloom and mountain glory—and must be pondered with fear, even if that fear is a nuanced delight. These categories and genres testify to the energy of the mind confronting the primordial energy of the natural world and in the end mastering it. Without the mind, Nature is inevitably the source of superstition, the Queen of the Night. For the aria (no. 14) in which the Queen demands that Pamina kill Sarastro—"Der Hölle Rache kocht in meinem Herzen"—Mozart has written music so fixed in its venom that the

---

8. Ernst Bloch, *Essays on the Philosophy of Music,* trans. Peter Palmer (Cambridge: Cambridge University Press, 1985), 234–35.

only future the Queen's superstition can have is to be defeated: Progress from nature to culture could not be envisaged for it.

Nature, adrift from the mind, expresses itself in blank repetition— The Queen's "Verstossen sei auf ewig, Verlassen sei auf ewig" issues only in the appalling irony of "Alle Bande der Natur." But when the mind is in charge, it gathers up all the energies of the natural world and converts them to itself. *Die Zauberflöte* is like *The Tempest,* in that respect, but with this difference: In *The Tempest,* Shakespeare has natural magic accruing to Prospero as power, Orphic in its quality and tone, Ariel its servant; in *Die Zauberflöte* the modern mind, practiced in the ways of science and enlightenment, exerts itself upon the natural world and appropriates its energies. This is shown in the scene in which Pamina, brought to Tamino, promises them happiness—"Sie mag den Weg mit Rosen streu'n." Accompanied by a bassoon solo, she tells Tamino that her father made the flute in a magic hour from a branch of a thousand-year-old oak while storm and thunder raged. Nature offers itself to mind, culture, harmony. So the mind acts in the world. Enlightenment is incomplete until total knowledge is achieved; that is why there is still a project for it. The mind in the mode of its success is called wisdom and is accompanied by the statutory Masonic virtues, the ability to remain silent being the first of them.

Angus Fletcher has studied this aspect of *Die Zauberflöte,* the opera as singspiel that "uses the alternate silencing of music by spoken voice, of spoken voice by music." The extreme reaches of *Die Zauberflöte* in this consideration are silence and thunder. The opera is not concerned with producing scenes of dramatic action, as in Italian opera, but scenes of transformation, a profusion of metaphors, oppositions not of character but of mode. Tamino is willing to be silent, and Papageno's mouth has to be padlocked to make him stop chattering. As in Masonic practice, silence "accumulates inner strength, almost as if it nurtured, or stored, courage and authority."[9] The rite of passage is through silence. It is in this relation to silence that Mozart turns sounds and instruments into personages; flute, bassoon, clarinet, glockenspiel, and strings become nearly as individual, and call for nearly as much moral attention, as the characters who sing and chatter

9. Angus Fletcher, *Colors of the Mind: Conjectures on Thinking in Literature* (Cambridge, Mass.: Harvard University Press, 1991), 207.

and scream. This is so much the case that an ideal performance of *Die Zauberflöte*, I think, would be a puppet show—not only because of the rapidity of the opera, its thirteen changes of scene (three in the first act, ten in the second). There is something absurd in the strivings of a stage designer and a director to cope with these. The true changes are musical, not theatrical; they are metamorphoses, not challenges to the carpenter. Nothing would be lost by having puppets move to the music.

Fletcher's description of the opera in relation to silence and speech is persuasive. He emphasizes that the three questions asked about Tamino by the priests of the Temple of Wisdom—"Is he virtuous? Can he maintain silence? Does he love his fellow-men?"—depend on the grand question they imply: Can Tamino remain quiet "in order to give mental space to the highest princely act, which is to think in an enlightened fashion"? But Fletcher wants to construe this question and the silence it requires as having religious force:

> The Masonic ideology underlying *The Magic Flute* deliberately hovers between religious and political conceptions of social bonding. *The Magic Flute* is a work of pre-Romantic equivocity, though it stresses the ritual foundation of political authority. To a degree the opera shows a conflict of raw power, in the mythic opposition of Sarastro to the Queen of the Night. Yet we are shown, in another sense, that a religious mystery—the Masonic initiation into wisdom—has the force of a higher law to overcome and dispel the irrational powers of the Queen.[10]

Where that second sense is alerted by *Die Zauberflöte*, I cannot discover. The Masonic initiation into wisdom seems to me to have no connection with religion: there is nothing numinous about it, no theology sustains it, no metaphysic; it is directed by pragmatics and pointed toward expertise. None of its ideological claims calls for any deeper response than we give to a notion in psychology or sociology.

A misinterpretation of Kierkegaard's essay on *Don Giovanni* seems to account for the prevalence of religious terms in considerations of Mozart's operas, and indeed of his entire music. In *The Classical Style* Charles Rosen says:

10. Fletcher, *Colors of the Mind*, 208.

Behind [this] essay . . . stands the idea that music is a sin: it seems fundamentally sound that he should have chosen Mozart as the most sinful composer of all. What is most extraordinary about Mozart's style is the combination of physical delight—a sensuous play of sonority, an indulgence in the most harmonic sequences—with a purity and economy of line and form that render the seduction all the more efficient.[11]

But this depends upon a casual definition of sin and a perfunctory idea of seduction. Kierkegaard makes it clear that sin does not arise in his philosophy of music, or it arises later, too late to thwart expression of the erotic-sensuous. Referring to Don Juan and the Middle Ages, he writes:

The Middle Ages had much to say about a mountain, not found on any map, which is called the mountain of Venus. There the sensuous has its home, there it has its own wild pleasures, for it is a kingdom, a state. In this kingdom language has no place, nor sober-minded thought, nor the toilsome business of reflection. There sound only the voice of elemental passion, the play of appetites, the wild shouts of intoxication; it exists solely for pleasure in eternal tumult. The first-born of this kingdom is Don Juan. That it is the kingdom of sin is not yet affirmed, for we confine ourselves to the moment at which this kingdom appears in aesthetic indifference.[12]

To this, a helpful editor adds a note: "By 'aesthetic indifference' S. K. means an undifferentiated (immediate, unreflective) aesthetic condition or stage."[13]

So why does Rosen want to talk of sin in relation to Mozart's music generally, and Fletcher to make *Die Zauberflöte* in any respect a religious work, Masonic and anti-Catholic of course? Both are reacting, I think, to Schumann's interpretation of Mozart as a composer of lightness, grace, and charm. Each of them wants to hear the music as the sounding of mystery, awe, sin, paradise lost. They are evidently not content, as Attali is, to talk of politics and the political economy of sound; they want to hear Jehovah. I cannot quote further chapter and verse from Fletcher, but Rosen asserts that it is only by recogniz-

---

11. Charles Rosen, *The Classical Style* (New York: W. W. Norton, 1972), 324.
12. Kierkegaard, *Either/Or*, 88.
13. Kierkegaard, *Either/Or*, 449.

ing "the violence and the sensuality at the center of Mozart's work" that we can comprehend his structures. "In all of Mozart's supreme expressions of suffering and terror—the G minor symphony, *Don Giovanni,* the G minor quintet, Pamina's aria in *Die Zauberflöte*—there is something shockingly voluptuous," Rosen claims. But voluptuousness is not the issue. Nor is shock. Indeed, another sentence in the same chapter shows that Rosen is of two minds about his sense of Mozart and wants to shift the terms of description. The word he wants now is "profound," though that word is just as hard to construe as "genius." Rosen is still talking about Schumann's conversion of Mozart's G Minor Symphony to charm: "It should be said at once that to reduce a work to the expression of sentiments, however powerful, is to trivialize it in any case: the G minor symphony is not much more profound conceived as a tragic cry from the heart than as a work of exquisite charm."[14]

If that were true, we could settle for exquisite charm and stop quarreling with Schumann. But Rosen himself, ten lines later, is describing the G Minor—I have just quoted the sentence—as the expression of suffering and terror. Earlier in the book, with the D Minor Concerto, K. 466, in view, he says that "it is one of the fullest realizations of that aspect of Mozart which the nineteenth century quite rightly named 'daemonic' and which, for so long, made a balanced assessment of the rest of his work so difficult."[15] I take it that Rosen means balanced between classical and Romantic affiliations, the demonic and the civil, the spiritual and the erotic-sensuous.

So we return with Rosen to Kierkegaard's vocabulary. "Don Juan," Kierkegaard says, "is the expression of the daemonic determined as the sensuous; Faust, its expression determined as the intellectual or spiritual, which the Christian spirit excludes."[16] *Die Zauberflöte* does not come into this reckoning. Kierkegaard thought it defective for "tending toward consciousness." I think he means that it sacrifices purely musical or erotic-sensuous values in favor of ideas. He means, too, that it exemplifies the aspect of Mozart that Wagner attributed to the arithmetician in him.

The question we have come to is this: Is the immediacy of Mozart's

14. Rosen, *The Classical Style,* 324.
15. Rosen, *The Classical Style,* 228.
16. Kierkegaard, *Either/Or,* 8.

music, its erotic-sensuous character, adequately heard—not, of course, accounted for—in a political, economic, and civil context? Or does it break through those boundaries and call for description in metaphysical or religious terms? It seems to me that Bloch's sense of the question is persuasive, and that he is justified in making a contrast between Mozart and Bach for his purpose. "In Mozart," he says, "it is the secular self, and in Bach the sacred self, which becomes the object." This is clarified by Bloch's reference to Mozart's "musical Hellenism"—his practice in the operas of moving between recitative and song and back again, concentrating in each character the emotion of a situation "without the ulterior motive of collectively storming away from the specific physical self and its moderate bounds." "Moderate" is hardly justified, except that Bloch regards Mozart's music as essentially an extension of chamber music rather than a full development of the resources of the symphony. The contrast with Bach turns upon the *St. Matthew Passion:*

> When Jesus says: "I say unto you that one of you shall betray me," and the disciples, excited and confused, cry in a most violent allegro: "Lord, is it I?" and then, after a wondrous pause, the congregation sings the chorale "It is I, I should atone," this moment in the *St. Matthew Passion* reverberates with the most intense feeling. Kierkegaard himself could not have found a more powerful sermon for this sense of being addressed *ad hominem,* for Christian action and the subjectifying of Christianity. In this way, then, the chorale's lyrical disposition overrides both the purely private lyricism of the characters in the story and the external drama . . . of the actual choruses. For the chorale, like some of the contemplative arias, is essentially the form of expression proper to a higher or theocratic community which dwells beyond events, so to speak.[17]

Bach's lyricism is ontological rather than psychological. It does not inhere in an individual but in a sense of life as such. Its narrative form is myth, sustained by providential power rather than by what we merely happen to know.

What about the Mass in C Minor? Is it not a genuinely religious work, and not a function of the Enlightenment? I cannot hear it as a religious work. It seems to me to be just as secular as *Die Zauberflöte* and to have been produced by transferring to choir stalls and pews

17. Bloch, *Essays on the Philosophy of Music,* 20.

the methods of the opera house. There is no sense, in the C Minor Mass, of the community that dwells beyond events. In *Die Zauberflöte,* expressiveness arises from the individual, psychologically considered, and returns there, but always under the governance of the Enlightenment. Sometimes the expressiveness is such that it is hard to count any aspect of it as a limitation. In those moments, Mozart's music is indeed prophetic: What it prophesies is the conviction that one's true life is private, lived in relation to oneself, soliloquy its form.

My misgiving begins at this point. I have given the impression that Mozart's music, being secular and humanist, presupposes that reality is entirely external. It would follow that the enlightened mind's business is to gain knowledge and to administer the world. Classicism in music and art supports that aim. Mozart is for the most part a willing adept of the classical style. But there are a few works, and in *Die Zauberflöte* a few moments, in which he intuits the inward, self-communing style we associate with Romanticism. In *The Philosophy of Money,* Georg Simmel has explained how this conviction of self arose and developed in the nineteenth century, how it came to be believed that one's true life is lived in relation to oneself.[18] This sentiment resulted in a split between one's public life, deemed to be inauthentic, and one's private life, the only true part of being alive. Pamina's aria, "Ach, ich fuhl's," is one of its supreme articulations. Tamino cannot speak to her, so she thinks he has abandoned her. The comic Papageno, his mouth full of food, cannot speak. Pamina's aria is technically addressed to Tamino: If he does not love her, she will find peace in death. But she really sings to herself; the eloquence is entirely inward. The aria is the most beautiful piece in *Die Zauberflöte,* incomparably poignant. The most heartbreaking moment in it is the change of tone and register for the repeated "so wird Ruhe, so wird Ruh' im Tode sein," leading to the descent from the sustained high G on the last *Ruh* to the low C-sharp quaver on *im*. The ideology of Enlightenment has nothing to say to such grief.

But the movement from the values of the Enlightenment to those of Romanticism is not abrupt. It is true, or at least a feasible hypothesis, that the Enlightenment was a project of knowledge as power, and that

18. Georg Simmel, *The Philosophy of Money,* trans. Tom Bottomore and David Frisby (London: Routledge and Kegan Paul, 1978).

it was more interested in the object of knowledge than in the mind that appropriated it. Romanticism involves a change of emphasis from the object to the subject. The mind that perceives becomes as interesting to itself as the object it perceives—more interesting, since the mind half-perceives and half-creates the apparent object of its attention. The "moment" of Romanticism is one in which the mind, engaged with an object, communes with itself and seeks a form to express its own processes. The object of attention is displaced; it participates in an experience and in one degree or another yields itself to the mind that engages with it. Knowledge is still the aim, but now it is the mind's knowledge of itself, often intuitive and divinatory rather than rational. Epistemology and ontology are displaced by psychology.

Marshall Brown has argued that Mozart is part of this Romantic or pre-Romantic story in a few strange works, notably in the introduction to the "Dissonant" Quartet in C Major, K. 465. Brown maintains that this work enacts reverie, a self-absorbed mode of consciousness, come upon as if prior to the thought of anything in particular; it is an instance of the generation of form from within. He associates it with dreaming, fantasy, pure duration, the dominance of a mood, the "qualitative progression"—to use Kenneth Burke's phrase—of tone poems. Beethoven's Bagatelles and his Choral Fantasia, Schumann's Piano Quartet, the prelude to Wagner's *Das Rheingold,* and Mozart's Fantasia K. 475 are other examples of music that expresses pure inwardness, conscious but conscious of nothing. Such works are characterized by harmonic and metric uncertainty, the diffusion of certitude and direction. The "Dissonant" Quartet features, as Brown says, "the gradual emergence of form out of the preconscious, indistinct, throbbing pulse of time."[19] It is not surprising that this quartet inspired the depiction of chaos at the beginning of Haydn's *Die Schöpfung.* In the last years of the eighteenth century the only way to present chaos or void was by evading the imperatives of classical form, refusing to establish a beat, setting meters in conflict. This is what Haydn does at the beginning of *Die Schöpfung,* before summoning Raphael to speak of formless earth and darkness on the face of the deep. Much the same procedure was necessary if a composer wanted to express the mind's brooding upon its own processes. The later

19. Marshall Brown, "Mozart and After: The Revolution in Musical Consciousness," *Critical Inquiry* (Summer 1981): 697.

movements of the "Dissonant" Quartet commit themselves to classical form, as if the solar myth had to be reasserted, but the introduction led not only to *Die Schöpfung* but also to the tone poetry of Wagner and Debussy.

So it is necessary to ask a different question. Not: Is Mozart's music entirely secular, was he a committed man of enlightenment, or had he indeed a religious sensibility? Bloch seems to me to be right about this. Rather: Do Pamina's aria and the introduction to the "Dissonant" Quartet reveal Mozart in the act of disavowing enlightenment, moving toward the inwardness, the organic form of Romanticism? That seems to be true, and it makes Mozart a transitional figure. But even a conclusion as undramatic as this one must be qualified. Mozart still associates order with the classical style. Just as Uriel, in *Die Schöpfung,* reports that God created light and divided light from the darkness, so Mozart divided form from chaos, and in turn divided the state of being conscious but conscious of nothing from the state of being conscious of something in particular, something out there in the world. The social character of his music depends upon this sequence. In the equivocal works, and especially in the Introduction to the "Dissonant" Quartet, what we hear is not a refutation of the Enlightenment but the misgivings a genius feels in committing himself to values he has not invented for himself.

2

How extraordinary was Mozart?

HOWARD GARDNER

I BEGIN by placing my cards on the table. I recall my ecstasy in May 1991 during the traditional undergraduate "reading period" at Harvard University, where I teach. At such times, WHRB-FM, the local radio station, features musical "orgies," during which the programmers devote long periods of time to the works of a particular artist, such as Bob Dylan or Béla Bartók, or to a coherent theme, such as "string quartets" or "operettas." To commemorate the two hundredth anniversary of Mozart's death, WHRB offered 220 straight hours of his music, proceeding essentially form K. 1 through to K. 626. For those of us who love Mozart, it was sublime. My only regret is that I had to miss portions of the orgy when traveling out of town, teaching class, or sleeping. As I remarked, having all of Mozart available at one's fingertips all of the time is the closest I can come to imagining Heaven. I was reminded of George Bernard Shaw's testimony on the topic of Mozart: "the only music yet written that would not sound out of place in the mouth of God."[1]

From one perspective, it is fun to write about a person about whom one has been enthusiastic for forty years. There is no need to motivate oneself, as I might have to if I were to consider, say, Sibelius or Bruck-

1. R. Taruskin, "Why Mozart Has Become an Icon for Today," *New York Times*, September 9, 1990, Section 2, 35.

ner. It is not that I do not respect those composers—it is just that their music suggests Purgatory to me rather than Heaven. On the other hand, offered an opportunity to comment on Mozart, I feel tempted simply to tell stories, to wax enthusiastic, to wave my hands. In an effort to avoid these temptations, I shall attempt to treat Mozart as a case that has come to my attention, rather than as a lifelong love.

A word, finally, about my credentials for discussing the case of Johann Chrysostom Wolfgang Amadeus Mozart. I am neither a musician nor an expert on Mozart, although I claim at least a modest amateur status in both cohorts. For the last twenty-five years, I have studied artistic and creative processes from the vantage points of cognitive and developmental psychology.[2] For the most part this work has been carried out with "normal subjects"—children with no special talent in the arts and no special claim on the label "creativity"—though I have in the course of my research encountered some youngsters who are remarkable.

Over the last few years, however, I have embarked on a new course of study, one far more relevant to the task at hand. In an effort to illuminate creative breakthroughs of the highest order, I have been studying seven "creators of the modern era"—individuals living in the shadow of 1900 whose ideas and practices were instrumental in shaping the consciousness of our century.[3] Deliberately choosing individuals from a disparate set of domains, I have been examining the lives and works of Sigmund Freud, Albert Einstein, Pablo Picasso, Igor Stravinsky, T. S. Eliot, Mahatma Gandhi, and Martha Graham. My purpose in this study has been twofold: (1) to discover which properties of the process of creation may be common to quite different realms of endeavor (and which may be "domain-specific") and (2) to determine whether such a study can help us to understand our own era better. As it turns out, both these missions have relevance to the case of Mozart.

While the differences between, say, Freud and Eliot are at least as striking as the similarities, it is the parallels across my set of creators

2. Howard Gardner, *Art, Mind, and Brain* (New York: Basic Books, 1982).

3. David Feldman, *Beyond Universals in Cognitive Development* (Norwood: Ablex, 1980); Gardner, *Creating Minds: An Anatomy of Creativity as Seen through the Lives of Freud, Einstein, Picasso, Stravinsky, Eliot, Graham, and Gandhi* (New York: Basic Books, 1993).

that prove most germane to this study. Taking account first of biography, I note that my seven creators came from backgrounds that, while hardly affluent, were reasonably comfortable. Their families were intact and supported their talented child. Of my septet, Picasso was clearly the most precocious; he began to draw seriously well before he started school and attained master status by early adolescence. But even those who started to create at a relatively late age had already shown distinct talent while they were still young children. By and large, the creators came from communities a bit removed from the central capitals of the world. It is therefore remarkable how rapidly they migrated to world-class cities such as Paris, Zurich, Vienna, and London, where they discovered and began to collaborate with other gifted young individuals and determined to spend their lives.

The facts of career development are quite striking. Independent of domain, it takes about ten years of intensive practice for the young individual to master the tools of his or her trade, to join the well-trained practitioners of a calling.[4] Naturally, the younger one begins, the younger one becomes a master: starting at four or five, Picasso became a master by his teenage years; Martha Graham did not begin to dance seriously until the age of twenty and was not a mature dancer until she was about thirty.

In the course of achieving mastery, most creators are highly productive. But no matter how productive and how precocious they are, it takes about ten additional years for them to achieve their most important and most dramatic breakthrough. I refer here to Freud's theory of the unconscious, Einstein's special theory of relativity, Gandhi's epochal strike and fast at Ahmedabad, and the artistic breakthroughs associated with Picasso's *Démoiselles d'Avignon,* Eliot's *Waste Land,* Stravinsky's *Sacre du printemps,* and Graham's *Frontier.* Generally speaking, another breakthrough occurs approximately a decade later, one that is broader, deeper, more comprehensive, and more integrally linked to earlier traditions in the domain. Most creators do not continue to realize breakthroughs at successive decade-long intervals. At least in certain domains, however, the possibility of continuing innovations remains as long as the creator is active and continues to confront challenges.

4. J. R. Hayes, *The Complete Problem-Solver* (Philadelphia: The Franklin Institute Press, 1981), passim.

Turning to aspects of human personality, I find that our creative individuals are remarkable—but also remarkably difficult—human beings. They are fiercely ambitious, single-minded, egocentric, unhesitant to sacrifice all in the service of their work. They may be capable of acts of great generosity, but fundamentally they are selfish or, perhaps more accurately, self-centered. It is risky to remain within the orbit of a creative individual, for one may well be used or tossed aside should the interests or passions of the creative individual happen to change. However, there are obvious rewards for remaining within that orbit; such individuals are tremendously lively, energetic, and stimulating.

Psychologists tend to direct their regard within the skin of the individual whom they are studying. After all, our jobs as investigators are simplified if we do not have to take into account contextual factors, ranging from significant other persons to the overall culture in which our subjects live. In this sense, the study of creativity has proved quite sobering for me. I have been struck by the strong needs felt by creative individuals for both psychological and substantive support during the periods of their creative breakthroughs. Feeling isolated, misunderstood, and on the edge, the creators become reliant on a person, or a small group, whom they can use as a sounding board and who can satisfy their temporarily heightened needs for love and understanding.

One has the feeling that, just as a parental figure teaches the infant about his or her language and culture, the aspiring creator is trying to teach a wholly new language to the person(s) to whom he feels closest. Albert Einstein had his Olympiad group and his life-long friend Michele Besso; Freud was highly dependent on his odd physician-friend Wilhelm Fliess; at the time of their most important breakthroughs, artists Picasso, Stravinsky, Eliot, and Graham were dependent, respectively, on Georges Braque, the Diaghilev Circle, Ezra Pound, and Louis Horst. Only Gandhi seems to have escaped the need for an intimate during his times of heightened exploration, though it is possible that the Sarabhai family played precisely this role during the pivotal mill-owners' strike at Ahmedabad in 1918.

No matter how special the brain, the personality, and the temperament "within the skin" of the creative individual, they all constitute but a single one of three essential components of any creative activity. Of equal importance to the individual in any creative achievement are two other factors: (1) the nature of the domain—the discipline or craft within which the individual is working—and (2) the nature of the field—the set of social roles and institutions that render judgments of quality with respect to the works or projects fashioned by the individual working in a domain.[5] Only when reasonable congruence prevails among the person, the domain, and the field does the possibility of creative achievement emerge. Put differently, even the most talented individual cannot function if he or she does not fit within a domain that exists (or is invented) during his or her lifetime, and if the quality of his or her work is not *ultimately* recognized by some field—some functioning set of experts.

In this context, it is instructive to compare the young prodigy with the creative genius on the eve of his great breakthrough. In the case of the prodigy, one might say, following David Feldman,[6] that the talent, the domain, and the field are in exquisite harmony. The gifts of the young Picasso and the young Mozart matched nearly perfectly with a domain that was valued during their youth.

On the other hand, tension inevitably is generated when an individual begins to issue new ideas or products. By definition, these novelties will stretch current practices of the domain and challenge the sensibilities of important portions of the field. (One inevitably recalls the critical comment of Emperor Joseph: "Too many notes, my dear Mozart, too many notes.")[7] Those individuals whom we ultimately prize as being creative are the ones whose innovations succeed in changing the definition of the domain and in altering the tastes of the field. A case like Bach becomes fascinating here, for he may be considered among the most remarkable talents of any era without his having fully satisfied the standard criteria for creative innovation.

My study reveals numerous other traits and processes characteristic of the creators of our era. These range from a capacity to mobilize the most current means of communication to a tendency to revert to a "neoclassic" vein after two decades of frank innovation. Suffice it to

5. Mihaly Csikszentmihalyi, "Society, Culture, and Person: A Systems View of Creativity," in R. J. Sternberg, ed., *The Nature of Creativity* (New York: Cambridge University Press, 1988); Gardner, "Freud in Three Frames," *Daedalus* (Summer 1986): 105–34; Gardner, "Creative Lives and Creative Works: A Synthetic Science Approach," in Sternberg, ed., *Nature of Creativity;* Gardner, "Creativity: An Interdisciplinary Perspective," *Journal of Creativity Research 1* (1988): 8–26.

6. David Feldman with L. Goldsmith, *Nature's Gambit* (New York: Basic Books, 1986), 11–15.

7. Taruskin, "Why Mozart Has Become an Icon for Today," 35.

say that, even among the most remarkable individuals of this century, it is possible to discover common features which might not have been entirely anticipated before the study.

Even though he lived well over a century before my group of creators, during a time and under circumstances that seem remote from world wars, instant worldwide communications, and air travel, Mozart was in many particulars a typical creative genius. Music, the art form in which he would ultimately make his contribution, was virtually a second language in his home. With a father who was an esteemed teacher and performer of music, a mother who was supportive, and a sister who was also precocious, it became a virtual certainty that this gifted young child would be drawn into the world of musical performance. That Mozart began to compose at an early age was perhaps more remarkable, though it was probably expected in his household; however, we should bear in mind that Mozart lived at a time when performers were typically improvisers and when the lines between composing and performing were less sharply drawn than in our era. Mozart stood out for the extent to which he was able to assimilate the idiom of other composers, such as Johann Christian Bach or Michael Haydn; but at the same time, and equally notably, he never simply imitated others. His apprenticeship proceeded smoothly and swiftly, and by his teen years he was producing highly competent works.

Although music was recognized as a creative art form in the mid eighteenth century, it was still considered primarily a professional trade. Individuals in the generation of Leopold Mozart—whose ranks included the redoubtable Franz Joseph Haydn—saw themselves as members of a guild. Part of the common expectation was that they would perform and create music on a regular basis within the court or group to which they belonged. Rather than enjoying the luxury—or enduring the pain—of waiting until inspiration struck, they were supposed to produce on demand. There is no question that Mozart was enormously productive; for twenty-five years, he turned out an average of twenty-five works a year, including many large-scale compositions such as operas, masses, oratorios, symphonies, and concertos. But more than a handful of musicians of his era—including the now infamous Salieri and the charmingly named Karl Ditters von Dittersdorf—were equally productive.

In the dimensions of his compositional output, Mozart seems to resemble other highly productive musical tradesmen of the period. By an impressively early age he had mastered the various genres of his time: the concerto, the symphony, the opera based on mythical stories. Mozart was able to seize upon musical motifs that occurred to him, or that were provided by others, and transmute these materials into powerful instances of the specific genre in which he happened to be creating. No matter his mood or the number of pieces on which he had recently been working, Mozart was able to rise to the occasion and provide a serviceable additional instance of the genre virtually on demand. Where he differed from others, of course, was in the degree of innovation that characterized each new composition and in the extent to which nearly all of his adult works were recognizable as being "Mozartisch." Mozart's language may not have been radically new, but it was instantly identifiable as his own.

There is no reason to think that Mozart was gratuitously nasty; no more so than Einstein, Freud, or Eliot did he exert any special efforts to be difficult or to induce pain. At the same time, like the other creators whom I have studied, Mozart was a prickly character. He was intensely involved in his own work. He concentrated on it to the exclusion of everything and everyone else, even composing in one room while his wife, Constanze, was giving birth in an adjoining one.

With time, Mozart gradually sacrificed the politeness which he had acquired as a young man, and increasingly he said what he thought to whomever he encountered. This candor came at a high cost. Unable to assume the court positions that he needed in order to live comfortably, he ended up isolated and impoverished. In this sense, Mozart became a casualty of the imperial era in which he lived; two hundred years later, Mozart's quirkiness and candor would have been more readily accepted—and perhaps even celebrated in a weekly news-magazine.

Long aware of his special gifts, Mozart does not seem to have had a strong need in his later years for other individuals, except perhaps as sources of nocturnal companionship or, less happily, as providers of financial support. As a youth, however, he was extremely close to his father, a closeness that served him well in many respects but that ultimately spawned tensions and caused unhappiness for both. Leopold sacrificed everything to the career of the "miracle that God made to happen in Salzburg" but expected at a minimum that Mozart would lead the career for which he had so painstakingly groomed him. While remaining superficially submissive to his father, Mozart gradually evolved his own ideas about musical composition, professional development, and style of life. As these notions began to clash with Leopold's conservative conceptions, the relation between father and son became strained, and Mozart gradually broke away from him.

If a single figure came to replace Leopold in Mozart's pantheon of heroes, it was Franz Joseph Haydn, his contemporary. From the time of their initial acquaintance in the 1770s, Mozart admired Haydn's music more than that of any other composer of the time. He was especially influenced by Haydn's talents as an inventor of string ensemble music. As he had done with favored composers during his England-based youth, Mozart took Haydn's compositional approach as a model, studied it carefully, and ultimately produced a set of six quartets that he dedicated to the Austrian master. Although many of his works seemed to come easily to the prodigious Mozart, these quartets posed a challenge even for him. Mozart found himself struggling with the counterpoint and poring over numerous drafts, unlike his customary manner of composition. One can read in these dedicative lines the filial respect Mozart had for Haydn:

> To my dear friend Haydn: A father, having resolved to send his sons into the great world, finds it advisable to entrust them to the protection and guidance of a highly celebrated man, the more so since this man, by a stroke of luck, is his best friend. Here, then, celebrated man, and my dearest friend, are my six sons . . . your approval encourages me more than anything else.[8]

I have suggested that, at least in many key respects, Mozart resembles other remarkable creative individuals of his time and of a later era. On the dimensions reviewed thus far, one can find other individuals of Mozart's era, or of our own era, with whom he shared salient characteristics: individuals as prodigious as Mozart, individuals as productive, individuals as personally pugnacious and troubled. One could say that Mozart stood out for his combination of these features—certainly few were as prolific *and* as prodigious *and* as prickly. But then it is hard to know how to quantify any of these dimensions, let alone

8. Howard Chandler Robbins Landon, "What Haydn Taught Mozart," *New York Times*, August 19, 1988, Section 2, 23.

how to sum or multiply them into an overall measure of extraordinariness.

One advantage of studying a set of individuals, even ones drawn from a different century, is that one evolves certain expectations of what a creative individual will be like. These expectations, in turn, permit one to notice when a newly examined individual stands out in various ways. In what follows I mention four areas where the case of Wolfgang Mozart may be unique.

Evenness of productivity, quality, growth

Even allowing for the fact that Mozart belonged to a guild whose membership entailed responsibilities for regular composition, the profile of output is truly arresting. Most artists' lives exhibit periods of ups and downs, of greater fertility and greater fallowness; but Mozart's creative output proved regular and predictable in quantity and quality across decades, virtually independent of what was happening in his personal world or in the wider world. In our time prodigies pass through so-called "midlife crises," as a result of which they cease to perform or compose for a while.[9] Following periods of breakthroughs there are often periods of consolidation. But these blips seem not to have afflicted Mozart. It is almost as if his brain had been set to produce a certain number of melodies and compositions per unit of time, and Mozart had simply followed the dictates of his nervous system. Moreover, for the most part, these compositions were so completely conceived cerebrally that he rarely had to undertake significant revisions. The string quartets may be the exception that proved this rule.

With regularity often comes predictability, if not boredom. What places Mozart in a unique category is the combination of evenness of productivity with work of steadily stunning quality and work that exhibits continued growth and development. An individual familiar with Mozart's mature style (say, after 1778) is able not only to recognize Mozart's work with a high degree of success but also to order Mozart's works with considerable accuracy. There are no sudden breakthroughs or regressions, but rather sustained and steady growth until

9. J. Bamberger, "Growing Up Prodigies: The Midlife Crisis," in Daniel Feldman, ed., *New Directions for Child Development* (San Francisco: Jossey-Bass, 1982), 17.

the very end. No external pressures drove Mozart to greater creativity; if anything, pressures were in the direction of greater mundaneness. It had to be Mozart's own sense of self-challenge, his own delight at the achievement of ever more comprehensive and complex works, that stimulated him over the years.[10] What we do not know is how Mozart would have changed had he lived another decade or two: Would he have become Beethoven or Brahms—or even more Mozartean?

Combination of childlike and adultlike characteristics

It is a virtual convention to remark on the combination of childlike and adultlike traits in creative individuals. Indeed, the biological concept of neoteny suggests that some individuals may be especially prone to retain the properties of the very young later in life. In my study of the creators of the modern era, I was struck by the extent to which the creators seemed mature while still young yet often retained into later life some of the more charming—as well as some of the more problematic—aspects of childhood.

But even when aligned with the childish antics of the elder Picasso, the fascination with puzzles that continued to animate Einstein, or the naked simplicity of the mature Gandhi, Mozart represents an extreme in his amalgam of the young and foolish on one hand with the mature and wise on the other. Of course, playwright Peter Shaffer has made this point central in his controversial *Amadeus*. But one need not have recourse to this work to be struck by the tendency of the grown Mozart to cavort like a small child, to engage in the most sophomoric name-calling, braying, and versifying, to play the bad boy in the salon and on the street.[11] Many individuals fail to grow up. But the same Mozart who wrote ridiculous notes to his cousin Baesle and who grunted like a barnyard animal at salons was able at the age of eleven to spend hours a day studying obscure texts on counterpoint and could compose an opera, *Apollo and Hyacinth,* in which he sensitively depicted homophilic sentiments.

It is tempting to write about this combination of childlike and adultlike behavior by resorting to psychodynamic concepts, but I pre-

10. Mihaly Csikszentmihalyi, *Flow* (New York: HarperCollins, 1990).
11. E. Blom, *Mozart's Letters* (London: Penguin, 1956), 63–64.

fer to think of the eccentric fusion in developmental terms. In my view, something about Mozart's precocious gifts and the severe demands imposed on him by his society jammed up the usual unfolding of developmental milestones. Expected to act like an adult from a very young age, and somehow able to pull off this personal and professional feat, Mozart had to forsake much of the unpressured playful and exploratory private air that is permitted a young child. But one cannot act beyond one's years perpetually; ultimately there will be costs. I see these costs as a stunted emotional development, detectable in other creative individuals, as in the prodigious Picasso, but most flagrantly manifest in the case of Mozart.

Rather than maturing gradually, then, Mozart retained the capacity to act at different ages or developmental stages, though he may not always have been in control of this process. If sometimes painful personally, this flexibility may have conferred a special power on his music. As Sir Charles Stanford commented: "When you are a child, Mozart speaks to you as a child. No music could be more simple, more childlike. But when you are a man, you find to your astonishment that his music, which seemed childlike, is completely adult and mature."[12]

Exquisite personal intelligences

That Mozart was in some measure stunted in the emotional sphere is not in itself surprising. Nor would such immaturity be thought a crippling handicap for most composers, who, after all, are expected to be innovative in the realm of sound. What is astounding, however, is that Mozart became an incomparable composer of *operas*—and one, moreover, with a special genius for characterization. All lovers of Mozart operas have their favorite arias and their most treasured operatic personalities. Suffice it to say that any composer who could capture in music the complex interpersonal ties among the characters in *Le nozze di Figaro*, the flawed personality and pathos of the character of Don Giovanni, and the shifting emotional configurations in *La clemenza di Tito* and *Così fan tutte* was a master of human character, one who

---

12. W. J. Turner, *Mozart: The Man and His Works* (New York: Doubleday, 1956), 316.

merits mention in the same company as Shakespeare, Goethe, or Keats.

To say that Mozart supplemented an expected (if unique) genius in musical intelligence with unanticipated gifts in the personal intelligences is simply to place a new label on what we already knew.[13] The puzzle concerns the source of such knowledge about the world of human beings in an individual who in many ways seemed so immature and so lacking in insight about himself. It is no denigration of Mozart's talents to say that, from early on, he was fascinated by the theater, by legends, by dramatic stories and personalities, and that he was able to master the traditional means of depicting emotions and stock characters: classical heroes, sly servants, hubristic nobles, and the like. These were part of the language of musical characterization of the era.

We have no reason to believe that Mozart possessed special insights into other persons in the manner exhibited by a gifted clinical psychologist, a political leader, or a salesperson. He often misread the effects upon others of his words and his actions, and he was not able to get others to do his bidding. Where Mozart went beyond the formulaic was in his capacity to observe human traits and behaviors *with respect to the artistic issues on his mind*. Then, drawing on these observations and understandings, he was able to capture in his musical creations those aspects of human speech, gesture or manner, and pathos that helped create convincing *individual* characters and *individually* effective works. In my terms, he expertly yoked personal and musical intelligences.

On the edge of modernity

Mozart's unique place in musical history can be readily appreciated if we compare him with Bach and Haydn, on one hand, and with Beethoven and Wagner, on the other. Bach and Haydn clearly belonged to a musical tradition in which one remained at one's assigned post for decades, producing works of quality for specific occasions. Theirs was a calling that involved responding to requests on the part of individuals deemed to occupy a superior social position. Just as clearly, Beethoven and those who followed him saw themselves as belonging

13. Howard Gardner, *Frames of Mind* (New York: Basic Books, 1983).

to a different professional order. They were freestanding artists, members of a guild that generated itself, answerable only to the demands of their own creative genius. To be sure, it was still necessary to earn a living; if one could get others to pay for what one already desired to do, so much the better. But one sought to live on one's own terms as much as possible, and one's calling took second place to no other.

Mozart's rather unhappy professional life serves as an emblem of a broader transition that occurred in the arts in the period between 1750 and 1850. The earlier period, still medieval in temper, was represented by Mozart's father, who saw himself as practicing an honorable trade, and by the events and practices of Mozart's own early years, when the composer sought to please the nobles and clerics of the day. By the latter years of his life, Mozart had turned his back on this ancient version of music-making. As he is said to have once noted with regret, he could no longer compose to satisfy others, so he was henceforth going to compose to satisfy himself. Mozart was not yet in a position to publish his own music, name his own price, or publicly berate those who sought to exploit or pervert his genius for their own gain. But he served as an important transitional figure in laying a foundation of independence and self-initiated creation, a foundation that made possible the studiedly Romantic lives of the Beethovens, the Wagners, and the Liszts who followed him in the next century. Wolfgang Hildesheimer has suggested that Mozart was not the first poor musical artist, but that he was the first free one, and that he was poor as a result of this freedom.[14]

However unusual Mozart may have been as a member of the fraternity of creative individuals, he is certainly unusual as an artist. I cannot imagine a human society where, following a period of familiarization with his music, Mozart would not be appreciated; and I believe that there will be a niche for him so long as human civilization continues. I have no new words for the celestial majesty of Mozart's music. I hope to have helped to place Mozart within the exalted company of creators in which he so clearly belongs by identifying some of the ways in which he resembles others and by noting four dimensions in which he may be distinctive.

14. Wolfgang Hildesheimer, *Mozart* (New York: Farrar, Straus and Giroux, 1982), 19.

As a closing thought, I offer a brief meditation on how the case of Mozart broadens our understanding of giftedness and creativity. To begin with, while there were prodigies before Mozart and there have been many since, it is not an exaggeration to maintain that Mozart defined the phenomenon of prodigiousness for the modern era. Mozart is the standard against which all prodigies are assessed, and this standard-setting goes beyond prodigies of performing and composing to prodigies in other domains. When Stephen Toulmin described Lev Vygotsky as the Mozart of Soviet psychologists, and contrasted him with the Beethoven-like Alexander Luria,[15] educated readers knew instantly what he meant.

Many prodigies do not grow up to become competent adult practitioners, let alone creative geniuses. What it takes to be a phenomenal ten-year-old is quite different from, *and in some ways inimical to,* what it takes to be a phenomenal thirty-year-old. The dutifulness of youth must give way to the grittiness of the adult years. Some prodigies, such as Mendelssohn or Picasso, make the transition. None has made it with the ease or completeness of Mozart. Once again, Mozart defines the genre and remains the standard of comparison.

In our era, it is commonplace to search for links between an individual's personal life history and the events and products of his creative activity. There have been psychobiographies of countless historical personages, and these include more than one study of Mozart.[16] But although Mozart's brief life had its moments of interest, its painful depths, and its occasional heights, all that we know of it provides scant insights into his music. As has often been noted, Mozart could write celebratory music when he was depressed and tragic music when he was elated. His *Jupiter* Symphony was written during a period of poverty, pain, and pessimism. He could work on a composition over many years, but he could also compose on demand.

Mozart remains among the most compelling arguments for respecting the distance between the personal life and the life of the creative mind. He takes a place alongside Shakespeare, Keats, and a few others who were capable of "negative capability"—of submerging their own personalities and entering wholly into the mind and spirit of other

15. Stephen Toulmin, "The Mozart of Psychology," *New York Review of Books,* 25, September 28, 1978, 51–57.

16. A. Esman, "Mozart: A Study in Genius," *Psychoanalytic Quarterly* 20 (1951): 603–12.

persons and other entities.[17] We might even say that, in a manner more reminiscent of a mathematician than of a poet, Mozart was able to submerge his persona throughout his entire musical development and to draw upon his life only to the extent that it served his aesthetic ends. Otherwise, his personal life never intruded.

Finally, Mozart stands out because he signaled, if inadvertently, the end of one major era of Western artistic history and the beginning of another. Until his time, the artist was closer to the artisan, subjugating his personality and his personal agenda to the nature of the assignment in an established genre. Within a decade or two of Mozart's death, the status of the artist had changed forever in the West. Artists defined their own projects and pursued their own agendas; other individuals were expected to accommodate themselves to the muse of each creative artistic genius.

This trend reached its apogee during the age I have been studying—the first decades of this century, the Modern Era. This period witnessed the most dramatic breakthroughs in various artistic and scientific forms—cataclysmic alterations that would have been unthinkable in Mozart's time but that had gradually become conceivable in an era that heard the *Eroica,* the *Symphonie Fantastique,* and the *Ring Cycle;* that saw the canvases of Claude Monet, Georges Seurat, and Paul Cézanne; and that read the texts of Karl Marx, Charles Darwin, and Friedrich Nietzsche.

Between the medieval atelier on one hand and the Romantic garret on the other, I believe that we may have witnessed the range of human creative milieus. In the wake of modernism and its postmodern blip, we have glimpsed the limits on individual breakthroughs—at least those unaided by technology. I suspect that we are reverting to a period in which creative activity will be less individualistic and less iconoclastic, more communal and more continuous with its past.[18]

In contemplating the range of creative stances, we may receive a final insight into the specialness of Mozart. Containing aspects of both traditional and modern forms of creativity, he can be understood and appreciated in an evolutionary as well as a revolutionary age. While at

    17. Walter Jackson Bate, *John Keats* (Cambridge: Harvard University Press, 1963), 260–61.

    18. C. Martindale, *The Clockwork Muse* (New York: Basic Books, 1990), passim.

any moment the stocks of Bach or Palestrina may move in inverse direction from that of Berlioz or Beethoven, Mozart veers equally in both directions. In this sense he is the most universal—as well as the most unique—of creative spirits.

3

Mozart and
the transformational imperative

DAVID HENRY FELDMAN

MY GOAL IS to discuss Mozart from the perspective of one who has spent several years studying child prodigies. My limited background in both music and the Mozart literature prevents me from trying to shed new light on specific questions about his life or work, such as what he might have thought and felt as he walked the narrow streets of Salzburg, what his impressions were as he approached the magnificent portals of the Castle Belvedere in Vienna or sat down to write to his father about his mother's death, or what musical ideas he might have been exploring when composing the Haffner Symphony.

I do not propose new interpretations of the facts, nor do I claim to have unearthed any new ones. My experience studying child prodigies enables me to highlight some features of Mozart's mind and emotions that strike me as noteworthy in relation to what I have seen in other prodigies.

I hope to stick as close to the known facts as possible, and I shall not alter events or change their sequence, as the playwright Peter Shaffer did so artfully in *Amadeus*. And unlike Shaffer and others who have tried to create a fictional Mozart to entertain an audience, I have no need to make my subject more interesting than he was.

I hope, nonetheless, that my interpretations are respectful of the facts as we know them and that they are consistent with what decades of careful scholarship have revealed about Mozart's life. The scholarly literature runs well into the hundreds of works, and I do not presume to claim mastery over even a small part of that literature. And so, given the considerable limitations on what I know (and even on what is more generally known) about Mozart, I shall try to present him neither as the Apollonian god he is often portrayed to be (as in the ridiculous statue in Vienna) nor as the uncouth, raunchy, ignorant, and uncivilized savant of *Amadeus*.[1] At best, I shall be able to capture only a few features of this most elusive of prodigies.

Before turning to the man, let me explain the words "transformational imperative" in my title. For several years I have been trying, as have a number of colleagues, to construct a framework for the investigation of creativity, particularly creativity in extreme cases.[2] One component of that framework is a notion that has been labeled "the transformational imperative," which I believe to be a uniquely human tendency to take intentional liberties with the world, and thereby to change it.

The framework assumes that all human beings participate in some way in this transformational process, although in widely varying ways and to widely varying degrees. It also assumes that some people are more highly disposed to transform than others, and that individuals vary within themselves in the degree to which they desire to transform. That is to say, someone might be very attached to a certain brand of cigar, while at the same time devote great energy to revolutionizing a field or discipline or social order. Freud was apparently like this.

In Mozart's case, I shall explore two manifestations of the transformational imperative that may add to our ability to explain some of the uniqueness of his gifts. The first manifestation is Mozart's inordinately strong tendency toward certain forms of wordplay, particularly the juxtaposition of words and word meanings, a ready flow of verbal doggerel, the transposition of syntactic and semantic rules, and a playful and mischievous orientation toward written language.

Mozart's second transformational tendency is more difficult to describe. It is his seeming sociability and wide involvement in the social

1. Robert Lewis Marshall, "Mozart/Amadeus: Amadeus/Mozart," *Brandeis Review* 5 (1985): 9–16.
2. David Henry Feldman, Mihaly Csikszentmihalyi, and Howard Gardner, *Changing the World: A Framework for the Study of Creativity* (New York: Praeger/Greenwood, 1994).

world, which at the same time he wished to transform. I believe that there was operating in Mozart a desire to transform the social world he so fully participated in, and that his way of trying to do so was through his music, particularly the operas.

It was from an effort to compare Mozart with other prodigy cases that his distinctive ways of manifesting the transformational imperative began to emerge. Mozart is often cited as the greatest prodigy of all time, yet less is known about his early development than the legend of Mozart would suggest. In fact, very little can be said with certainty about Mozart's first three years of life, and relatively little about our subject from ages three to five. For a music prodigy, the years from three to five are almost always crucial.[3] This is in contrast to prodigies in some other fields, such as art or mathematics or writing, in which the emergence of extreme talent does not usually occur until the age of ten or later.

Nonetheless, there is no doubt that Mozart's musical talent appeared early and powerfully. His older sister Nannerl's music lessons (her real name was Marianne) with their musician father probably provided the opportunity for three-year-old Wolfgang to begin playing the clavier and the violin. Once launched, there was, as is typically true in extreme prodigy cases, no stopping the process of musical development.

Prior to age three almost nothing is known about Wolfgang's early development. We know that his mother nearly died in childbirth; he was her seventh child, though only two survived. We also know that the family's general circumstances in Salzburg were modestly comfortable. But modern studies in developmental psychology place critical importance on early experience, and about Mozart's earliest experiences we are largely ignorant. This places a severe constraint on our ability to interpret the case.

What we know with reasonable certainty about the Mozart family and their life in Salzburg begins with Leopold's letters to his family, friends, and business associates during the travels first undertaken when Wolfgang was six and Nannerl was eleven. These tours, designed to promote the children as musical "wonders of God," were often the

3. David Henry Feldman, *Nature's Gambit: Child Prodigies and the Development of Human Potential* (New York: Teachers College Press, 1991).

fate of prodigies in the seventeenth and eighteenth centuries in Europe. As it happened, the musical education the travels provided for the eager young Wolfgang was probably the best that could have been designed at the time. He was exposed to some of the greatest musical talents of his day, he was able to meet and play with several virtuoso performers, and he witnessed the compositional craft as exercised by some of its most able practitioners.

As is true for all prodigies, Mozart's successful development depended upon the marshaling and deployment of specialized resources over several years, a feat that was accomplished *en passant* as the boy and his family made their way from city to city, from religious and noble court to court, and from musical experience to musical experience. Leopold was himself a music teacher of some distinction, and he devoted his full energies to the preparation of his children in music. For most prodigies, having at least one parent devote full time to the child's preparation is a prerequisite to adult success. That Leopold happened to be a gifted music teacher and a musician was fortuitous; no doubt it contributed to Wolfgang's rapid movement into the world of practicing performers and composers.

Leopold's depth of commitment and degree of ambition for son Wolfgang (it became clear quite early that the boy was the more promising musician) led to later complications as Wolfgang struggled to break free from the physical and emotional ties that bound him to his father, a struggle that all children face but that is especially intense and complicated when it is played out in prodigies. Although Peter Shaffer's portrayal of Leopold as a humorless, relentless, meddlesome, and ultimately pathological influence on Wolfgang is overdrawn and in places inaccurate, there is no doubt that he was the most important human influence in Wolfgang's life.

Usually a parent's power is diluted when the prodigy enters the world of his chosen field and becomes attached to his teachers and mentors. Leopold played both roles—parent and mentor—for an unusually long period in Wolfgang's life, and consequently the inevitable breaking away was profoundly difficult for both father and son. By the time most prodigies reach the age of twelve or so, their parents realize that they must give over the child to those who can better help him or her along the way toward adult achievement. In many cases, especially in music, this process begins earlier.

In one of the cases I studied most closely, a musical prodigy some-

times compared with Mozart, the transition from all-powerful parent
to teachers-as-partners had occurred by about age eight.[4] Another
transition took place in this boy about two years later, when he
changed course and began to prepare for a career in violin performance rather than in composition. This led to his emotional and musical
allegiances' being distributed among several teachers. By the time he
was sixteen, Nils Kirkendahl (a pseudonym) was enmeshed in the
world of Juilliard, other musicians, teachers, and students. He no
longer lived at home. Although still very close to his parents, he had
begun a process of separating from them that would make the transition from student to professional musician, from boy to young man,
less abrupt and difficult than was true for Mozart. And indeed,
Kirkendahl has had a relatively smooth entry into the professional
world of the concert violinist.

There are a number of other qualities that Mozart shares with prodigies in music and in other fields. These include: (1) a history of family
interest in, and commitment to, the domain in which the prodigy will
perform (although only one generation's interest in Mozart's case);
(2) being the first-born or only son (although this is changing as more
girls are encouraged to excel in various fields); (3) an ability to focus
energy and maintain a near-total commitment to reach the highest
levels in a domain (in Mozart's case, perhaps most clearly demonstrated in his tendency to compose in spite of tremendous distractions
and pressures, including while his wife gave birth); and (4) a period
of at least ten years of work before performance at the highest levels
is achieved. (Contrary to myth, Mozart's early compositions were not
major works; the first that seems to belong securely to the modern
repertoire is the "little" G Minor Symphony, K. 183, which he wrote
when he was seventeen.)[5] Further, the musical prodigy arouses ambivalence and jealousy, as Mozart surely did among his colleagues in
musical circles of Vienna, and is a mixture of child and adult, as Mozart was all his life, including often in his music.

Without going into detail about each of these qualities, suffice it to
say that Mozart conforms well to the profile of the child prodigy, a
profile that has now become fairly clear as a result of studies of several
cases in and out of music. Of course, Mozart was more than a typical

---

4. Feldman, *Nature's Gambit*, 123–48.

5. H. C. Robbins Landon, ed., *The Mozart Compendium: A Guide to Mozart's Life and
Music* (New York: Schirmer Books, 1990), 392.

child prodigy; he was a composer of transcendent gifts. He did not simply master existing forms in his domain (another feature of prodigies); he gave them new form and meaning through his continuous exploration and innovation.

And so Mozart was and was not a typical prodigy. He was not typical in the fact that he had a successful adult career. Regrettably, most prodigies do not fulfill their promise in adult accomplishment. Even those who do have successful careers generally do not inspire festivals and conferences and concerts and performances all over the world two centuries after their death. As Kurt Pahlen wrote: "Others may reach heaven with their works, but Mozart, he comes, he comes from there!"[6]

Although it is beyond our capability to explain what would lead someone to exclaim that Mozart's music was God's own, two qualities of this prodigy that do stand out may shed some light on why Mozart was different from all other prodigies. These qualities contrast with what is typical in prodigies, if the word "typical" can be used at all in the context of such a rare phenomenon.

Remarkably, there have been few studies of Mozart from within the psychological research community. There is not a single major piece of research on his *development*. Perhaps the field recognized that it was simply not up to the task. With the availability of several recent theoretical and empirical advances, however, it should now be possible to study Mozart without distorting the uniqueness of his story.[7]

Having spent some time in the Mozart literature over the past year, two aspects of Mozart's character struck me, neither of which is characteristic of the child prodigies I have studied.[8] These two qualities may have had something to do with how Mozart approached his mu-

6. Wolfgang Hildesheimer, *Mozart*, trans. Marion Faber (New York: Vintage Books, 1983), 15.

7. Mihaly Csikszentmihalyi, "The Domain of Creativity," in M. Runco and R. Albert, eds., *Theories of Creativity* (Newbury Park: Sage Publications, 1990), 190–212; "Society, Culture, and Person: A Systems View of Creativity," in R. Sternberg, ed., *The Nature of Creativity* (New York: Cambridge University Press, 1988), 325–39; David Henry Feldman, *Beyond Universals in Cognitive Development*, 2d ed. (Norwood: Ablex Publishing, 1994); Howard Gardner, *Frames of Mind* (New York: Basic Books, 1993); Dean Keith Simonton, *Genius, Creativity, and Leadership: Historiometric Inquiries* (Cambridge: Harvard University Press, 1984); Doris Wallace and Howard E. Gruber, *Creative People at Work* (New York: Oxford University Press, 1989).

8. For examples, see Feldman, *Nature's Gambit*.

sical tasks, although I am not qualified to make any direct link. What I can say is that I have not seen these qualities in any other prodigy, musical or otherwise.

Mozart was, first of all, the most social being by far of any prodigy I have encountered. His circle of acquaintances, friends, relatives, associates, colleagues, and cronies far exceeded that of anyone in the literature of extreme talent. Secondly, he was given to making innumerable changes and transformations in speech, writing, and music. He was an inveterate tinkerer, perhaps the greatest musical tinkerer of all time. The first quality, that of seeming sociability, does not in any obvious way bear directly on the nature of his composing, although it may have affected it. His verbal transformational tendencies, though, seem quite directly relevant to his compositional approach.

Neither of the qualities I will be describing is unknown to Mozart scholars. Indeed, it was from wonderfully rich source materials that the two qualities—sociability and verbal transformation—emerged for me. But what is noteworthy is that they are not common qualities of prodigies. It is also true that the two qualities to be emphasized here are not at all straightforwardly interpreted. Was Mozart truly a social being, or was his gregariousness a substitute for or response to something else? To some degree, it appears that Mozart was indeed a very social being, while in other senses he appears isolated from his fellow human beings.

Of his seemingly endless tendency to transform whatever came his way, we may ask whether the tendency can be reconciled with the fact that he apparently invented no new musical forms. Mozart respected both the means of producing music and the various musical forms that were available to him, even as he pushed constantly at the boundaries and limits of what could be achieved through these means and forms.

As we shall see, these two qualities—a kind of extreme sociability on one hand and an unbounded need to transform on the other—led to paradoxical tensions in Mozart's life, paradoxes we shall not be able to resolve but can at least try to describe. The qualities can be illustrated by example.

The first example, revealing both Mozart's wide number of acquaintances and his tendency to verbal transformation, is found in the postscript that he added to his mother's letter to his father, written when Mozart was about to turn twenty-three: "I can't write anything sensible today, as I am rails off the quite. Papa be annoyed not must. I that just like today feel. I help it cannot. Warefell. I gish you good wight. Sound sleeply. Next time I'll sensible more writely."[9] The rest of the postscript mocks the prevailing custom of sending greetings to virtually every acquaintance, providing a good example of Mozart's playful yet searing humor and his tendency to generate variations:

If I could find some more room, I would send 100,000 compliments from us 2, I mean, from us two, to all our good friends: particularly to the A's:—the Adlgassers, Adretters and Arco (Count); B's:—Herren Bullinger, Barisant and Berantzky; C's:—Czernin (Count), Cusetti and the three organ pumpers [*Calcanten*]; D's:—Herren Daser, Deibl and Dommeseer; E's:—Mlle Barbara Eberlin, Herr Estlinger and all the asses [*Eslin*] in Salzburg; F's:—Firmian (Count and Countess and their little molly-coddle), young Franz and the Freihof of St. Peter's; G's:—Mlle, Mme and the two MM. Gilowsky and the Councillor too; also Herren Gretry and Gablerbrey; H's:—the Haydns, the Hagenauers, Theresa Hollbrey: J's:—Joli (Miss Sallerl), Herr Janitsch the fiddler and Hagenauer's Jakob; K's:—Herr and Frau von Kusinger, Count and Countess Kuhnburg and Herr Kassel; L's:—Baron Lehrbach, Count and Countess Lutzow, Count and Countess Lodron; M's:—Herren Meisner, Medlhammer and Moserbrey; N's:—Nannerl, our court ninny, Father Florian, and all night watchmen; O's:—Count Oxensturn, Herr Oversee and all the oxen in Salzburg: P's:—the Prexes, Count Prank, the Lord High Cook, and Count Perusa; Q's:—Herren Quilibet, Quodlibet and all quacks; R's—Father Florian Reichsigel, the Robinigs, and Maestro Rust; S's:—Herren Suscipe, Seiffert and all the sows in Salzburg: T's:—Herr Tanzerberger, our butcher, Theresa and all trumpeters; U's:—the towns of Ulm and Utrecht and all the clocks [*Uhren*] in Salzburg, especially if you put an H in at the beginning; W's:—the Weisers, Hans the Wurstmaker and Woferl; X's:—Xantippe, Xerxes and all whose names begin with an X; Y's:—Herr Ypsilon, Herr Ybrig and all whose names begin with a Y; and lastly, Z's:—Herr Zabuesnig, Herr Zonca and Herr Zezi at the castle. Addio. If I had room I would write something more, at least my compliments to my good friends. But it is impossible, for I don't know where I could work them in.[10]

9. Hildesheimer, *Mozart*, 115.
10. Hildesheimer, *Mozart*, 114–15.

Remember that Mozart had to put all of this down on paper with a quill pen. It must have taken the better part of an hour just to write it out; given his facility, it probably was done on the fly. Mozart must have felt pleasure in the sheer absurdity and wackiness of the exercise he had laid out for himself. And he carried it through to completion, from *A* to *Z*. Once launched on this zany course, Mozart sustained it to the end.

There are many other examples of association chains in Mozart's writing, barely harnessed into semi-coherence. As Wolfgang Hildesheimer says:

> His active verbal fantasy comes to dominate, triggered by the slightest excuse. His compulsive delight and ease in association are capable not only of producing euphony and rhythm with disparate and seemingly arbitrary combinations of sound but also of keeping the connotations always in mind. In writing he yields himself up to the flow of words, going far beyond the comprehensible, reveling on, intoxicated by the sounds and the continually changing meanings they suggest.[11]

Mozart seemed to have an almost boundless enthusiasm for variation, juxtaposition, elaboration, surprising shifts of meaning, and unexpected twists and turns of phrase.

I am of course not the first to remark on Mozart's verbal prankishness, nor on the connection between his letter writing and his music. Hildesheimer, among others, has made quite a point of it. If there is something to be added, it is simply that this connection is very *unusual* among prodigies. More typically, a prodigy's performance within his or her domain stands quite apart from other qualities of mind, or at least it seems to. What is striking about Mozart is that the tendency to alliterate, generate transformations, transpose, and twist meanings seems to have parallels in his musical inventions. Reciprocally, his letters—especially those in which he is called upon to respond to crisis or pressure—often seem to resemble not genuine responses but musical compositions with stock passages. To my knowledge, there is no other case in the literature with this specific profile.

As mental abilities go, Mozart's capacity to generate and transform would seem quite modest but for the fact that this very ability has been used as a measure of creativity for the past forty years in the field

11. Hildesheimer, *Mozart*, 119.

of creativity research. These so-called creativity tests have had little success, however, and do not seem to be able to predict real-world creative performance with any significant degree of accuracy.[12]

A typical question on one of these tests might be: "How many ways can you think of to use a paper clip?" or "Suppose the world were covered with fog and you could see only people's feet. What would be the consequences?" The ability measured in one of these tests is called verbal fluency, a kind of rapid-fire facility with generating alternatives. People who do well on this test not only tend to be facile with words but also seem to have a critical, sarcastic, mocking attitude toward established rules and customs. We can imagine Mozart, in the right mood (say after a good game of billiards), setting records for performance on this test.

It is puzzling that Mozart seems to provide new evidence that an all but discredited test for creativity is valid after all. But we can solve the puzzle if we recognize that Mozart's verbal facility was an *adjunct* to his musical talent—was harnessed to it—rather than the wellspring of that ability. If Mozart had verbal faculties alone, we might continue to enjoy his limericks or know about his Jabberwocky, but we would not be celebrating the majestic compositions that are still being played throughout the world.

It should be emphasized that, in Mozart's case at least, his unbounded verbal facility reflected a remarkable tendency toward transformation using existing grammatical rules, analogues of which can probably be found in his compositions. Even though verbal facility *per se* is not tantamount to creativity, as the tests assert, this ability can be of real value when wedded to a great talent for music. Since there is at least a partial analogue between musical composition and speech— that is, both are made up of many single units tied together intricately and sequentially—some of the abilities that are used in one can be used in the other. Mozart was sometimes criticized for producing music that was too intricate and unusually complicated, that had "too many notes," as Emperor Joseph said, a characteristic consistent with verbal fluency.

For all his verbal facility, however, Mozart's actual writing, in what-

12. David Henry Feldman, "Faulty Construction," *Contemporary Psychology* 15 (1970): 3–4; also Michael A. Wallach, "Creativity Testing and Giftedness," in F. D. Horowitz and M. O'Brien, eds., *The Gifted and Talented: Developmental Perspectives* (Washington, D.C.: American Psychological Association, 1985), 99–123.

ever form, does not compare with his music. His poetry, for example, was amateurish, as is revealed by this poem written when his pet starling died:

> A little fool lies here
> Whom I held dear—
> A starling in the prime
> Of his brief time,
> Whose doom it was to drain
> Death's bitter pain.
> Thinking of this, my heart
> Is riven apart.
> Oh, reader! Shed a tear,
> You also, here.
> He was not naughty, quite,
> But gay and bright,
> And under all his brag
> A foolish wag.
> This no one can gainsay.
> And I will lay
> That he is now on high,
> And from the sky,
> Praises me without pay
> In his friendly way.
> Yet unaware that death
> Has choked his breath,
> And thoughtless of the one
> Whose rime is thus well done.
>   Mozart, June 4, 1781[13]

Even allowing for awkwardness in translation, it is difficult to imagine that we are dealing here with the same mind that ten days later wrote *Ein musikalischer Spass* ("A Musical Joke"), K. 522, a tour de force that caricatures the most prominent composers of the day. He was also at the time working on the score of *Don Giovanni*.

And so we must distinguish between a set of capabilities that can be *used* in the service of more profound purposes, as was the case with Mozart, and these same abilities being identified with the creative

---

13. Hildesheimer, *Mozart*, 206–7.

process itself. Mozart's transformational tendencies were powerful and pervasive, and these tendencies made a significant contribution to his overall ability to compose. But it was his unparalleled musical facility, his ability to generate music as naturally as the rest of us generate speech, that made it possible for his broader transformational talents to be put to good use.

Let me turn to the second striking discrepancy that sets Mozart apart from other prodigies. He was perhaps the most *social* prodigy of all time. This contrasts with the other cases I have studied, in which the children and their families tend to be all but cloistered; the parents carefully and often warily control contact from the outside. There is a kind of bunker mentality that sometimes pervades the households of several of my cases. This condition of social isolation was also evident in Michael Deakin's account of a family of four prodigies in his book *The Children on the Hill*.[14]

Especially during the earliest years, families of prodigies tend to see their role as one of organizing and directing the course of the child's preparation in the chosen domain. This requires careful control of access and vigilant surveillance of those who are allowed access. I sometimes felt that parents of my prodigy subjects believed they could not afford to make a wrong move—that they bore a tremendous responsibility to protect and nurture their children's exceptional talent, and that there were few outsiders whom they could bring safely into the inner circle.

The Mozarts as a family stand in stark contrast to this image, and Wolfgang in particular appears to be almost singularly gregarious among the great talents of Western civilization. The family lived in Salzburg near St. Peter's Church, a center of social, religious, and commercial activity (an open-air market still operates in the courtyard between the house where Mozart was born and the church), and enjoyed frequent contact with people in many walks of life. They were on particularly good terms with the owners of their house, the Hagenauer family. From quite reliable accounts of what life in the city was then like, one gets a sense of a vital and close community, albeit one with a clear social hierarchy.

Although Leopold was unremittingly ambitious, as parents of prod-

---

14. Michael Deakin, *The Children on the Hill* (Indianapolis: Bobbs-Merrill, 1972).

igies tend to be, and although he devoted his life to promoting his son's development and career, as such parents must do, the level of sociability in this particular case is highly unusual. Leopold of course knew that Wolfgang's success depended upon securing audiences and establishing relationships with the nobility and with church leaders, and he assiduously courted every avenue of access. Mozart's father was fairly skillful at social interaction and derived satisfaction from his ability to make his way upward toward the more privileged classes in Salzburg and then in all of Europe.

The Mozart family was solidly middle class and well established when Wolfgang was born in 1756, and it remained so throughout his life. Indeed, contrary to the legend that Mozart died in poverty, he enjoyed a comfortable bourgeois life right up to the time of his death. Mozart expected to live well, and sometimes did so in spite of not having sufficient resources to support his tastes in expensive clothes, horses, and sweets. Part of this tendency to enjoy the creature comforts of the day (we might describe it as upper-middle-class today) was a continuous set of social activities.

Mozart's social life was almost dizzying at times. He did not always enjoy the many social events and obligations he participated in, especially when he was unhappiest in Salzburg and looking for a way to escape to Vienna or almost anywhere else. But whether these occasions were endured or enjoyed, Mozart's life was filled with people to a degree not seen in any other prodigy case.

To convey the flavor of what daily life was like for Mozart at two different times—one when he was busy, happy, and productive, the other when he was miserable and less productive—consider two excerpts taken from his Vienna letters. The first was written on December 28, 1782, during the period when he had successfully launched his career as an independent performer, teacher, and composer:

> Mon Très Cher Père!
> I must write in the greatest haste, as it is already half past five and I have asked some people to come here at six for a little concert. Altogether, I have so much to do that often I do not know whether I am on my head or my heels. I spend the whole forenoon giving lessons until two o'clock, when we have lunch. After the meal I must give my stomach an hour for digestion. The evening is therefore the only time I have for composing and of that I can never be

sure, as I am often asked to perform at concerts. [The rest of the letter deals with musical matters.][15]

We see clearly in this excerpt, and in numerous letters written during these years, that Mozart was caught up in the musical world of Vienna, which was itself highly social. These were probably his happiest years.

His last two years in Salzburg were an earlier and less happy period. Following are excerpts from his sister Nannerl's diary, which he himself took over writing occasionally, with devilishly comic consequences. As we shall see, there are signs of Mozart's transforming and transposing tendencies, along with his signature mocking humor. Here are some passages written between August 13 and August 21, 1780, when he was twenty-four:

The 12th: at half past eight, church. Then to Lodron and Mayr. Afternoon Katherl at our house. And Fiala. Thunderstorms and heavy rain.

The 13th: at 10 o'clock to the cathedral for the 10:00 Mass. Then to Surgeon-Katherl's. Herr Wirtenstadter contributed the target. Barber-Katherl won. Played Tarot cards with the Tarot cards. At 7 o'clock took a walk in the Mirabell gardens just the way, in the Mirabell gardens, one takes a walk, as one take it, took, as one takes. Rainy, but no rain. Little by little . . . the skies clear! . . .

The 17th: at 9 o'clock to church. At Lodrons' and Mayrs'. Afternoon at Katherl Gylofsky's. My brother came with Schachtner. Afterward, Papa came too. Rain. With Katherl at the home of Mlle the Saint, who picks her nose with her big toe.

The 42nd: at half past 8, to Gylofsky. To the cathedral. At 10 o'clock to Lodron. At 3 o'clock we three went to watch bowling at the Stieblbrau. At half past five a walk. Fine weather. Birds of a feather.

The 52nd: at the Augustiner. At 1 to church 7 o'clock went. Lodron at our house in the afternoonish. We went to Fiala's. At 3 o'clock six of us went walking, welking, wulking, wolking, wilking. It day a fine was.

The 62nd: apud the contessine de Lodron. Alle dieci e demi I was in the templo. Afterward at Mayrs'. Post prandium signorina Catherine chez us. We havemus joues Tarot cards. At sept heures we

15. Emily Anderson, ed., *The Letters of Mozart and His Family* (New York: W. W. Norton, 1966), 476.

took a walk in the horto aulico. We had the most pulchras tempestas imaginable.

The 72nd: at 10 o'clock in the cathedral. Heard the 10:00 and 10:30 Masses. Afterward paid a call on the Robinings. Fiala contributed the target, I won. Played Tarot cards. At quarter past six Count Thurn at our house. At 7 o'clock took a walk with Papa and Bimperl. Fine weather. A bit of rain in the afternoon. But then fine again. A party and music in Mirabell today. At 10 o'clock Pinsker and two violists played a *Nachtmusik* for us.

The 82nd: a half to niney, blow one out behindy in church. At quarter past nine, blow one out behindy at Mayrs'. The Chief Purveyor. Afternoon to Lodron's. Young Weyrother at our house. At half past five took a walk in the Dietrichruhe gardens. Fine weather.[16]

Although there are other things of interest in these passages, including Mozart's well-known preoccupation with digestive functions and scatological humor, they convey the variety and frequency of Mozart's social contacts (technically, his sister's contacts in the present example). During this period, Mozart found his social obligations increasingly burdensome, his professional duties oppressive, and his life very much in need of changing. But the changes he desired did not reduce his social contacts; they only reconfigured them and moved them to a new venue.

Another way of making the point about the extensive social world within which Mozart functioned is to note that, in the introduction to a list of the major characters in Mozart's life that appeared in the book *The Mozart Compendium,* Malcolm Boyd wrote: "Mozart enjoyed a wide circle of friends, acquaintances, relatives, colleagues and pupils—so wide, indeed, that one sometimes wonders how he found time to compose."[17]

There follows a list of about 150 family names, from Adamberger to Yppold. Since a family name often included several individual members, the list actually includes several hundred entries. Clearly, Mozart's circle was wide. His music was always central, of course, but the musical world he participated in—and to some degree constructed—was a highly social one.

16. Hildesheimer, *Mozart,* 134–35.
17. Malcolm Boyd in Robbins Landon, ed., *The Mozart Compendium,* 41.

This apparent sociability in Mozart must be balanced against what seem to be peculiar relationships with people. Wolfgang Hildesheimer's well-known biography, although deservedly controversial,[18] is perhaps best when it deals with Mozart's lack of social understanding, his naiveté, and his blindness to the inappropriate. Despite its being speculative, much of Hildesheimer's report is plausible, at least to this observer of prodigies and other extremely gifted cases. Hildesheimer writes, "He [Mozart] himself, however, never had sufficient sensitivity to assess how people responded to him. Approachability and inaccessibility were qualities that Mozart did not register in his relationships; in the realm of human contact he was always a helpless foreigner."[19] Another of his observations reinforces this point: "Mozart's reticence about personalities is so striking that it inclines us to think he saw in his fellow-man only what was relevant to him, the musical side of the personality."[20] And finally: "In Paris he became an adult (if we can apply that term to him), and as an adult he did not have any deep ties to others, except, later on, to his wife, Constanze."[21]

There are also many examples of Mozart's misunderstanding of social situations. For example, he routinely overestimated how impressed people were with his work, or how loyal, committed, or reliable they were. Inappropriate requests and outrageous replies to his father are legion. These included a request for support of a trip to Italy with Aloysia Weber and a truly out-of-touch response to his father's objections to his plan to marry Aloysia's sister, Constanze.

Even his relationship with Constanze, which was without question very significant to Mozart, is not straightforward. It appears, as Hildesheimer suggests, that he decided he must fall in love with Constanze. His too-pure, self-imposed code of honor and his naiveté allowed him to be put in a compromising position by Constanze's mother. A misguided sense of responsibility, along with his powerful emotional and sexual need to be close to *someone,* led Mozart to become the self-appointed protector and savior of the Weber family.

From these feelings, and no doubt others, Mozart built a set of attitudes, beliefs, and practices that he followed as if they defined a

18. Cf. Maynard Solomon, review of *Mozart* by Wolfgang Hildesheimer, *Musical Quarterly* 69 (1983): 270–79.

19. Hildesheimer, *Mozart,* 95.
20. Hildesheimer, *Mozart,* 26.
21. Hildesheimer, *Mozart,* 75.

role in one of his operas. He created the role of adoring and attentive husband, and he tried his best, in his fashion, to play it. By all accounts, he played it well.

But what did it all mean to Mozart? The question is very difficult to answer. I suspect that Hildesheimer is not far off when he says that Mozart was a "helpless foreigner" in the world of human relationships. If so, why was he so thoroughly involved in social affairs, and why was his set of social relationships as rich and complex and apparently important to him as it was?

These questions are beyond our ability to answer, but Mozart's passion for opera may at least provide a clue. It is well known that he wanted most to write opera. To compose in that genre, one must have some experience with the social world. Because Mozart's own sensibilities and aspirations (although not always his behavior) were those of a pure-hearted, idealistic, and noble man of the highest honor, and because he wanted his opera scores to reflect some of those ideals, he could not achieve his goals in isolation from others, however distant he may have felt from them.

There were of course many practical reasons for Mozart to learn how to function in the world. His success as a musician depended upon appropriate, well-crafted interactions with those who controlled musical resources and set artistic policy. Contrary to the image portrayed in *Amadeus,* Mozart tried hard to behave properly. Only when it came to music did he find it nearly impossible to compromise and to control his behavior. It would not have occurred to him that anyone would have expected otherwise or been offended by his musical judgments, however harsh.

What seems true is that Mozart was so pure of heart and spirit, so extreme in his sense of duty and honor, so canonical in his sense of good and evil and right and wrong, so susceptible to flattery, so completely certain of his musical sensibilities, and so guided by the distilled emotions of music, particularly of opera, that he experienced the social world in a decidedly peculiar way. It was as if Mozart looked out at the world through eyes that perceived only the simplified and somewhat contrived emotions of opera, and behaved as if opera conveys how the social world actually functions.

Herein lies another paradox. If Mozart was the most social of prodigies—someone who needed constant social contact to sustain his musical momentum—he was also possibly the least able to make his way in the world. When he broke with his father and moved to Vienna (as he inevitably had to do), he lost contact with the only voice that could have guided him in a world he had experienced only obliquely. Without the compass his father provided (however heavy-handedly), and because Constanze was either unable or unwilling to replace Leopold in this role, Mozart most likely became increasingly unable to negotiate his way among his fellow human beings.

The composing went on, of course, and several of the splendid operas were written during the later Vienna years: *Don Giovanni, Così fan tutte,* and *Die Zauberflöte.* Yet consider this letter to Constanze sent from Vienna to Baden on June 12, 1791:

> Dearest, Most Beloved Little Wife!
> Now why did I not get a letter from you last night? So that you might keep me even longer in anxiety about your baths? This and something else spoilt the whole of yesterday for me. I went to see N. N. in the morning, who promised me, parole d'honneur, to call on me between twelve and one in order to settle up everything. So I could not lunch with Puchberg, but had to wait at home. Well, I waited until half past two. He never came, so I sent a note to his father by our servant. Meanwhile I went off to the "Ungarische Krone," as it was too late to get lunch anywhere else; even there I had to take my meal *alone,* as all the guests had already left. You can imagine the sort of lunch I had, worried as I was about you and annoyed with N. N. If only I had someone to console me a little. It is not at all good for me to be alone, when I have something on my mind.[22]

There is little question that Mozart needed companionship, that he drew sustenance from those around him. Nor is there any question that he was an attentive husband and father. What is not so clear is how his contacts with others played themselves out in his composer's mind. Here we can note only that he was more extreme in his need for social contact than most people, and among great composers he was the most social of all. It seems reasonable to suppose that his sociability, however peculiar, must have had some impact on his compositional processes.

---

22. Anderson, ed., *The Letters of Mozart,* 954.

But it is also possible that Mozart's relations with people were incidental to his composing. There are certainly those who believe that he carried on his work regardless of what was happening in his life, and that his compositional output was unaffected by the events going on around him. If this is so, then Mozart's extreme sociability can be seen as a distinctive quality of his personality, important because it is Mozart we are talking about, yet unimportant in relation to his unique musical gifts. But because there are so few clues to the mystery of Mozart's genius, and because he was so different from other composers in displaying an extravagant (if somewhat strange) sociability, this line of inquiry merits attention in the future.

It was the French cultural anthropologist Claude Lévi-Strauss who observed that we know next to nothing about the difference between those many minds that do not "secrete music" and the very few that do. Why someone would find it necessary to create music is a question we are unable to answer well at any level. If we are not able to explain why *anyone* composes, even less can we explain why the music of this one man, Mozart, has captured a permanent place in our hearts and stands among our civilization's most treasured artifacts.

It was also Lévi-Strauss who asserted that modern science crumbles when faced with the challenge of explaining music. He added that explaining the impact of music is the most significant challenge facing the scientific and scholarly communities, for the explanation of music is a prerequisite to progress in all disciplines. It can be ignored no longer. In his words: "Music itself [is] the supreme mystery of the science of man, a mystery that all the various disciplines come up against and which holds the key to their progress."[23]

In sum, then, we have seen how the study of exceptionally gifted individuals can help provide a context for the study of a particular extreme case. By comparing what is known about child prodigies in music and other fields with what is known about Mozart, it becomes possible to see two qualities that set him apart from other prodigies. Whether these two qualities—an extreme tendency to transform words and meanings in writing, and an extreme sociability that resulted in imaginary social worlds—help explain Mozart's uniqueness remains to

---

23. Claude Lévi-Strauss, *The Raw and the Cooked*, trans. John and Doreen Weightman (New York: Harper and Row, 1969), 18.

be seen. Of course, they do not begin to explain why Mozart was blessed with compositional talents of perhaps unprecedented range and delicacy. We may feel we know Mozart a bit better after considering these characteristics, but we have hardly begun to understand how and why he composed, much less how and why he composed so magnificently.

4

On the economics of musical composition in Mozart's Vienna

WILLIAM J. BAUMOL AND HILDA BAUMOL

Perhaps in this neglected spot is laid / Some heart once pregnant with celestial fire, / Hands, that the rod of empire might have sway'd, / Or wak'd to extasy the living lyre.

Thomas Gray, "Elegy Written in a Country Church Yard"

Believe me, my sole purpose is to make as much money as possible; for after good health it is the best thing to have.

Mozart to his father, Vienna, April 4, 1781

THE PRIMARY OBJECT of this chapter is to help explain the extraordinary confluence of composers whose activities centered in Vienna around Mozart's time.[1] These included Gluck, Haydn, Dittersdorf, Salieri, Beethoven, Schubert, and, of course, Wolfgang Amadeus Mozart. We shall suggest some possible reasons for this phenomenon and describe the underlying economic causes that had a profound effect on music and musicians, taking particular note of the

1. We are deeply grateful for comments and suggestions to Edward T. Cone, Timothy Guinnane, Richard Kapp, Arno Mayer, John J. McCusker, and Maynard Solomon. We are particularly indebted to Dr. Julia Moore, who saved us from some embarrassing mistakes on matters musical or historical—fields in which our standing is strictly that of amateurs (in both the original and the current senses of the word). Of course, none of these can be held responsible for our conclusions, and Dr. Moore in particular takes a different view from us on Mozart's finances. We are also very much indebted to New York University's C. V. Starr Center for Applied Economics for facilitating our work on this chapter.

economic and political climate that characterized Mozart's period of residence in Vienna—the decade 1781–91. Finally, we have been unable to resist some discussion of several recent revisionist targets, in particular the denial by a number of scholars of the widely held vision of a Mozart beset by grinding poverty.

Our central purpose, however, is to help account for the period's extraordinary abundance of musical talent. Why at the end of the eighteenth century? Why in the Holy Roman Empire and its associated lands (the Germanic states, Bohemia, Hungary, and Italy)?

Obviously, economic and political conditions cannot create talent, but they certainly can either inhibit it or provide opportunities for its exercise. Our main hypothesis is intended to narrow the pertinent geography—to account for the striking level of composing activity emanating from Germany and Italy. This hypothesis suggests that the political division of the Holy Roman Empire and the Habsburg possessions into many petty states worked to produce the circumstances (notably substantial demand and a profusion of jobs) that help to explain the profusion of musical productivity. It is our secondary hypothesis that in the Empire, as in England and France, the rising prosperity of the eighteenth century—the first stirrings of the industrial revolution and associated developments such as the rise in the wealth and position of the small body of the bourgeoisie as consumers of culture—contributed to the demand that underlay the creation of a free market in musical composition. Through this development, demand helped to elicit supply.

Although much private support continued, the composer was beginning to take control of his own professional life. By the second half of the eighteenth century, demand for the work of the composer derived from two sources: the continued patronage of royalty and nobility, and the emerging free market. The resulting availability of employment opportunities served to attract into the profession many who would otherwise have sought to earn a living elsewhere. Among this profusion of composers many, predictably, proved to have no outstanding talent. But among the group there were the few who, as the poet put it, might otherwise have been "born to blush unseen and waste their sweetness on the desert air."

The last ten years of Mozart's life, the period when he lived in Vienna, are arguably one of the most dramatic periods in history. The decade encompassed the end of the American Revolution, the adoption of the Constitution of the United States, the widely accepted date of the beginnings of the industrial revolution in England (including the development of Watt's improved steam engine), and the first years of the French Revolution. Its intellectual life was shaped by such luminaries as Rousseau, Voltaire, Franklin, Hume, Samuel Johnson, Adam Smith, Goethe, and Schiller.

Germany, as a result of its fragmentation, had a comparative advantage in the supply of two products: composers and royalty. It contributed a striking number of European monarchs of great ability, domineering personalities with at least nominal allegiance to the ideas of the Enlightenment: Gustav III of Sweden,[2] Catherine the Great of Russia, Frederick the Great of Prussia, and, by no means least, Joseph II of Austria, Mozart's emperor. But that was by no means all. George III of England derived from Hanover, as everyone knows, and while Louis XVI was obviously not (primarily)[3] Teutonic, his queen, Marie Antoinette, was the younger sister of Joseph II.

Despite their great inherited power, the monarchs' efforts to hold together a liberalized modification of the old order were to be undermined by the French Revolution and other disturbing circumstances. The enlightened rulers sought to preserve their vestiges of absolute power by using the bourgeoisie as a counterpoise to the aristocracy, whose influence they sought to curtail. The bourgeoisie, somewhat expanded and enriched by the first stirrings of the industrial revolution, though still very small in number by modern standards (see below), used this opportunity to acquire for themselves benefits suited to the wealth they were accumulating.

Economic historians suggest that considerable portions of the Habsburg territories, and the Austrian lands in particular, which included Vienna, were highly prosperous at the end of the eighteenth century, at least in relative terms. Their per capita incomes were probably well ahead of Brandenburg (Prussia), and very likely higher than France. Only England and the Low Countries may have been in a superior

2. The assassination victim of Verdi's *Un ballo in maschera*.
3. Of course, royal marriage patterns made it difficult to say of any monarch that he had no significant amount of German blood. Among the ancestors of Louis XVI there was, for example, Anne of Austria, wife of Louis XIII and mother of the Sun King, she whose association with the Duke of Buckingham is the focus of *The Three Musketeers*.

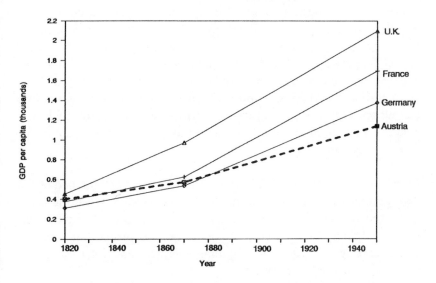

Figure 4.1. Per capita GDP of the United Kingdom, France, Germany, and Austria in 1970 dollars, 1820–1950. (Source: Maddisson 1982, 8)

position. As Figure 4.1 shows, according to Maddison's widely respected estimates[4] (which, unfortunately, begin only in 1820), Austria's relative prosperity continued well into the nineteenth century, and it fell behind only as the industrial revolution gathered full steam in France and Germany. Here it is important to recognize that, in each country where it occurred, "the" industrial revolution was a gradual process for which there is no defensible starting date. In England, some historians argue, it had its beginnings at least as early as the seventeenth century, and probably before that, so the conventional starting date of about 1760 has little significance. In Austria, it is supposed not to have been under way until well into the nineteenth century, but that too is at best valid only as a suggestive characterization.

Austria is reported to have been, in Mozart's time, one of the largest iron producers in Europe (easily outproducing England), and to have had the largest single ironworks in the world, as well as the most

4. Angus Maddison, *Phases of Capitalist Development* (New York: Oxford University Press, 1982), 8.

important textile firm in central Europe.[5] Such sources brought great wealth to well-placed members of the nobility and the small group of the upper bourgeoisie of Vienna and the nearby territories, among them Hungary and Bohemia (including Prague). They spent liberally, running their courts and mansions in a lavish style that included the services of many composers and performers. At the same time, because real wages, and those of musicians in particular, were relatively low, a given real expenditure could purchase much more than today in the way of musician service.

Mozart's emperor, Joseph II, was perhaps the most enlightened of the "enlightened despots" of the era.[6] Like Frederick the Great, he was a dedicated amateur performer of chamber music, but, unlike the latter, Joseph admired German culture and sought to promote it—for example, through his efforts to encourage German opera at the expense of the fashionable opera of Italy.

Joseph's remarkable measures of liberalism included an attempt to introduce universal and compulsory education, virtual abolition of censorship, steps toward the ending of serfdom, (near) abolition of the death penalty, and elimination of the most oppressive restrictions upon Protestants and Jews. Had the emperor not had a fatal attraction to military activity (probably stimulated by admiration and envy of Frederick the Great), for which he apparently had little talent, he might have been remembered universally as a prime contributor to the spread of the rule of law and modern standards of freedom and public welfare. Unfortunately, the Turkish war, his Vietnam, proved fatal to him, to his achievements, and to his reputation. The war, incidentally, was probably responsible in part for Mozart's financial difficulties during his two very troubled years, 1789–90 (the years when Mozart repeatedly sought to borrow money), his income having been made precarious when the emperor and part of the music-supporting nobility left Vienna, at least some of them for the front. Concurrently, a sharp but short-lived inflation that may have doubled prices (Figure 4.2) is likely to have cut severely into the purchasing power of Mozart's income.[7]

5. David P. Good, *The Economic Rise of the Hapsburg Empire 1750–1914* (Berkeley: University of California Press, 1984), 20–21.

6. See, e.g., S. K. Padover, *The Revolutionary Emperor* (New York: R. O. Ballou, 1934).

7. Figure 4.2 is based on information from Mary Sue Morrow, *Concert Life in Haydn's*

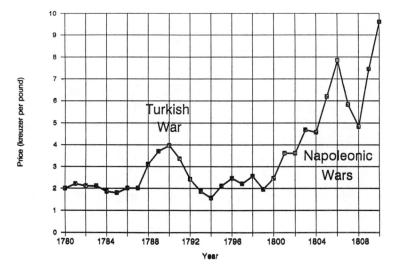

Figure 4.2. Bread prices in Vienna, 1780–1810. One florin = 60 kreuzer. (Source: Morrow 1989, 115)

Despite his enlightenment, Joseph retained a degree of despotism and felt it appropriate to intervene in a variety of activities in ways that hardly contributed to his popularity. Though he intended to abolish the death penalty, when a nobleman was found to have killed an old woman for her wealth, Joseph condemned the murderer to an execution medieval in its cruelty. He prohibited ballet during opera performances (though he was persuaded, apparently by da Ponte, to

Vienna: Aspects of a Developing Musical and Social Institution (Stuyvesant, N.Y.: Pendragon Press, 1989), 115. Figure 4.2 reports only the price of bread, serving, *faute de mieux,* as a crude indicator of inflation. Unfortunately, Julia Moore's excellent index of food and rent prices in "Beethoven and Musical Economics" (Ph.D. dissertation, University of Illinois, 1987), surely as accurate as the surviving data permit, begins only in 1790. The use of bread prices is particularly suspect since, as in some other countries in Europe at the time, bread prices were controlled by government because rising bread prices often threatened disorder and revolution. However, this suggests that the rise in bread prices during the Turkish war is apt to provide an underestimate of the general rate of the war inflation, with the government permitting a doubling in bread prices only when it could no longer hold them back. This suggestive use of bread price is the only way that Figure 4.2 is employed in this chapter. Its sole purpose is to apply, to Mozart, Moore's cogent argument about Beethoven—that one cannot understand his real income without taking into account the role of inflation.

make an exception for *Le nozze di Figaro*). He forbade the wearing of corsets for reasons of health and, for the same reasons, promulgated the highly unpopular restrictions on burial practices that apparently form the basis for the legend that Mozart was given a "pauper's burial," a subject we shall consider in slightly more detail later.

Characteristically prudent in his expenditures, Joseph seems to have had a strong desire to keep Mozart in Vienna, but to do so at the lowest possible expense. So although he rewarded Mozart with commissions and a stipend, they seem not to have been overly generous.

During Mozart's decade in Vienna, the city was probably the largest and the wealthiest in the German lands. Still, its population of nearly a quarter of a million was only about half that of Paris and less than one-fourth of London's. Vienna then had somewhat fewer inhabitants than Baton Rouge or Rochester or Tampa has today. As the location of the main court of the Holy Roman Emperor, the city attracted both nobility and ambitious members of the rising bourgeoisie—and that, in turn, meant business opportunities for composers, tradesmen, and others who served the wealthy, as well as for those who provided goods and services to the latter in the multiplier chain of expenditure.

Vienna lagged behind other capitals in forming societies organized for the purpose of presenting public concerts, and it lacked an adequate concert hall. Instead, the Viennese depended on the two imperial theaters. The leading one was the *Burgtheater*, which probably held between 1,600 and 1,700 persons (the Haymarket in London is reputed to have held 4,000), and the other, smaller one was the *Kärntnerthortheater*. Both were "under the jurisdiction, at least theoretically, of the Emperor. Their connection with concert history derives from the fact that religious practice dictated that no staged drama, spoken or sung, be presented during Advent and Lent."[8] The custom arose of providing musical performances during those periods as a substitute for the usual presentations of drama, and thus, in Vienna, music performances were presented at these premises only six weeks of the year, and musicians had to make do with much smaller makeshift rooms and parks for the rest of the year.

For whatever reasons, by the end of the century musical salons were the basis of musical life in Vienna. This included the significant dil-

8. Morrow, *Concert Life in Haydn's Vienna*, 38.

ettante movement, in which amateurs from various social strata, including the very highest, gave music performances and often hired professionals (Mozart among them) to participate. There was much music-making in the home at all economic levels and at gala occasions, and professional musicians were hired by those who could afford them to provide after-dinner music and other services.

The sizes of the special groups from which consumers of musical services were largely drawn have been estimated. Moore cites Johann Pezzl's estimate that the aristocracy constituted 1 percent of the population of Vienna, while the middle class came to 2.5 percent of the total.[9] This means that the middle class of that time could not offer anything resembling a mass market for music, but it could add substantially to the audience provided by the even smaller aristocratic portion of the population.

Toward the end of the eighteenth century, when the 25-year-old Mozart settled in Vienna, that city could hardly claim to be the unchallenged music capital of Europe. Paris and London provided a greater number of lucrative musical opportunities and higher fees, and they were more attractive to a number of composers, such as Handel, Gluck, and Haydn. Vienna had neither a public concert hall nor a friends-of-music society, but it held the advantage of proximity to the sources of supply of musical talent, which at the time flowed predominantly from Italy and from the great number of German and Habsburg non-German centers (especially Hungary and Bohemia). Among the most noteworthy were places such as Berlin (where Frederick the Great employed C. P. E. Bach), Salzburg, Munich, Leipzig, Stuttgart, Prague, and Mannheim. Nevertheless, Vienna, as the seat of empire, was surely the focus of musical life in the German lands, so it is not surprising that most of the great composers of this part of the world eventually made their way to that city.

Mozart's Vienna decade is noteworthy as a watershed in the economics of music and, in particular, of composition. This surely was the period of transition from the universal system of private patronage to the beginnings of a market mechanism under which the product of the composer and the performer became a commodity that could be

9. Julia Moore, "Mozart in the Market Place," *Journal of the Royal Musical Association* 114 (1989): 34.

bought and sold, the prices ranging from niggardly to spectacularly generous, depending on what the composer or performer could command in the marketplace. Mozart was among the first in Vienna to turn his talents as composer and virtuoso pianist into a commodity. He usually composed on commission or to advance his career, and he seldom composed without a commercial incentive.

His letters affirm this repeatedly, as in the quotation at the beginning of this chapter. Such statements, however, may well exaggerate Mozart's dedication to money-making, perhaps having been intended to reassure his father and to stem the flow of stern fatherly advice. In a private conversation, Edward T. Cone reminded us that Mozart wrote pieces for his own family: four-hand sonatas that he played with his sister, violin sonatas that he played with his wife, and pieces he wrote for his pupils. Thus, as is to be expected, his objective was not quite undeviatingly pecuniary.

Haydn provides perhaps the most telling example of the transition to market mechanisms. When he was freed from Esterhazy patronage by the death of his sponsor, his income leaped from the modest level at which it had been held for many years to the spectacular earnings he received in England (sweetened by the honors conferred on him by the ancient universities). By our calculations, the British market mechanism made him the equivalent of a 1990 millionaire in the United States. When Mozart died in 1791, arrangements were being made for him to follow Haydn to London, where he probably would have found the way open to comparable earnings.

Some profound changes helped to make such musical entrepreneurship feasible at this time. One was the gradual replacement of the old *Kapelle* arrangement by hired, professional musicians, a replacement that had begun approximately with the Seven Years War (1756–63). Under the old system the musical demands of a noble household were supplied by a cadre of household servants led by a kapellmeister, who was little more than a servant himself. Working, probably, for a royal or noble patron or a prince of the church, the kapellmeister was responsible for all musical activities—composing, performing, overseeing musicians, giving musical instruction, and so on. His compositions were not his own property but belonged to his master, and he had to seek permission to accept outside commissions or even to resign from the service of the master. Sometimes he had additional assignments, as when even as famous a kapellmeister as

Karl Ditters von Dittersdorf is believed to have had to wait on tables every other night.[10]

The reasons for the decline of this system may have been rooted in fashion as well as economics. Early in the eighteenth century the most aristocratic patrons of music had established *Kapellen* in their own households, in which servant-musicians were organized to provide all musical needs, including the most elaborate productions. The *Kapelle* system was largely replaced in the latter part of the eighteenth century, when it became fashionable to maintain only smaller *Harmonien,* to be augmented by hired musicians. Concurrently, there emerged dilettante concerts in which amateurs (often members of the highest aristocracy) performed in private salons along with professional musicians hired for the occasion, sometimes of the caliber of Mozart himself.

The imperial court had abandoned its reliance on the *Kapelle* under Maria Theresa and limited its support of music mainly to opera. Moore comments that it seems "a particular source of prestige when adopted by a given social class quickly lost its prestige among the next higher social class. By the middle of the eighteenth century, the Imperial court could outshine the private musical performances of aristocratic households only in the area of full-scale opera productions; therefore, the Imperial court virtually abandoned those forms of music that no longer represented its special status. Were the four music-loving emperors who preceded Maria Theresa born music-lovers, or were they conditioned to love music by the fact that they reigned during a period when the Imperial court could command musical resources far superior to those of the aristocracy in general?"[11]

While the long process of decay of royal theaters and the disbanding of large private musical establishments proceeded, those composers and musicians who were partially or entirely displaced declared themselves for hire. They earned their livings in new ways. Public concerts featuring their own works and charging admission began to be organized either by the composer for his own benefit or by one of the new public-concert societies. Musicians also gave lessons, had their own works published for sale to the public, and accepted commissions and part-time employment.

10. Moore, "Beethoven and Musical Economics," 66.
11. Moore, "Beethoven and Musical Economics," 100.

Publication began to expand, though so slowly that significant proceeds seem to have largely benefited Mozart's estate rather than himself. The popularity of the new *galant* style of composition, as opposed to the difficult contrapuntal style, increased the feasibility of amateur musical performance. This led to a great demand for published compositions of varying levels of difficulty. The emergence of the music-publishing industry facilitated wide dissemination of the composer's product. The composer, of course, profited from the sale of his work, for which the publisher made a fixed payment. The new publication arrangement also served to advertise the composer's work at home and abroad.

This was the situation when Mozart, having figuratively thumbed his nose at Salzburg's archbishop and been physically booted out in return, went to Vienna, where he found the opportunities for support through patronage only modestly rewarding.[12] He then augmented his earnings by private enterprise, with noteworthy financial success, as we shall see. By the time of Beethoven, reliance on the market was far greater, and although Beethoven still benefited from private patronage, severe inflation had cut deeply into its value.

The eighteenth century brought with it a spate of inventions—the "wave of gadgets" that underlay the industrial revolution. Musical instruments also benefited from this trend. Mozart, one of the earliest virtuoso pianists, had the advantage of improvements that were being made in keyboard instruments. Before the emergence of the forte-piano in the second half of the century, the organ, the clavichord, and the harpsichord were the only keyboard instruments available.

> The clavichord was simple and cheap to construct, and it allowed the player an intimate control over the intensity and quality of its sound. Sensitive gradations of tone, even a vibrato—the *bebung*—could be achieved. But the clavichord was quiet (it could hardly be heard from a few yards away), and therefore a private instrument. The harpsichord, by contrast, was sufficiently loud and brilliant for hall, theater and church, but could not produce subtle gradations of volume.[13]

---

12. In 1787, however, he was appointed to the post of Imperial Chamber Musician, largely a sinecure, at a fairly generous stipend of 800 florins per year.

13. Cyril Ehrlich, *The Piano: A History,* 2d ed. (Oxford: Clarendon Press, 1990), 11.

Closson reports, "From the moment that Mozart in 1777 discovered the pianos of Stein, he definitely gave up the harpsichord. Haydn did the same . . . so did Beethoven."[14] Bie concurs that "Mozart, the first world-virtuoso, the idol of the concert hall, thinking only of sound-effects in the great halls, never hesitated for a moment between clavicymbal and piano."[15]

The piano helped to expand the market for the composer's efforts in at least two ways. First, it made concert performance possible before larger audiences. Second, as pianos entered an increasing number of private homes, the demand for (new) music also rose. Thus, the evolution of the technology of musical instruments was yet another influence that expanded the free market available to composers and increased the demand for their services in the second half of the eighteenth century.

Low wages, as we suggest farther on, stimulated the production of plays and the demand for playwrights' services in renaissance London. In eighteenth-century Germany, the demand for musicians' services, generated by the profusion of courts and princes, was also reinforced by low wages (although it is impossible to estimate the value of the perquisites that accompanied them). No doubt remuneration varied for each individual case. At the lowest rung, a musician such as Haydn's brother, the tenor Johann Evangelist, might receive (aside from his servant's compensation in kind) starvation wages of 60 florins per annum—roughly equivalent to a wage of $4,000 today, and half the income of a poorly paid schoolteacher.[16]

It is, of course, dangerous to take such figures literally, since so large a proportion of the earnings of musicians and others was paid in kind—food, lodging, etc. Moreover, many musicians were paid far better. But still, if the producer was economical, musical services could be provided at far lower relative cost than today. For example, we know that, in 1791, on the occasion of the coronation of Leopold II, Joseph's successor, the impresario Domenico Guardasoni, undertook to produce *La clemenza di Tito* for under 7,000 florins. This was less

14. Ernest Closson, *History of the Piano* (London: Paul Elek, 1947), 85.
15. Oscar Bie, *A History of the Pianoforte and Pianoforte Players,* trans. and rev. E. E. Kellett and E. W. Naylor (New York: E. P. Dutton, 1899), 131.
16. Volkmar Braunbehrens, *Mozart in Vienna* (New York: Grove Weidenfeld, 1990), 127, 129.

than twenty times the monetary salary of a high school teacher in Vienna at the time. Included in this sum were composer's fees, costumes, scenery, performers' salaries, and candles (no minor outlay).[17] The example is not meant to deny that extravagant production could be very expensive, sometimes ruinously so to a minor ruler.[18] But it does mean that the activity could be carried out at astonishingly low cost when compared (in real terms) with the outlays required today.

Not only the possibility of economical presentation of musical performance stimulated demand for the composers' work. The advent of the *galant* style of musical writing, with its expressiveness and avoidance of contrapuntal complexities, also made attendance at operas and concerts more popular, and facilitated amateur performance and the demand by amateurs for new compositions.

Musical activities were also sought out as a matter of honor and prestige. "Music, especially instrumental music, then, was a highly honorific indoor sport in Vienna: any Viennese understood that it was something the best people cultivated in a big way. . . . If music was eminently socially correct . . . it would not fail to be impressive to the bevies of newly rich and newly noble. They could think to better themselves cheaply by aping their betters, so they too assiduously cultivated their musical talents and interests."[19]

Moore quotes from the letters of a Count Franz Anton von Sporck, who, while professing himself a music lover, was induced to engage an opera company "after I learned that Princess Schwarzenberg was to take a cure only a mile from here on her husband's estate. . . . I hoped that the illustrious princess would remain in the vicinity for the entire summer."[20]

The fact that audiences generally were prepared to listen only to *new* music, usually to works written no more than a decade earlier,[21]

17. H. C. Robbins Landon, *Mozart's Last Year, 1791* (New York: Schirmer, 1988), 88–89, 116–17.

18. On this, see, e.g., Alan Yorke-Long, *Music at Court* (London: Weidenfeld and Nicholson, 1954), 7, 60–61, 71.

19. Arthur Loesser, *Men, Women and Pianos* (New York: Simon and Schuster, 1954), 119.

20. Moore, "Beethoven and Musical Economics," 95–96, quoting from Daniel Freeman, "The Opera Theater of Count Franz Anton von Sporck in Prague 1724–35" (Ph.D. dissertation, University of Illinois, 1987), 52.

21. The expected impermanence of musical works is underscored by the fact that they were often written with particular performers in mind. There are many examples in Mozart's writings, and he was known to criticize performances because they were not given by the

additionally stimulated the demand for music and music composition. It is true that societies of "ancient music" had been formed in London and Vienna in an effort to save the works of such composers as Handel and Bach from oblivion, but these "ancient" works were only about thirty years old—closer in time to Mozart's Vienna than, say, those of George Gershwin are to our New York. Moreover, these were esoteric activities, of interest only to highly dedicated amateurs and professional musicians. It consequently required the constant efforts of living composers to compose enough new works to keep the market supplied.

We turn next to the main subject of our study—influences that led to the extraordinary profusion of composing talent in the Habsburg Empire during Mozart's period and the neighboring decades. One can, of course, never determine all the causes of such a phenomenon, even if such a listing were conceivable. However, it is our basic contention that the fragmentation of the Holy Roman Empire and the attendant circumstances go a considerable way toward explaining the incentives for composition in Vienna at the end of the eighteenth century.

In a sense, we are suggesting that the opportunities for Bach, Telemann, Gluck, Haydn, Mozart, and Beethoven have their origin in Canossa in 1077, when Henry IV's submission to Pope Gregory served to perpetuate the dismemberment of Germany, and in the submission in Venice, precisely one century later, of Frederick Barbarossa to Pope Alexander, which confirmed this fate. In the eighteenth century, the Holy Roman Empire included roughly 1,800 more or less independent German states (to be contrasted with the fewer than two hundred states on the entire planet recognized by the United Nations in 1990). It is certainly true that effective power resided in perhaps a half-dozen to a dozen major secular and ecclesiastical dominions, but the fact is that Germany and Italy, unlike France and the United Kingdom, were subdivided into a multitude of petty states, each with its

performer for whom the composer intended them. He describes his attendance at a Holzbauer opera in Mannheim thus: "[The prima donna, Madame Wending,] is always indisposed and, what is more, the opera was not written for her, but for a certain Danzi, who is at present in England; consequently it is not suited to her voice, but is too high for her" (Mozart to his father, November 14–16, 1777, in Emily Anderson, trans., *The Letters of Mozart and His Family* [London: Macmillan, 1938], vol. 2, 549–50).

own provincial capital and each with its own small court in which boredom was a principal concern of the ruler and musical activity frequently served as the main antidote.

> Each [of the many states of the Holy Roman Empire] was headed by an absolute sovereign princelet, who . . . strutted about, affectionately coddling his ornamental army, his hunting apparatus, and his little orchestra. . . . Of the kings and dukes, the greater and richer ones maintained their own opera establishments. These were very expensive, fancy luxuries, requiring incredibly luxurious stage machinery. . . . Princelets who could not afford their own operas contented themselves with keeping little chamber orchestras.[22]

Here, of course, some principalities were more equal than others. Mannheim was a major focus of musical activity, with its own "style" and magnificent orchestra. Wittenberg and Dresden were great musical centers, and Berlin was not far behind.[23] Vienna and Prague were the main centers in the Habsburg possessions. Germany, Bohemia, and Hungary were flooded with composers and musicians, many, undoubtedly, very minor talents and long deservedly forgotten, but their sheer number was surely astonishing.

As we have already noted, old music was almost never played, and programs consisted of newly composed music, often by the court composer. This made for an abundance of employment opportunities for a host of composers and musicians spanning the full range of ability. It is well known that many of the court musicians were treated as servants. In many cases, in order to qualify for employment as a servant, the candidate was expected to display some musical skills. It also seems obvious that the necessity to practice these skills, often in the company of extremely accomplished musicians, served to hone them to a higher level. It is even reported (though it may strain credulity) that, in Bohemia, "every schoolmaster was expected to compose, rehearse, and perform at least one mass each year."[24]

We conclude that this profusion of outlets for the work of the composer served in a manner analogous to the bush leagues in baseball today, attracting the prospective superstars, along with a horde of less talented aspirants, into musical composition rather than the other, of-

22. Loesser, *Men, Women and Pianos*, 4–7.
23. On all this, see, e.g., Yorke-Long, *Music at Court*.
24. Braunbehrens, *Mozart in Vienna*, 295.

ten vastly different, occupations of their ancestors. The courts that valued music the most and were willing to spend the most money picked off the best.

We can hardly claim that anything approximating proof is provided by the evidence offered here for the hypothesis that the availability of a very large number of composers' posts brought forward many practitioners of the art, among them some geniuses who might otherwise never have written any music. Yet we believe that this line of reasoning, coupled with that of the following pages, is sufficiently persuasive to convince dispassionate observers that it constitutes a substantial part of the story.

In an era in which sons often followed the occupations of their fathers (as did Bach and his own numerous sons), what else can have led these great German composers to seek a career other than the ones traditionally pursued by their forefathers? In the absence of an enormous demand for the services of composers, one might never have suspected that the son of a forester (Gluck), the son of a wheelwright and distinguished town official (Haydn), and the grandson of a bookbinder and a government official (Mozart) were potential giants of musical composition.[25] The implication is that although suitable economic circumstances are in themselves hardly sufficient to elicit an abundance of musical genius, they may constitute a necessary condition for that result. As we have said before, economics can hardly be the entire story, but neither can its role be denied altogether. And surely it is plausible that many of those entering the labor market would turn to careers for which they thought themselves suitable in professions where there existed opportunities for employment.

The role of economics in such matters is eloquently expressed in another context by G. V. Plekhanov, the noted defender of historical materialism. He observes:

> In order that a man who possesses a particular kind of talent may, by means of it, greatly influence the course of events . . . the existing social order must not bar the road to the person possessing the talent which is needed and useful precisely at the given time. . . . Napoleon would have died as the barely known General or Colonel Bonaparte had the old order in France existed another seventy-five

25. H. C. Robbins Landon, *Mozart: The Golden Years, 1781–91* (New York: Schirmer, 1989), 11.

years. In 1789 . . . Augereau was a fencing master; Lannes was a dyer; Gouvion Saint-Cyr was an actor; Jourdan was a peddler; Bessières was a barber; Brune was a compositor; Joubert and Junot were law students; Kléber was an architect. . . . Had the old order continued until our day it would never have occurred to any of us that in France at the end of the 18th century, certain actors, compositors, barbers, dyers, lawyers, peddlers and fencing masters had been potential military geniuses.[26]

We have already seen evidence suggesting strongly that the political fragmentation of Germany (and Italy) provided opportunities for musicians that France and England did not offer. Despite the considerable musical activity in Paris and London, much of the talent seems to have been imported. Opportunities for native musicians must have been very limited because France and the United Kingdom had no secondary cities with a thriving musical life. Lyons and Rouen were not Mannheim, and York and Glasgow were not Berlin. One is led to surmise that the incentives for young job seekers to turn to music were far more modest than in Germany.

Perhaps the case can be made more plausible by an analogy.[27] The reason for the profusion of memorable composers in Germany toward the end of the eighteenth century clearly has its counterpart in the large number of great playwrights in London during the reigns of the first Elizabeth and James. Marlowe, Jonson, and Shakespeare are only the most notable of these figures. Once again, economics surely cannot have created their genius, but it can be argued with some degree of plausibility that it gave them their opportunity.

The Phelps Brown–Hopkins index of real wages is a carefully constructed and widely used set of statistics based on the records of the building wages of manors in southern England and of the ancient universities.[28] That index, extending back to the thirteenth century,

26. G. V. Plekhanov, "The Role of the Individual in History," in *Fundamental Problems of Marxism* (New York: International Publishers, 1969), 169–70.

27. This section is based on material provided in W. J. Baumol and Mary I. Oates, "On the Economics of the Theater in Renaissance London," *Swedish Journal of Economics* 74 (March 1972): 136–60.

28. The index was constructed by E. H. Phelps Brown and Sheila V. Hopkins for the years 1260 to 1954. See their "Seven Centuries of the Prices of Consumables, Compared with Builders' Wage-Rates," in E. M. Carus-Wilson, ed., *Essays in Economic History* (London: Edward Arnold Ltd., 1962), vol. 2, 179–96.

shows clearly how the plague and its decimation of the labor force raised real wages to levels unduplicated until the end of the nineteenth century. But with the accession of Henry VIII, there began the great Tudor inflation, which lasted nearly one and a half centuries, and which eroded the purchasing power of wages, bringing them, by the decade of Shakespeare's greatest productivity, to the lowest level in the entire seven centuries covered by the statistics. Undoubtedly, wages of theater builders, costume makers, and actors followed a similar pattern.

The consequence for the economics of play production was dramatic. Today it takes well over a year for a nonmusical play to recoup the expenses of its production; before World War I, it required a run of less than two months to break even. However, at the time the Globe Theater was in operation, if a play ran for two weeks it was a great and profitable success. Low wages made a labor-intensive activity like theatrical production relatively cheap, and the result was that the demand for new plays was enormous. Producers had to maintain a stable of playwrights. They even resorted to the services of playwriting committees, which were sometimes ordered to grind out new plays in a matter of days if the previous production proved to be disappointing commercially. With so much opportunity it is easily imagined that persons in search of employment would turn to the dramatist's occupation, and that out of the large number of entrants into the craft a small number who might otherwise never have been suspected of possessing talent would turn out to be extremely capable—in some cases, even able to write for the ages.

As has been argued, a different but equally powerful set of influences stimulated the market for composers' services in the Holy Roman Empire in the second half of the eighteenth century and, arguably, led many of those in search of gainful employment to turn to this activity. We may surmise that the bulk of those who did so might well have gone into forestry, farming, or bookbinding. But surely it was from among those many that society found those few whose works would endure.

Thus, it is our conclusion that a combination of circumstances helps to explain the profusion of great composers in Vienna at the time. Among those circumstances, perhaps the most important was the fragmented state of the Empire, which added greatly to the number of job opportunities for composers—and created an ideal situation for

Mozart and others to pioneer abandonment of the old retainer system and to become music entrepreneurs.

This completes the discussion of our central topic. But we cannot end without commenting briefly on some of the romantic legends that have grown up about Mozart, most of which have been dispelled by biographers such as Braunbehrens and Robbins Landon,[29] and then more extensively on the recent revisionist literature about Mozart's life and economic circumstances.

We have already alluded to the circumstances that inspired the tale of Mozart's "pauper's burial." Joseph II, as an enlightened ruler, decreed that for reasons of sanitation, economy, and rationality, burial Masses would be celebrated in Viennese churches, and that the bodies would then be transported in (reusable) wooden boxes on special carts to mass graves outside the city limits. Not many people chose to argue with the emperor, and it became the custom to conclude the burial service at the church rather than to follow the funeral cart on its long trip to the burial ground. Only members of the highest nobility managed to avoid this sort of "pauper's burial," and so it is true that Mozart, along with the wealthy bourgeoisie, did not escape it. (Incidentally, it was customary to dig the bones out of the mass graves after a number of years and deposit them in the ossuaries that tourists still visit in Vienna, so that the cemetery grounds could be used again.)

The evidence also leads one to spring to the defense of Constanze against the accusation that she was a silly, uncaring woman. It is true that Mozart's father disapproved of the marriage and that her family may have been opportunists, but the deep affection displayed in Mozart's letters to her (not one of her letters to him is preserved), the intelligence and care with which she oversaw posthumous publication of his works (with unwillingness to accept lucrative offers that threatened shoddy publication), and her contributions to the material for Nissen's biography of Mozart all make the traditional depiction of her as less than bright extremely questionable.

Only those whose total knowledge of Mozart's life is limited to attending the play or movie *Amadeus* can believe that Salieri poisoned Mozart. Actually, when the deed was alleged to have been committed,

---

29. See Braunbehrens, *Mozart in Vienna,* and Robbins Landon, *Mozart's Last Year, 1791* and *Mozart: The Golden Years, 1781–1791.*

Joseph II had died, and his successor, in a great economy sweep, had fired Salieri and abolished his post, to which Mozart may conceivably once have aspired.

It is difficult to picture Mozart as an unmannered lout when we know the company he kept, which included some of the most distinguished people in Vienna. Further, the profusion of common themes in his librettos, written by different librettists, surely indicates that he must have taken a substantial role in their writing. An example is the recurrence of the theme of the exploitation of servants by masters and the superior intelligence, leadership, and/or morality of the servants (Blonde in *Die Entführung,* Susanna and Figaro in *Le nozze,* Despina in *Così,* and even, to some degree, Leporello and Zerlina in *Don Giovanni*). Another illustration is the repeated appearance of the theme of forgiveness. The point is that the operas, from several librettists, are rare in their literary sophistication, something that can be accounted for only by an influence they shared in common. They all clearly show the hand of a talented and powerful intellect, one with clear ideas about human nature, justice, marriage,[30] and the appropriate role of humor.

We are also inclined to concur with Julia Moore's educated guess about Mozart's character: "I would describe him rather as high-spirited, energetic, hard-working, fun-loving, absolutely assured of his talent and impatient with the lesser talents of most fellow musicians, and usually buoyant in the face of adversity."[31]

We turn next to a discussion of Mozart's economic circumstances. During his decade in Vienna, he earned a good deal of money, and for some years now it has become increasingly clear that, whether or not his income placed him in the most affluent portion of the middle class—a subject still disputed—it surely put him well above the poverty

30. "People of noble birth must never marry from inclination or love, but only from interest and all kinds of secondary considerations. Again, it would not at all suit a grandee to love his wife after she had done her duty and brought into the world a bouncing son and heir. But we poor humble people can not only choose a wife whom we love and who loves us, but we may, can and do take such a one, because we are neither noble, nor highly born, nor aristocratic, nor rich." (Mozart to his father, February 7, 1778, in Anderson, trans., *The Letters of Mozart,* vol.2, 690–91).

31. Julia Moore, "Review Essay: Mozart Mythologized or Modernized?" *Journal of Musicological Research* (1991): 22.

level.[32] However, the magnitude of his earnings seems not to have been evaluated defensibly in terms of today's dollars. We shall attempt to provide such a translation. Specialists have designed methods that do the job in a rough and ready manner, and we employ one such method, of earnings equivalents, to portray in 1989 terms where Mozart's income placed him in the hierarchy of earnings in Vienna in the mid-1780s.[33]

Over a century ago, Otto Jahn provided the then currently known evidence on Mozart's recorded earnings during his decade in Vienna.[34] (For a careful review of what is known and what is not known about Mozart's income, see Steptoe.)[35] Jahn's figures on Mozart's income are all (more or less) documented and, apparently, were not disputed until very recently. After Volkmar Braunbehrens took them over as the basis for his calculations, Julia Moore examined the figures more critically and took issue with the inclusion as income of such things as Mozart's borrowings and a 2,000-florin figure that Mozart men-

32. See Braunbehrens, Robbins Landon, and the data provided by Moore, "Review Essay," 21.

33. The task of interpreting Mozart's eighteenth-century income in today's terms cannot be carried out unambiguously, given the vast differences in consumption patterns and living standards. Two different conversions of 1786 florins to 1989 dollars can be used to present a fuller picture. In the first method, one compares the *purchasing power* of a unit of currency today with that of the eighteenth century. The figure obtained in this way is an estimate of the number of 1989 U.S. dollars required to purchase a market basket of consumer goods that is roughly equivalent to a market basket that could have been bought for one florin in Vienna in 1786.

A second method of conversion, the one we have used in this essay, provides an *earnings-equivalent* comparison. This takes into account both the change in the purchasing power of money and the rise in average standards of living. It gives us the ratio of the number of dollars earned by a "typical" worker in 1989 to the comparable earnings figure for 1786. It does so by adding to the information used in the calculations of the preceding paragraph an estimate of the rise in real wages over the 204 years in question. This approach to 1989-dollar translation of a 1786 florin is to be interpreted as the number of dollars an American must earn in 1989 to be in the same relative position, vis-à-vis an "average worker," that the earner of a given number of florins would have been in Vienna in 1786. By this method we conclude that a florin of Vienna in 1786 can be interpreted as equivalent to some seventy 1989 U.S. dollars. This figure will be used to determine in 1989 terms where Mozart's income placed him in the hierarchy of earnings in Vienna.

For further explanation of the mechanics of the methods of conversion, please consult the authors.

34. Otto Jahn, *Life of Mozart*, trans. Pauline D. Townsend (London: Novello, Ewer, 1891).

35. Andrew Steptoe, "Mozart and Poverty: A Re-Examination of the Evidence," *Musical Times* 125 (April 1984): 196–201.

tions in 1791 as an expected receipt in a letter seeking to borrow money—a receipt for which absolutely no confirming evidence appears to exist. Our calculations are based on her figures rather than those of Braunbehrens.[36]

These figures must be interpreted with considerable caution because they represent only the *documented* portion of Mozart's income. In addition, they represent only gross income, with no deductions for professional expenses (we discuss his expenses below). Many sources of income, including publication fees, payments for lessons, private concerts, payments for the composition of some operas, and so on, have been omitted because we do not know the precise amounts Mozart received for them. However, for many of the omitted items we do know the customary fees and the amounts Mozart had received for other similar activities. For example, we know that for *Le nozze* he was paid 100 ducats or 425 florins (equivalent, roughly, to a wage of $30,000 in 1989). Yet because we do not know his fee for *Die Entführung,* this fee is sometimes treated as though it were zero.

Mozart had five principal sources of income: patronage, performance, music lessons, publication, and commissions. His income from patronage in Vienna was principally the sinecure stipend, 800 florins per year, granted by the emperor in 1787. The grant came late in Mozart's life, and the amount, though hardly negligible, was far smaller than others, such as Gluck, had received.

Mozart probably earned a large part of his income as a virtuoso pianist. He played often at the all-important private salons, where most of the music-making took place, and where "Mozart . . . maintained a dizzying schedule of private appearances at his zenith in the mid-1780's."[37] Payment was at the discretion of the host and probably varied greatly. He composed twenty-six pianoforte concertos, considered to be among his greatest works, for performance at his own concerts. He organized subscription series of three or more concerts,

36. Still, it should be noted that for the years 1783–91, Moore's figures total only 11 percent less than Braunbehrens's—his average annual figure for the known portion of Mozart's income during those years is 1,928 florins, while hers is 1,711. We also use her figures for only the years 1783–91, ignoring 1781–82, the first two years of Mozart's residence in Vienna, because the available information is so poor that the known portion of his income for those years seems a ludicrous underestimate of his total income. For example, no payment for *Idomeneo* (1781) or for *Die Entführung* (1782) is included in Moore's figures for those years.

37. Morrow, *Concert Life in Haydn's Vienna,* 18.

aided at least sometimes by perhaps the first private impresarios, Philippe Jacques Martin and Ignaz Schuppanzigh. Such concerts were held in the inadequate private facilities that existed in Vienna. Mozart claimed to have 174 subscribers for one such projected series, and his series of six concerts in the Mehlgrube attracted 150 subscribers.[38] They may have been extremely lucrative.

How much did he earn at public concerts? Here Morrow's careful scholarship comes to our aid:

> Generalizing . . . is impossible. . . . If the circumstances were right, one performance could bring in 1,000–1,500 gulden [florins] or more (two to three times the court orchestra concertmaster's annual salary). Even a half-empty hall at Jahn's [Ignaz Jahn, the Court Caterer, rented out for concerts the hall in his restaurant in the Himmelpfortgasse] would have brought in 400 gulden and left ca. 250 gulden after expenses. The situation in Vienna offered musicians a good chance to make money, if they had the business sense and the talent to take advantage of it.[39]

We have more evidence on how much Mozart could earn at his peak as concert performer. His father, in a letter to his daughter on February 16, 1785, wrote of "his first subscription concert, where there was a vast concourse of people of rank. Each person pays one *souverain d'or* (13½ gulden) or 3 ducats [$900 today] for the six Lenten concerts. . . . For the use of the room he pays only one half a *souverain d'or*."[40]

It was the opinion of Otto Jahn that Mozart did not earn much from publication of his works in that "the music trade of the day was small and insignificant; indeed, the first impulse was given to it by the publication of an edition of all Mozart's works soon after his death. During his life . . . compositions were more often copied than printed; and the composer was obliged to keep careful watch lest copies should be distributed which were . . . never paid for."[41] He points out that such caution was not in Mozart's nature, but adds, "He was careful only of his concertos . . . not allowing any one to play them who chose." Certainly his letters reflect this view.

38. Morrow, *Concert Life in Haydn's Vienna*, 51.
39. Morrow, *Concert Life in Haydn's Vienna*, 139.
40. Quoted in Robbins Landon, *Mozart: The Golden Years, 1781–1791*, 125.
41. Jahn, *Life of Mozart*, 293.

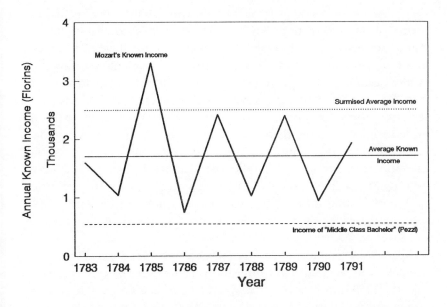

Figure 4.3. Mozart's known income, 1783–91. Moore's calculations, omitting undocumented income. (Source: Moore 1989)

Mozart insisted on the high price for lessons of six ducats (some $1,800 in 1989 wage equivalent) for twelve lessons, to be given one a day. The work was limited to the winter season and was a highly undependable source of income. Some teachers—Clementi, for example—charged more than Mozart for lessons, but Mozart's fee was far above the norm.[42] It is possible that he resorted to private teaching when he was in great need of money. Such lessons may have been his principal source of income before the premiere of *Die Entführung* in 1782, his first great popular success.

For composition Mozart also received fees toward the high end of the customary scale, normally 100 ducats per opera. He probably sometimes received more, but not as much as Paisiello at his most popular.

The jagged curve in Figure 4.3 reports Moore's calculations of Mozart's *documented* income, year by year, for the period 1783–91.[43]

42. Steptoe, "Mozart and Poverty," 197.

43. The data in Figure 4.3 for Mozart's *known* income are from Moore, "Mozart in the Market Place," and generally constitute a downward revision of the data first docu-

Its considerable volatility is probably attributable to the haphazard nature of the information that survives as much as to changes in the market for his services. Braunbehrens calculates that if we add to these figures reasonable evaluations of Mozart's undocumented income, his average earnings during his Vienna years can be conservatively estimated at 3,000–4,000 florins per year.[44] We adopt a far more conservative guess for purposes of comparison. We assume (without evidence) that no more than two-thirds of his total income is included explicitly in the documentation provided by the surviving papers, and therefore comes to some 2,500 florins. It should be emphasized, however, that these figures can, at best, be accepted as reasonable estimates of Mozart's *gross* income, because they do not deduct unavoidable professional expenses, whose magnitude has proved very difficult to estimate.

Mozart's average annual *documented* income during the years 1783–91 can be calculated from Moore's data to have been a bit more than 1,711 florins,[45] and we have estimated his total income to have averaged 2,500 florins. This can be translated, very approximately, into a real-wage equivalent in 1989 dollars of some $175,000, which would put Mozart well inside the upper 5 percent bracket of U.S. family incomes.

If the guess at Mozart's average annual income is considered too shaky, one can perform a similar calculation upon the average of Mozart's *known* income figures as reported by Moore—somewhat in excess of 1,700 florins. Performing the same calculations as before, this figure translates into a real-wage equivalent of about $120,000. This clear underestimate of Mozart's income—1,700 florins—does not amount to vast wealth, but it is surely far from grinding poverty.

mented by Otto Jahn in his 1856–59 biography of Mozart. Also in the graph, for comparison, are three horizontal lines. The lowest shows Pezzl's estimate of the annual income required by a (lower) middle-class bachelor. The middle line is the average of the known income figures reported by Moore for the years in question. The top line depicts our guess about the magnitude of Mozart's average income, documented and undocumented.

44. Kraemer proposes a figure well above 10,000 florins for Mozart's annual income, but that far exceeds every carefully calculated estimate, and from the evidence it seems highly implausible (Uwe Kraemer, "Wer hat Mozart verhungern lassen?" *Musica* 30 (June 1976): 203–11). Steptoe's estimate is that the average figure was slightly *less* than 3,000 florins ("Mozart and Poverty," 198). But this excludes earnings from private performances, which were probably not negligible. In any event, since just the documented portion of his income averages nearly 2,000 florins, it is implausible that the total was far below 3,000 florins.

45. Our reason for omitting the years 1781–82 is given in note 36.

Again, 1,700 florins came to more than five times the 300-florin income that was the top of the scale for a high school teacher at that time. If we assume that the average teacher received as much income again in kind (such payments were common practice then), and that Mozart received absolutely no such nonmonetary remuneration,[46] the *known and documented portion* of Mozart's income alone would have come to more than 2.8 times (1,700 = 2.8 × 600, approximately) that of the teacher. Thus, if Mozart were in the same income position relative to a New York City high school teacher today, whose top salary is $50,000, he would have to earn more than 2.8 times that amount, or nearly $150,000 per annum! This comparison, which cannot be considered more than a suggestive guess, illustrates that our translation of Mozart's income into today's dollars is based on a comparison of Mozart's income with the earnings of others in Vienna at the time. It also suggests that Mozart's earnings put him well into the bracket of the middle class of his Vienna, where, according to Pezzl's guidebook, the 1786 budget of a typical middle-class bachelor (actually, a rather impecunious middle-class bachelor) amounted to some 550 florins—that is, well under 25 percent of our conservative guess about Mozart's average income.

There is an abundance of other evidence that supports this general conclusion about Mozart's secure middle-class status, though the numbers just suggested should not be accepted as more than gross approximations. (It is also important to note that there has just emerged, through the careful scholarship of Dr. Moore, a re-revisionist position maintaining that the recent studies concluding that Mozart's income was substantial are an exaggeration, if not worse.)

It is true that there were periods when Mozart was in financial difficulties. In part, this was attributable to his high standard of living. In addition, the two years (about 1789 to 1790) in which he seems to have been seriously strapped coincided with an expensive illness of Constanze's and a period probably characterized by high inflation and reduced demand for musical services by the court and by that part of

---

46. As a matter of fact, Mozart did receive some nonmonetary income which, at least in earlier years, was likely to have been substantial. Thus, Moore ("Mozart in the Market Place," 22, note 10) cites Angermüller's report that "the Mozart family returned from their European concert tour of 1763–66 with nine gold watches, 12 gold snuff boxes, countless gold rings with precious stones, earrings, necklaces, miscellaneous gold objects and *galanterie* clothing worth perhaps 12,000 fl[orins]."

the nobility who were occupied with the Turkish war. Clearly, the inflation considerably (if temporarily) reduced the purchasing power of Mozart's earnings. (Figure 4.2, which shows the price of bread as reported by Morrow for the period 1780 to 1810, includes all of Mozart's time of residence in Vienna.)[47]

Steptoe, in his review of the evidence (1984), also notes that, in the years when Mozart appears to have been in financial trouble, he suffered a sharp drop in the number of his concert appearances, which may well be, to some degree, attributable to the dispersion of the court and the fall in demand resulting from the war.[48] There may also have been a general drop in Mozart's popularity caused, perhaps, by overexposure on the Viennese concert stage, as Steptoe proposes. Certainly Mozart undertook several onerous trips between 1785 and 1791, possibly to duplicate his Viennese success in other cities. Unfortunately, they seem to have been only mildly remunerative, if at all.

It is noteworthy that by 1791, Mozart's last year, Constanze was apparently no longer taking the cure, the Turkish war was over, prices appear to have returned to their prewar level, and the documented part of Mozart's income was higher than its 1783–91 average. Offers were arriving from England and Russia, and honorary pensions were being gathered to attract him to Amsterdam and Hungary.[49] Had he but lived, his financial troubles might possibly soon have vanished[50]

47. The figures are in kreuzer per pound of bread; a florin was equivalent to 60 kreuzer. By our calculation, bread sold at a wage equivalent of about two 1989 dollars per pound. That is, an average income earner in Mozart's Vienna worked about the same time to earn a pound of bread as it requires an average American worker to earn two dollars today. Incidentally, because it ends in 1810, the graph only begins to show how much more serious was the inflation with which Beethoven had to deal. It was only after 1810 that Austrian prices really exploded (perhaps more than thirty-fold between 1795 and 1817), and the bankrupt Austrian government debased its currency on a 5-to-1 ratio in 1812 (see Moore's very careful analysis in "Beethoven and Musical Economics"). Naturally, this severely eroded the 4,000-florin annual stipend that had been granted to Beethoven in 1809 by the archduke and two princes. Like many others at the time, Beethoven resorted to the courts and sued the creditors of the bankrupt Prince Lobkowitz and the estate of the dead Prince Kinsky. In 1815 he was awarded partial adjustment for the debasement of the currency by the government (but no adjustment for the severe inflationary erosion [see Moore, "Beethoven and Musical Economics," 3, 126–27]). All of this evidence supports Moore's contention that Beethoven's financial problems were very real and severe. It certainly suggests that there is as little basis for the widespread skepticism on Beethoven's financial complaints as there is for the equally common view that Mozart was chronically impoverished.

48. Steptoe, "Mozart and Poverty," 196.

49. Braunbehrens, *Mozart in Vienna*, 141.

50. Mozart was well aware of the irony in the fact that all this came too late. During

(perhaps only to rise again during the terrible inflation of the Napoleonic wars, as happened to Haydn and Beethoven).

It is reasonable to surmise that Mozart, like so many businessmen today, experienced cash-flow problems. No doubt he was pressed for payment for expenditures connected with his musical activities, and we know that at least some of his receipts came in very slowly. He had probably borrowed a substantial amount while establishing himself in Vienna and for various other purposes, though it is interesting that he did not leave a particularly large burden of debt on his death— less than 2,000 gulden.[51] By his final year, however, his finances appear to have been under somewhat better control,[52] and he had reason to expect in the next year to follow Haydn to London, where the latter had been able to earn far more than Mozart earned in Vienna, even in his most prosperous periods.[53]

As Mozart ran his own business, so to speak, it is interesting to consider his professional expenses. One component may have been the necessity of adequate premises. Robbins Landon observes that Mozart's name was on every tongue in Vienna in 1784, and that, after the great success, including the financial success, of one academy concert, "the Mozarts urgently required a new and much larger apartment, where they could accommodate the constant presence of copyists, pupils, and the complicated organization needed to deal with academy concerts, subscription invitations, and so on. . . . The move was to be made . . . to splendid, very expensive, and spacious quarters,

---

his final illness, according to his first biographer (Georg Nikolaus Nissen, Constanze's second husband), Mozart wrote, "Now . . . when I could compose freely and independently whatever my heart dictates! I must leave my family . . . in that moment when I would be in a better condition to care for them. . . . " (cited in Robbins Landon, *Mozart's Last Year, 1791*, 153).

51. Braunbehrens, *Mozart in Vienna*, 424.

52. However, a document has turned up indicating that only a month before his death, Mozart was sued by Count Lischinowsky, later a patron of Beethoven, for the considerable sum of 1,435 florins and 32 kreuzer. The claims of either side in this case, or its outcome (if it ever did reach a hearing), are unknown, since all other documents related to the case have disappeared. On this, see Von Walther Brauneis, ". . . wegen schuldigen 1435 f. 32 xr' Neuer Archivfund zur Finanzmisere Mozarts im November 1791," *Mitteilungen der Internationalen Stiftung Mozarteum* 1991, 158–63.

53. The known income of Mozart's last year, 1,925 florins, is well above the average. However, he was still plagued by debt and he may have lost a costly lawsuit, so that although the future seems to have looked promising, as already noted, his financial difficulties undoubtedly were not quite over.

for which the rent was 460 gulden [florins] p.a. [per annum] (compared with the 150 gulden for his previous flat)."[54] That is, he was now paying a rent equivalent to $30,000, measured in 1989 U.S. wages. It should be said that rents in Vienna were very high, and this was less than rents paid by many of Mozart's friends—highly compensated actors, opera singers, and members of the nobility and the wealthy bourgeoisie. Keeping up with them must have been a strain on the Mozart budget.

Pianos were also costly. Mozart reports that Stein's price for his higher-quality pianos was no less than 300 gulden (over $20,000 in wage equivalent). This was the same as his father's base annual income. Mozart also undoubtedly increased the outlay on his pianoforte further by having it fitted with a complicated pedal board "built like the fortepiano, with similar hammers, dampers, etc., but the keys are much enlarged and so disposed that they can be played with the feet."[55]

As we have seen, there is no reason to suggest that Mozart was economical in most of his outlays. Jahn refers to his "thoughtless liberality." His love of costly clothing was probably carried to extremes. On April 16, 1785, Leopold wrote to his daughter that Madame Lange and Wolfgang had intended going with him to Munich, but nothing was likely to come of it, "although each of them has now had six pairs of shoes made, which are all standing there now."

Bär carefully reviews much more such evidence, both on Mozart's outlays and on expenditure patterns in Vienna at the time.[56] He concludes that the family must have been spending approximately 2,000 florins per year. However, he does not include medical expenses (including Constanze's six pregnancies), maintenance of a horse, attendance at the theater (of which Mozart was extremely fond), and books and musical scores, among other things.

The itemization of Mozart's estate, which there is good reason to believe was deliberately undervalued (as it might be today), also suggests that his expenditures were rather generous. His estate contained many suits of expensive clothing, many porcelain figures and boxes, a

54. Robbins Landon, *Mozart: The Golden Years, 1781–1791,* 119–20.

55. Quoted in A. Hyatt King, *Mozart in Retrospect* (London: Oxford University Press, 1955), 245.

56. Carl Bär, "Er war . . . kein guter Wirth: eine Studie über Mozarts Verhältnis zum Geld," *Acta Mozartiana* 25 (April 1978): 30–53.

billiard table, and four couches with matching upholstered chairs that normally appeared only in the estates of the very rich.[57] He was certainly a liberal spender in some ways, but it does not follow that such outlays were excessive in light of his income level, and certainly not compared with those of his friends and acquaintances. We have already observed that the 2,000-gulden debt he left on his death was not a huge amount for one who had been so liberal a spender. Perhaps he paid off some of his debts when the money rolled in again in 1791.

Let us end with Steptoe's illuminating summation: "The financial difficulties Mozart encountered later in his life were almost inevitable for an artist reliant on irregular sources, who was in ill-health and somewhat unpopular at the same time. It is not necessary to infer that Mozart and Constanze were profligate or, as is often claimed without evidence, that Mozart gambled his income away in order to account for their predicament. She in particular has received an excessive degree of blame. Her supposed thriftlessness and caprice are hard to reconcile with her financial shrewdness as a widow."[58]

---

57. Beethoven's estate included only one couch. But that is not all we can learn from a comparison of the two estates. According to Moore ("Beethoven and Musical Economics," 452–54), Mozart's clothing and furniture were valued, respectively, at 55 and 229 florins of 1791, while the corresponding figures for Beethoven were only 37 and 57 florins of 1827. But this vastly underestimates the true difference because it ignores the probably more than twentyfold inflation in prices that occurred between 1791 and 1827. When corrected for this, in 1827 florins, we must estimate the value of the clothing in Mozart's estate at more than 1,100 florins and his furniture at more than 4,500 florins of 1827—that is, more than 80 times as great a value as Beethoven's.

58. Steptoe, "Mozart and Poverty," 200.

5

Mozart as a working stiff

NEAL ZASLAW

SEVERAL YEARS ago, I attended a conference sponsored by the Vienna Philharmonic Orchestra. The theme of the conference concerned the connections between the orchestra and various composers, and I had been asked to discuss Mozart's relations with the Viennese orchestras of his day. In the course of my talk, I revealed in passing that I (and, I might have added, many others studying Mozart) believe that he probably rarely completed a work for which there was no anticipated need. I speculated that because Mozart was usually extremely busy and because composing was in any case a demanding activity, some urgency would have been required before he found the time and energy to compose a piece, and that the motivating force was probably most often his need for cold, hard cash, of which he was perpetually short.[1]

I suppose I must have been at least subliminally aware that, in saying such things, I was being provocatively anti-Romantic, but I was quite taken aback at the vehemence with which my remarks were attacked. The moderator of the session took it upon himself to denounce me from the chair. If memory serves correctly, the gist of what

---

1. Neal Zaslaw, "Mozart's Viennese Orchestral Music and Its Relation to His Viennese Orchestras," in Otto Biba and Wolfgang Schuster, eds., *Klang und Komponist: ein Symposion der Wiener Philharmoniker* (Tutzing: Hans Schneider, 1992), 149–56.

he said was something like this: "Mozart's music could not and should not be compared with the music of such contemporaries as Dittersdorf, Vanhall, Hofmann, or Gyrowetz, because, whereas they were ordinary composers, Mozart was an original genius. Mozart's music belonged only to the highest spheres of creativity."

Hearing this tirade, I replied, as politely as I could, to the effect: "If I understand you correctly, Professor, then we disagree profoundly. Mozart's music ascended into the higher ether only in the course of the nineteenth century. During his lifetime, it was right down on the ground along with that of the other composers." In the discussion that followed this exchange, it seemed to me then that most of the older Germans and Austrians agreed with the moderator, while the younger German-speakers and the English-speakers apparently thought that what I had said made perfectly good sense. What interests me today is why the matter should be the cause of such strong emotion—a question to which I shall return in due course.

In asserting that Mozart had a practical purpose for each piece he wrote, I meant it in the broadest possible sense. Sometimes there was a formal commission, like that for the *Requiem,* or the *scritture* he received for most of his operas. At other times Mozart may have felt a general need, such as an upcoming series of Lenten concerts, which would please patrons more if they contained some new piano concertos. It could also occasionally have been a matter of speculation, as with the nearly completed opera *Zaide,* which Mozart and his father hoped to peddle to one of the new "national" theaters springing up in the 1770s, in which German plays and operas were to replace Italian opera and French *opéra comique.* It may have been to celebrate his sister's name day, or to please his patron Michael Puchberg, out of gratitude and friendship—and in the hope that Puchberg would go on lending him money. Or it may have been the sociable desire to entertain himself and his friends with a scatological canon or a *commedia dell'arte* skit for carnival. Publication may have been the goal, as with the six mighty quartets dedicated to Haydn or the three modest children's songs from Mozart's last year. In some cases—for instance, the charming flute and harp concerto of 1778, or the astounding pieces for mechanical organ of 1791—Mozart heartily disliked the commissions but urgently needed the payments that awaited their completion. As I remarked in my troubling Viennese talk, Mozart did not compose because he was inspired, although inspiration may be why he composed so well. I think it fair to state that, for each of Mozart's more than 800 finished compositions about which we know anything of its origins, some such motivating force can be identified.

But what of the hundreds of Mozart's works about whose origins we know either absolutely nothing or merely a date of creation? Might Mozart not have written some of these out of "pure inspiration," "from inner necessity," or "for posterity" (as the expressions go) rather than to satisfy an immediately practical goal? Let us take the best-known case of this sort—that of the last three symphonies—and subject it to closer scrutiny.

Generations of music lovers have been brought up (as I was) on Alfred Einstein's elegant book, *Mozart, His Character, His Work,* first published in 1946 and still widely available in paperback. Born in Munich in 1880 and the leading Mozart scholar of his generation, Einstein came to the United States in 1938, fleeing the Nazis. He taught at Smith College and died in California in 1952. Here is how Einstein's classic book introduces us to Mozart's last three symphonies:

> To the summer of 1788 belong the three last symphonies Mozart wrote, in E flat (K. 543), G Minor (K. 550), and C Major (K. 551)—all composed within the unbelievably short space of about two months. We know nothing about the occasion for writing these works. It is strange that Mozart should have written symphonies during the summer. Perhaps he hoped to be able to give some "Academies" [concerts] during the winter of 1788–89, and these plans fell through just as those for the following years did. . . . It is possible that Mozart never conducted these three symphonies and never heard them. . . . But this is perhaps symbolic of their position in the history of music and of human endeavor, representing no occasion, no immediate purpose, but an appeal to eternity. [In writing them, Mozart followed] an inner impulse.[2]

Einstein's remarks represent a distillation of attitudes to the last three symphonies found in many earlier German-language biographies and commentaries; and his book was, and remains, so influential that

---

2. Alfred Einstein, *Mozart, His Character, His Work* (London: Cassell, 1946), 234. For a recent attempt to sustain Einstein's point of view against mine, see Andrew Steptoe, "Mozart and His Last Three Symphonies—A Myth Laid to Rest?" *Musical Times* 132 (November 1991): 550–51.

this passage has been quoted or, more often, paraphrased—with or without acknowledgment—in hundreds of program notes written for concerts, recordings, and broadcasts. And not merely paraphrased, but simplified: Einstein's cautious "perhaps," "it is possible," and "nothing is known" harden into certainties, and we are repeatedly informed that Mozart *did* write these symphonies from inner necessity, that there *were* no concerts in the offing, and that Mozart *never* conducted or heard them.

It may be acceptable for Sherlock Holmes to base a brilliant deduction on the fact that the dog did not bark, but according to the rules of logic, it is impermissible to argue from the absence of evidence. If nothing is known, nothing may be concluded. But we do know a bit more than nothing about Mozart's last three symphonies. And since the writing of history, or of biography, is neither more nor less than telling stories by linking the known facts to form a plausible but hypothetical narrative, let us try a new story—mine this time, instead of Einstein's. Here is my story.

In the mid-1780s Mozart was in great demand for piano and composition lessons, for new works, and for public and private concerts in Vienna. From his vigorous freelance activities, he earned a solidly upper-middle-class income, living in expensive, beautifully appointed quarters, dressing elegantly, retaining a servant, and owning his own carriage. As the decade wore on, however, Austria fell into a foolish war with Turkey, the economy slid into a depression, and many of Mozart's noble patrons were either at the front or hiding on their country estates. The theaters were closed, many musicians were let go, and Viennese musical life declined precipitously. Predictably, Mozart's income suffered, and, apparently because he either could not or would not adjust his lifestyle in proportion, he began to accumulate debts, which he covered by a series of loans from his Masonic brother Michael Puchberg and others.

In the summer of 1788, Mozart must have been laying plans to deal with his financial crisis. He hoped to put on a series of three subscription concerts that autumn and eventually to arrange a visit to London where, his British friends Michael Kelley, Nancy and Stephen Storace, and Thomas Attwood assured him, he could make a lot more money than in Vienna. For both these plans, new symphonies would be needed. Thus we are not surprised to see entered into the catalogue of his works that Mozart kept at that time three new symphonies, one in E-flat on June 26, one in G minor on July 25, and one in C major on August 10.

Two weeks later, on Sunday, August 24, a Danish visitor to Vienna, Joachim Preisler, called on the Mozarts. Mozart improvised at the piano for what Preisler called "the happiest hour of music that has ever fallen to my lot." While that was happening, as Preisler noted in his diary, Mozart's wife, Constanze, "cut quill-pens for the copyist." We know that Mozart had copying done at home so that he could see to its correctness and, especially, to prevent copyists from stealing his works by making illicit copies for their own use.

It may have been a few weeks after the copyist was hard at work that Mozart wrote an undated letter to Puchberg begging for yet another loan:

> I dare to implore you to help me out with a hundred gulden until next week, when my concerts in the [Trattnerhof] Casino are to begin. . . . I take the liberty of sending you two tickets which, as a brother, I beg you to accept without payment, seeing that, as it is, I shall never be able adequately to return the friendship which you have shown me.

Subscription concerts were private events and, as such, were not advertised or reviewed in the Viennese newspapers, nor were there posters; we know about such concerts only in those rare cases in which Mozart or a member of his audience happened to mention them in a letter or diary entry. As for the concerts mentioned in the undated letter to Puchberg, if Mozart had reached the point of having tickets printed, we can reasonably assume that he had signed up a sufficient number of subscribers for the concerts to be put on, and that they were indeed put on.

The G Minor Symphony was in any case certainly performed soon after its completion, because the new versions Mozart prepared, of a single passage in the andante and of the woodwind orchestration of all four movements, would have been created only for a specific purpose, and these new versions are written on paper of the same date as the paper of the original manuscript. Furthermore, Mozart's own set of orchestral parts, containing emendations in his hand, survives in the library in Graz.

Although the tour to London never materialized, Mozart did travel in Germany, giving public orchestral concerts in Dresden and Leipzig in 1789 and in Frankfurt and Mainz in 1790. Each of these concerts contained at least two symphonies. Finally, a symphony by Mozart was included in a public Viennese concert of April 16, 1791, and repeated the next day: I can see no reason for supposing that Mozart would not have performed his last three symphonies at these five public concerts, and of his private concerts we shall never have an adequate accounting.

The very idea that Mozart would have written three such symphonies, unprecedented in length, complexity, and seriousness, merely to please himself or because he was "inspired" flies in the face of his known attitudes to music and life and the financial straits in which he then found himself.

Here endeth my story. I think it accounts for the possibly relevant facts surrounding Mozart's last three symphonies better than the traditional story does, but if anyone can tell me a more convincing story, I will happily abandon mine.

"If you have not got pupils," Leopold Mozart wrote to his son in 1778, "well then compose something more. . . . You must try to sell a work or two to some engraver or other. You must have money in order to live. And if your pupils are in the country, what other way is there for you to make money? You really must do something!" (August 13). "My desire and my hope is to gain honor, fame, and money," his son replied in 1781 to another importuning letter (May 16). "Believe me when I say that I have changed completely. Apart from my health I now think that there is nothing so indispensable as money" (May 26). Poor Mozart! Money was indispensable, and there never was enough of it. And there was probably more behind his claim that he had "changed completely" than simply his desperate need to fend off his father's criticisms with lies or wishful thinking. Many of Leopold Mozart's letters written to his son during the latter's early twenties contain accusations of laziness and disorganization. And even if Leopold's standards were unfairly high for a young man who was accustomed to being cared for and closely directed by his parents, there seems to have been some firm basis in reality for Leopold's accusations. Nonetheless, after settling on his own in Vienna at the age of twenty-five, Mozart's productivity was prodigious. Even given our necessarily incomplete documentation, the number of commissions, concerts, lessons, social events, compositions, and publications he was involved in during his last decade boggles the mind. And do not forget, he did not have a publicist, manager, or secretary, but ran all of this, so to speak, out of his hip pocket.

Even the disillusioned and disappointed Leopold Mozart was forced to acknowledge this state of affairs when he visited his son in Vienna for some ten weeks at the beginning of 1785. A series of letters reporting his stay to Mozart's sister, Nannerl, reveals that the father was discomfited by the son's lavish standard of living and stunned by the incessant rounds of musical and social activity.

So Mozart was worked hard in his childhood by his father and in his maturity by himself. If he did occasionally brag in his letters of his exceptional fluency in composition, simply to have written down all his works was a Herculean labor, without having also conceived them. Mozart occasionally boasted about his fluency in performance too, reporting to his father, for instance, that when he played for one Georg Friedrich Richter, Richter exclaimed, "Good God! How hard I work and sweat—and yet win no applause, and to you, my friend, it is all child's play." To which Mozart replied, "Yes, I too had to work hard, so as not to have to work hard any longer" (April 28, 1784). This reminds us of an anecdote about Bach, who, when asked how he composed so well, is said to have responded, "I have had to work hard; anyone who works just as hard will get just as far." Even though, to be true, the second half of Bach's assertion would have to be amended to "anyone *with my degree of talent* who works just as hard will get just as far," the first half stands as a healthy corrective to misty-eyed statements about "genius" and "creativity."

Why *do* many of Mozart's biographers so badly want him to have composed out of some inner necessity rather than to pay the rent? The short answer is: They still view Mozart through the purple-tinted lenses of Romanticism. There are many complex aspects to this conundrum, and I would like to emphasize two that seem central, which I shall call the *Amadeus* myth and the snobbery-of-those-who-have-never-had-dirt-under-their-fingernails syndrome. Recall the scene near the end of the film *Amadeus*, in which Mozart on his deathbed is struggling to finish the *Requiem*. For some reason—I cannot imagine why—Salieri is alone with Mozart and trying to help him. Observing Mozart continuing to compose the *Requiem* even as his physical strength ebbs, Salieri concludes that Mozart is an *idiot savant*—an obscene punk whom God has inexplicably chosen as his mouthpiece for divine music. This view of Mozart's creative process can be traced back to a notorious forgery—a letter published in 1815 in a widely read Leipzig music magazine, the *Allgemeine musikalische Zeitung*. In this letter, which purports to be a reply to an unnamed baron who has inquired how he composed, "Mozart" is made to write:

> When I am, as it were, completely myself, entirely alone, and of good cheer; say traveling in a carriage, or walking after a good meal, or during the night when I cannot sleep; it is on such occasions that my ideas flow best and most abundantly. *Whence* and *how* they come I know not, nor can I force them. Those ideas that please me, I retain in memory, and am accustomed, as I have been told, to hum them to myself. If I continue in this way, it soon occurs to me, how I may turn this or that morsel to account, so as to make a good dish of it, that is to say, agreeably to the rules of counterpoint, to the peculiarities of the various instruments, &c. All this fires my soul, and provided I am not disturbed, my subject enlarges itself, becomes methodized and defined, and the whole, though it be long, stands almost finished and complete in my mind, so that I can survey it, like a fine picture or a beautiful statue, at a glance. Nor do I hear in my imagination the parts *successively*, but I hear them, as it were, all at once. . . . When I proceed to write down my ideas, I take out of the bag of my memory, if I may use that phrase, what has previously been collected into it, in the way I have mentioned. For this reason, the committing to paper is done quickly enough, for everything is, as I said before, already finished; and it rarely differs on paper from what it was in my imagination.[3]

Even though this letter itself was denounced as a forgery by Mozart's most important nineteenth-century biographer, Otto Jahn, and has since been repeatedly denounced by other scholars, its substance has become deeply entrenched in Western writings not just about Mozart's peculiar gifts but about the very nature of artistic creation. So permit me briefly to rehearse what we know, from reliable sources, about Mozart's creative process.

We know that Mozart sketched. Many of his sketches were thrown away by Mozart during his lifetime or by his wife after his death, but quite a number have survived, and many of these have now been pub-

3. *Allgemeine musikalische Zeitung* 17:34 (August 23, 1815), cols. 561–66; trans. *Harmonicon* 35 (November 1825): 198–200.

lished in the appendixes of the various volumes of the *New Mozart Edition* (*Neue Mozart-Ausgabe*). We know that Mozart often composed with extraordinary speed and fluency but that there were also times when he was stymied, as he himself reports in his letters. A number of pieces were put aside incomplete; some remained that way, while others Mozart returned to months or years later and completed. Most of Mozart's autograph manuscripts are fair copies and contain few corrections; some do show second thoughts and hesitation. (A good example of the last is the C Minor Piano Concerto, K. 491, a facsimile edition of which has been published.)[4]

Despite an extraordinary ability to remember music and to manipulate musical ideas in his head, Mozart required a keyboard instrument when he was at work on compositions of any scope. This little-noticed fact is evidenced in two letters to Mozart's father, one written by his mother from Paris on April 5, 1778, the other written by himself from Vienna on August 1, 1781. Given Mozart's well-documented ability to work in his head, I suspect that the keyboard may have been necessary in the earliest and latest stages of creation: in the earliest stages, during which Mozart may have used his extraordinary gift for improvisation to generate ideas, and in the final stage, during which he could have tried the nearly finished piece to learn if the sounds as realized had the same feel and effect as the sounds as imagined.

Finally, when in his genuine letters Mozart described to his father how he was progressing on a project, the tone and contents are at stark variance with those of the 1815 forgery. Whereas in 1815 pseudo-Mozart is dreamily receiving ideas whence he knows not, in 1782 working on *Die Entführung,* real-Mozart is concerned with concrete matters of craft and the effects that well-calculated rhythms,

---

4. *Mozart: Piano Concerto in C Minor, K. 491, with a Foreword by Watkins Shaw and a Critical Introduction by Denis Matthews* (Kilkenny, Ireland: Boethius Press, 1979). An important recent monograph, Ulrich Konrad's *Mozarts Schaffensweise: Studien zu den Werkautographen, Skizzen und Entwürfen* (Göttingen: Vandenhoeck und Ruprecht, 1992), demonstrates that we have sketches for one in ten of Mozart's completed works (to say nothing of the sketches that survive for unknown and fragmentary works). Likewise, a recent article, Robert L. Marshall's "Clues to Mozart's Creativity: The Unfinished Compositions," in Peter Ostwald and Leonard S. Zegans, eds., *The Pleasures and Perils of Genius: Mostly Mozart* (Madison, Conn.: International Universities Press, 1993), 145–54, shows that for every four completed works by Mozart there survives one fragmentary work—that is, a work for which he began a fair-copy full score (not simply sketches) that he abandoned before completion.

textures, melodies, and harmonies will have on performers and listeners. Mozart's utterances about such matters have been conveniently gathered together and intelligently annotated in a new book.[5] Taken as a whole, Mozart's vivid remarks obliterate the 1815 forgery and the *Amadeus* myth based on it, substituting a well-focused reality for a blurry fantasy.

As for the snobbery of those who have never had dirt under their fingernails, it reminds me of some fiction I read a long time ago (I do not recall where) in which a group of characters was described as so primitive that they did not know how to acquire money except by working for it. And to many Romantic minds there was apparently something corrupting or demeaning about creating for money rather than out of "pure" inspiration, like the difference between love and prostitution. Mozart's attitude to money, which was something else entirely, has been summed up by Robert Marshall in *Mozart Speaks:* "Mozart by no means despised wealth. . . . But to be respectable and respected, wealth had, indeed, to be *gained*—that is, *earned* by virtue of one's talent and achievements—and not merely inherited."[6] And herein, I believe, lies the locus of cultural concerns that caused the outcry when I gave my anti-Romantic talk in Vienna: people cannot bear the thought that society might have treated an "original genius" like Mozart so badly that he was, so to speak, forced into artistic prostitution to survive, having to peddle his wares on the filthy streets of musical commerce. In the absence of evidence to the contrary— and sometimes even in the presence of such evidence—these people would prefer to imagine Mozart dreaming of posterity rather than of his unpaid rent.

Certainly the idea that exceptionally creative persons should be freed of ordinary responsibilities to pursue their work unimpeded by worldly concerns is of long standing. It was behind the more enlightened aspects of the patronage given by the Catholic Church in the Middle Ages, by Renaissance princes, by Orthodox Jewish communities to Talmudic scholars, and by the Princeton Institute for Advanced Study and other modern think tanks and artist colonies. To Romantic minds, a gifted composer was not a highly skilled craftsman

5. Robert L. Marshall, *Mozart Speaks: Views on Music, Musicians, and the World* (New York: Schirmer, 1991).

6. Marshall, *Mozart Speaks,* 161.

but an inspired genius to whom society owed something—and who would, in return, elevate culture by creating "masterpieces" for posterity. Mozart probably would have laughed at this. He was certainly well aware of his worth and had some sense that his music might have importance beyond the immediate occasions for which it was created. But the Romantic attitude would have astonished him, as he bent his every effort to craft pieces for the here and now, carefully calculated to fit the performers, suit the occasion, have an effect upon the listeners, and earn himself further commissions.

Mozart did write more than once that a reason for desiring financial security was that he found it hard to compose when he was upset and could therefore be more productive if he did not have to worry about money. This perfectly sensible and understandable sentiment was, however, expressed in the context of his being unable to imagine a time when he would not have to compose to support himself, and so wishing to make that process as painless and as successful as possible.

Under ideal circumstances—with a commission that appealed to him, with prospects for an excellent and prestigious performance, with the promise of adequate compensation—Mozart doubtless got intense pleasure from composing. It was probably not merely to fend off his father's criticisms of laziness in one of their interminable tiffs during his adolescence that Mozart called composing his "sole delight and passion." Nonetheless, we do not know, nor will we ever know, whether Mozart would have gone on composing at his usual rate—or even at all—had he become wealthy and no longer needed to sell his music to put bread on the table.

6

The challenge of blank paper:
Mozart the composer

CHRISTOPH WOLFF

MY TITLE MAY SOUND inappropriate and disrespectful to some, perhaps even blasphemous, but its provocation is deliberate. How could anyone propose that Mozart was challenged by paper—and by blank paper at that? Only a musicologist could come up with such an idea, you might say. Musicologists, alas, have somehow earned a reputation as people more closely involved with paper than with music. I hasten to say that I wish neither to confirm this notion in any way nor to discredit my discipline. On the contrary, I should like to argue that consideration of this seemingly ill-chosen subject matter opens up perspectives that will actually increase our appreciation and understanding of one of the most extraordinary and creative minds that ever lived, and bring us a little closer not only to the composer's working desk but also to his artistry and his very special musical language.[1]

The prevailing popular image of Mozart the composer is of the prototypical musical prodigy, a genius blessed with heavenly gifts, who

---

1. This chapter, originally delivered as a public lecture, with recorded musical examples, in Washington, D.C., in November 1992 for the Harvard Graduate Society for Advanced Study and Research, has been adapted from "Musikalische Gedanken und thematische Substanz: Analytische Aspekte der Mozart-Fragmente," *Mozart-Jahrbuch* (1991): 922–29; and "Vollendet und fragmentarisch: Über Mozarts Schaffen der letzten Lebensjahre," in Thomas Albert and Gisela Jaacks, eds., *Jahrbuch für Alte Musik*. (Wilhelmshaven, 1992), vol. 2, 61–87.

effortlessly created works of great beauty, deep expression, and exemplary perfection. This image actually has its origins in the late eighteenth century (and was vehemently advanced by none other than Mozart's father), but it has been increasingly embellished in subsequent generations down to the present day. Audiences everywhere are familiar with Peter Shaffer's *Amadeus,* which effectively juxtaposes Mozart, the divine genius, and Salieri, the most powerful figure of Vienna's musical establishment at the time. The thrust of the play is summed up in Salieri's words at the very end: "Mediocrities everywhere—now and to come."

The basic idea of Shaffer's play goes back 150 years to a dramatic poem by Alexander Pushkin, "Mozart and Salieri," written in 1830. One passage from the poem clearly articulates the force of Mozart's genius as felt by a Romantic poet:

> *Mozart* (having just played a newly composed piece):
> Well, do you like it?
> *Salieri:* What profundity,
> What boldness, and what art of composition!
> You, Mozart, are a god and know it not!
> *I* know it.
> *Mozart:* Bah! Really? Perhaps I am.

There is absolutely no question about Mozart's musical gifts, which set him clearly apart from the Salieris of his day and later times—though Salieri was an eminent composer indeed in his own right, who deserves much more credit than he is ordinarily given. Still, Mozart is in a category by himself. But what is it that makes him so special? Of course, we shall never be able to describe adequately Mozart's (or, for that matter, any other composer's) artistic impulses, let alone trace the roots of his inspiration. The psychology of creativity appears to be a rather nebulous sphere that resists critical scrutiny, and, in the final analysis, the nature of creativity cannot be confronted without a fair measure of speculation, which I shall resist. Let me turn instead to historically trustworthy and informative sources that permit us to examine Mozart's compositional methods. For Mozart, composing usually meant painstakingly hard work, often an extremely strenuous and time-consuming task that did not at all resemble the business of a stenographer merely recording what appeared to be divine musical messages.

For Mozart himself, the origin of his creative prowess and native genius was clear. In a letter to his father he stated in 1778, at the age of twenty-two, in quite a self-assured manner: "I am a composer and was born to be a Capellmeister. I neither can nor ought to bury the talent for composition with which God in his goodness has so richly endowed me (I may say so without conceit, for I feel it now more than ever)."[2] A few months earlier, he had told his father, in a somewhat enraged mood, that the elector in Mannheim "has no idea what I can do. . . . I am willing to submit to a test. Let him get together all the composers in Munich, let him even summon a few from Italy, France, Germany, England, and Spain. I undertake to compete with any of them in composition."[3] Although Mozart understood his musical talents as God's gift, he realized that he had to put them to work in a competitive environment.

Because we are discussing Mozart the composer specifically rather than, more generally, Mozart the genius, let us pursue—without going into a great deal of technical detail—aspects that shed some light on both the creative process and the resulting work of art. Of course, Mozart's immense productivity in a relatively short life of not quite thirty-six years makes it difficult to do justice to the subject. Therefore I would like to limit the exploration primarily to Mozart's later years and focus on a number of representative examples that help illuminate facets of his compositional methods and aesthetic goals. By "later years" I mean the last decade of his life, which he spent in Vienna, after splitting with the archbishop of his native Salzburg in 1781 at the age of twenty-five.

In Vienna Mozart worked primarily as a freelance musician, though he received a minor permanent appointment as chamber composer to the emperor in 1787 and, in the spring of 1791, the year of his death, a written promise of an appointment as kapellmeister at St. Stephen's Cathedral. Over the span of thirty years his productivity and creative output were remarkable; the works number 626 in the chronological catalogue assembled in 1864 by Ludwig von Koechel. According to Koechel, 370 works were composed before the Viennese years, and 256 between 1781 and 1791—figures that, in principle, still hold true today.

2. Emily Anderson, trans. and ed., *The Letters of Mozart and His Family,* 3d ed. (New York: W. W. Norton, 1989), 468.

3. Anderson, trans. and ed., *The Letters of Mozart and His Family,* 398.

Example 6.1. Minuet in F Major, K. 1a (beginning).

Example 6.2. Gigue in G Major, K. 574 (beginning).

In order to give a quick, albeit superficial, feel for both the chronological span of Mozart's musical output and a clearly noticeable change in his style, I propose two sharply contrasting examples, both compositions for keyboard: Example 6.1, Minuet in F Major, K. 1a

(1761), and Example 6.2, Gigue in G Major, K. 574 (1789). Both pieces belong to the genre of dance, and both are quite short; the innocent naiveté of the minuet cannot really be compared with the highly refined complexity of the gigue. Nevertheless, these two examples clearly and effectively indicate the overall direction of Mozart's development as a composer; the second example, with its sophisticated texture, is typical of Mozart's compositional tendencies in his late period—or better, later years.

We all recognize that the implications of the terms "later years" or "late period" vary from case to case. Applied to Haydn, Mozart, or Beethoven, they mean considerably different things, primarily because each of these composers reached a different age. Mozart died at age thirty-five but began his career as a wunderkind. Hence, the notion of a late period of work as a wise and penetrating epilogue to a long life's oeuvre can be applied to both Haydn and Beethoven but hardly to Mozart. In fact, Mozart's last works do not represent an endpoint at all. On the contrary, the final three symphonies signify the beginning of a clearly new symphonic approach. His last operas, especially *Die Zauberflöte,* represent a similarly new beginning in operatic composition. It is difficult, if not illegitimate, to imagine what course the history of music would have taken had Mozart been able to continue to fill the empty pages of his thematic catalogue[4] and to compose alongside Beethoven.

Consider for a moment the meaning of the several dozen unfilled pages in Mozart's musical diary (Figures 6.1 and 6.2), his thematic catalogue: pages of ruled but otherwise blank paper that he had clearly intended to fill—a mainly external challenge he had set for himself in 1784 in order to maintain and keep track of a steady, ambitious course in composition. Figures 6.1 and 6.2 show pages used and unused.

Mozart's thematic catalogue represents perhaps the most touching document of a remarkable creative life cut short, but it is by no means the only one, and probably not the most important one either. It is well known that Mozart left at his death the torso of a major work of sacred music, a requiem commissioned by a wealthy nobleman, but it is not generally known that he also left an abundant number of unfinished compositions, varying in length from one or two bars to sev-

4. Albi Rosenthal and Alan Tyson, eds., *Mozart's Thematic Catalogue: A Facsimile* (British Library, Stefan Zweig MS 63) (Ithaca, N.Y.: Cornell University Press, 1990).

Figure 6.1. *Verzeichniss aller meiner Werke*, fols. 28v–29r. (Stefan Zweig MS 63, British Library, London)

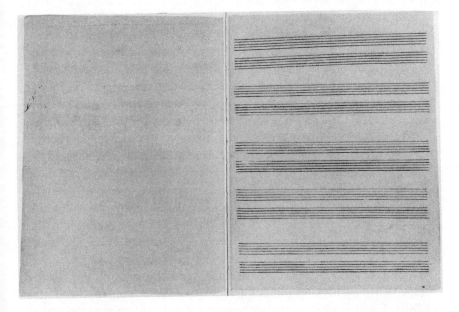

Figure 6.2. *Verzeichnüss aller meiner Werke*, fols. 29v–30r. (Stefan Zweig MS 63, British Library, London)

eral dozen, and in several cases to more than 100 measures. They extend over practically all the genres of interest to him. We know of no precedent for such an artistic legacy in the history of music. Constanze Mozart, who preserved the unfinished works after her husband's death, considered them important and exemplary documents of Mozart's artistry, comparable to (as she put it) "fragments of classical [i.e., ancient Greek] authors"[5]—a remarkable reference to Mozart's classical stature long before the use of the term "classicism" to designate a period of musical style.

Some sixty manuscripts originating from the estates of Constanze Mozart and her son, Wolfgang Amadeus Junior, are housed in the Salzburg Mozarteum.[6] The many fragments—well over 120 pieces—

5. Wolff, "Musikalische Gedanken und thematische Substanz," 922.
6. Most but not all extant fragments are transmitted in the Mozarteum manuscript collection. For more detailed information, see Alan Tyson, *Mozart: Studies of the Autograph Scores* (Cambridge: Harvard University Press, 1987), chapter 11: "The Mozart Fragments

invite investigations of various kinds. In particular, the fragments offer insight into the working methods and procedures of the composer, complementing the information provided by the autograph scores of the finished works. They may also illuminate the genesis of some finished compositions, particularly in instances that relate to specific cancellations found in the autograph scores. Some fragments document the scrapping or discontinuance of a projected work. The C Minor Mass, K. 427, of 1783 figures among the most prominent examples, but no less representative is the beginning of the G Minor Quartet, K. 587a/Anh. 74, a work terminated most likely in the fall of 1789, when Mozart filled the manuscript leaf with sketches for *Così fan tutte*.

But the fragments include first and foremost a large body of initiated works that were intended to be completed. The most significant as well as extensive example of this kind is, without doubt, the *Requiem*. Though there are also traces of less prominent compositions from Mozart's last year, the majority of the fragments by no means originate from 1791. They basically extend throughout the Vienna years, with perhaps slight culmination points in the mid and late 1780s. For the most part, they represent works that were interrupted rather than broken off—in other words, compositions the composer intended to finish. Alan Tyson demonstrated that some pieces among the finished works, notably the piano concertos K. 449 and K. 595, existed for some time as fragments—clearly constituting "work in progress" that was taken up at a later point.[7]

On the basis of my examination of the quartet fragments, I have suggested elsewhere that Mozart apparently kept a pragmatic filing system for his unfinished works. Although the system as such cannot be reliably reconstructed, he probably kept the various genres apart. At any rate, the simple fact that he did not discard so many unfinished pieces strongly indicates his interest in preserving the material. The fragments "on file" may well have served him as an ingenious mnemonic device, recording musical ideas and compositional concepts that he could easily return to—for purposes of completion, stimulation, or consultation.

The fragments are not to be understood primarily as documenting

in the Mozarteum, Salzburg: A Preliminary Study of Their Chronology and Their Significance"; also Robert L. Marshall, "Mozart's Unfinished: Some Lessons of the Fragments," *Mozart-Jahrbuch* (1991): 910–14.

7. Tyson, *Mozart: Studies of the Autograph Scores,* 150.

creative exuberance—an undeniable Mozartean phenomenon, of which the *finished* works provide far better and more eloquent evidence. Rather, they corroborate an intrinsic feature of Mozart's mature style—that is to say, the manifold implications of the inventive genius challenging himself with critical choices and making well-calculated and deliberate compositional decisions. The skeletal structure he notated on the music paper provided only the rough outlines of the piece; its compositional elaboration required considerable additional work. Facsimiles such as Figures 6.3–6.6 are representative of the principal types of fragments.[8]

Type 1: One-line notation (almost exclusively the melody in the upper voice), without indication of accompanimental voices. This occurs in compositions with secondary, that is, harmonically implied and unspecific, accompaniment. Examples: Contredanse in B-flat Major, K. 535b/Anh. 79; Horn Rondo in F Major, K. 522a/Anh. 108 (Figure 6.3).

Type 2: Notation of upper voice with bass, in order to indicate a specific harmonic, contrapuntal, or rhythmic-metric function of the bass line. Examples: Piano Concerto Movement in C Major, K. 502a/Anh. 60 (pedal point); Piano Concerto Movement in D Minor, K. 537b/Anh. 61 (complementary accompaniment) (Figure 6.4).

Type 3: Notation of upper and bass parts with occasional indication of other voices in order to indicate transitional passages, sequence of voice entries, etc. Examples: Piano Concerto Movement in A Major, K. 488c/Anh. 64; Piano Concerto Movement in D Major, K. 488a/Anh. 58 (Figure 6.5).

Type 4: Complete notation of all parts. This occurs when and where only the fully developed score affects the unequivocal resolution of texture, obbligato accompaniment, and character of a composition. Examples: virtually all trio, quartet, quintet, and keyboard fragments (Figure 6.6).

The outline was usually written down quite fast. For example, when at work on the opera *Idomeneo*, Mozart wrote to his father: "I must write at breakneck speed." And in the following sentence he explains why he had to write so fast: "Everything has been composed, but not yet written down."[9] That means that the substance of the work had been basically conceived and shaped entirely in his head; he then

---

8. Wolff, "Musikalische Gedanken und thematische Substanz," 922–29.
9. Anderson, trans. and ed., *The Letters of Mozart and His Family*, 702.

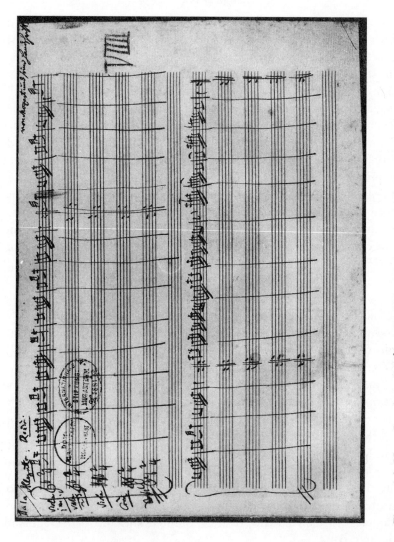

Figure 6.3. Horn Rondo in F Major, K. 522a. (Internationale Stiftung Mozarteum, Salzburg)

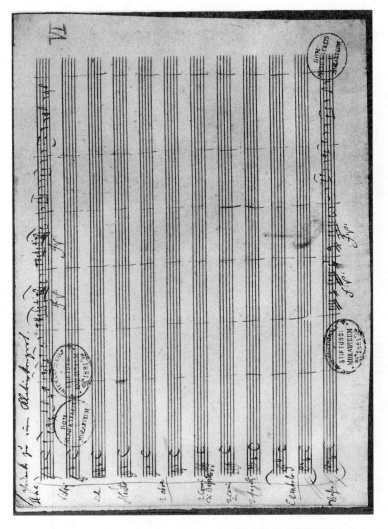

Figure 6.4. Piano Concerto Movement in D Minor, K. 537b. (Internationale Stiftung Mozarteum, Salzburg)

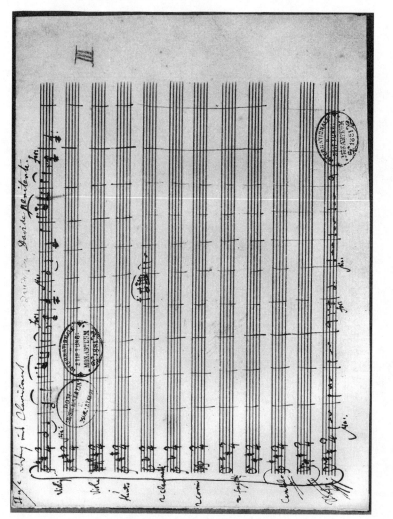

Figure 6.5. Piano Concerto Movement in D Major, K. 488a. (Internationale Stiftung Mozarteum, Salzburg)

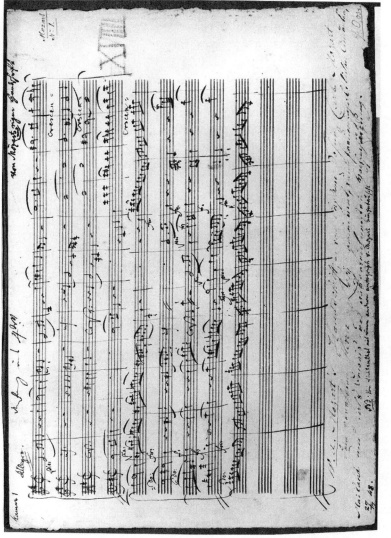

Figure 6.6. Quartet Movement in E Minor, K. 417d. (Internationale Stiftung Mozarteum, Salzburg)

needed to write down quickly the outline of the piece in order not to forget his ideas. The fleshing out of these ideas then required a second run-through, using watery ink for easy erasure.

Here, then, is the import of my title. Mozart had no trouble at all coming up with musical ideas, formulating them in his head, and thinking out a complete piece. In most instances he was eager to quickly preserve on paper the outlines of his thoughts. But the act of filling the blank sheets of paper with more than the bare skeleton required considerable additional compositional effort. In other words, what came easily into his mind took great and, at times, extraordinary pains to shape into a finished work.

For Mozart, the act of composition unfolded in a way that reveals significant differences from other composers. Let us briefly compare him with Bach and Beethoven. Bach apparently shaped the thematic material in his head (we know of no thematic sketches) and probably thought carefully about the general compositional consequences resulting from his choice of musical substance before putting anything on paper. He then wrote out the piece in a highly systematic manner and completed the score accordingly—that is, he generally worked out all parts of a composition more or less simultaneously, measure by measure or section by section. Beethoven, on the other hand, found it extremely difficult, at times even agonizing, to develop a musical idea into a suitable theme. He hesitated to settle on a final solution, and this procedure of elaboration typically extended over the entire composition, well beyond the invention of the thematic substance.

Actually, the compositional methods of these three composers were uncommonly sophisticated. Each of them strove deliberately for artistic perfection: Bach by constructing a musical piece in a steady and systematic fashion; Beethoven by constantly weighing his musical options at virtually every step during the creative process and gradually calibrating the shape of his final version; and Mozart by thinking through the outline of the entire work in advance, quickly formulating an incipit as a memory aid, drafting a skeleton score of the whole piece, and then filling in the missing and often elaborate details.

This approach to musical composition, however, was not characteristic of Mozart until approximately the late 1770s. Then, around 1780, and particularly with his move to Vienna, intricacies and complexities in his music become progressively more perceptible. *Idomeneo* and *Die Entführung*, as well as the first quartets of the set later dedicated to Haydn (especially K. 387) and the new type of piano concerto (K. 413–415), provide striking evidence in this regard.

Curiously, coinciding approximately with the beginning of the thematic catalogue of 1784, composing became an increasingly difficult task for Mozart. There are many reasons for this: his emancipation from Salzburg and, even more important, from his dominant father; the difficulty of winning independence and artistic freedom; the inner drive to achieve his goal. The pace of creating new works slows down; structures and textures display greater complexity and sophistication; the harmonic language shows more differentiation. In general, the intellectual dimensions of musical composition increase significantly, and hence the act of composition takes a lot more time. In 1785, when Mozart dedicated to Haydn a collection of string quartets that he had worked on for over three years, he expressly stated that these pieces "are, indeed, the fruit of a long and laborious study."

It is hard to define, or find a common denominator for, the musical style of Mozart's later years. Let us consider, however, the role of varied instrumental colors to enrich the musical structure and broaden its expressive scope. I would like to do this on the basis of an example taken from a piano concerto, the genre that provided Mozart in the mid-1780s with much ground for experimentation and exploration after he had made the unprecedented decision to use as an accompanying body the full opera orchestra, not just a string ensemble with the traditional two pairs of winds. For example, the opening statements of every one of Mozart's piano concertos from K. 450 (March 1784) on were designed to give the composer the possibility of exploring the rich and colorful resources of the orchestra. In this way, each piece presented at the very beginning its highly individualized coloristic profile.

Before turning to the question of Mozart's refined instrumentation of his musical ideas, let us consider the composer's point of departure—the formulation of the fundamental substance, the germinal cell, that is the basis of each musical piece. There is the very special instance of the simple tune that forms the point of departure for the final movement of the K. 453 piano concerto (1784). On May 27, 1784, Mozart notated in his account book the opening four measures of the melody of this variation setting as picked up quite competently by his little singing bird, a starling, and he added the remark, "That was nice!"

Clearly, most of Mozart's melodic inventions go well beyond the capability of even the most accomplished singing bird. Yet this striking example presents a case in point: a rather rudimentary idea could serve as the basis for an eventually extremely sophisticated compositional structure. Mozart lets the material evolve gradually. Variation 1 has the entire orchestra presenting the principal tune with a simple, straightforward chordal accompaniment. The tune itself, as well as the setting, is formed like a poetic quatrain (4+4+4+4 measures; lines 1–2 and 4 end with an emphatic five-note figure that serves as a "rhyming" device).

Variation 2 introduces the solo piano with a delayed, subtle string accompaniment in which the strings elegantly "sneak in" by contrapuntal means.

Variation 3 introduces the piano with systematically alternating wind and string accompaniments.

Variation 4 combines soloistically treated winds with the piano.

Variation 5 brings a mode switch (to G minor) and subjects the tune and its accompanimental material to intensive contrapuntal manipulation.

Variation 6 reintroduces the orchestral tutti and presents it in juxtaposition with the solo piano.

This highly abbreviated characterization of the opening six sections of the finale of K. 453 will have to suffice. However, Mozart's unique treatment of the orchestra, as seen in this particular example and in his novel approach to the genre of piano concerto in general, represents only one of his many compositional innovations. But it is clearly among the most important, especially as regards the composer's aesthetic goal to individualize the qualities of a single work, to give the piece its own unmistakable identity.

This pursuit of new and undiscovered horizons plays a major role in Mozart's last period of work, which represents without question an unprecedented point of culmination in his creative career. But it was not meant to be the end; it was, rather, a new beginning. Works from the final months of his life, such as *Die Zauberflöte*, the Clarinet Concerto, or the *Requiem*, stand as significant points of departure to truly new horizons. The picture is meaningfully complemented by the large repertoire of works-in-progress that is documented by Mozart's file of pieces composed in his head but notated only in skeletal form—because the burden of putting the material on paper in polished form had become ever more overwhelming, and because he was too self-critical a composer to risk turning out mediocre work. But as the fragments demonstrate, the composer's ambitious plans were fatefully reversed: What was to be an extraordinarily promising new beginning turned into an absolute end.

7

Marianne Mozart:
"Carissima sorella mia"

MAYNARD SOLOMON

IN EARLY YEARS, Mozart and his sister, Marianne (known familiarly as Nannerl), were as one flesh, one spirit. They were "the Mozart children," living and working together for common goals within the family enterprise, studying, traveling, and performing as symbiotic members of a single organism, sharing every life experience, from participating in triumphal events to watching each other hover on the brink of death. At three, Mozart was inspired to study music by watching his father's instruction of Marianne, who was five years older; he wanted to be like her. As children, they shared a secret language, were together the leading citizens of their jointly invented fantasy kingdom of Rücken—he its king, she his queen. In his hilarious mock entries in Marianne's personal diary, Mozart sometimes actually became her, assumed her personality, thought her thoughts, and wrote them down as if they were her own. The bantering intimacy of their earliest surviving letters, during Mozart's Italian journeys, at once masks and reveals the depth of their attachment. He sends her "a hundred kisses or smacks on your marvelous horseface,"[1] conveys outrageous greetings to her "from Catch-me-quick-and-then-you-have-me and from Don Cacarella, especially from

---

1. Emily Anderson, ed. and trans., *The Letters of Mozart and His Family*, 2 vols., 2d ed. (Macmillan: London and New York, 1966), I:115, February 17, 1770, Letter 80a.

behind."[2] He continues to play the imposter king to her queen: "I hope, my queen, that you are enjoying the highest degree of health and that now and then . . . you will sacrifice for my benefit some of your important and intimate thoughts, which ever proceed from that very fine and clear reasoning power, which in addition to your beauty, and although from a woman, and particularly from one of such tender years, almost nothing of the kind is ever expected, you possess, O queen, so abundantly as to put men and even graybeards to shame."[3] On occasion, he plays father as well: "Tell me, little girl, where have you been, eh?" or, writing to his sister and mother, "Addio. Farewell, my children."[4]

Mozart's adolescent letters to Marianne are replete with references to amatory matters, she acting as his intermediary with several of his Salzburg crushes and he chiding her on breaking hearts: "One thing distresses me, and that is that you have made Herr von Mölk sigh and suffer so frightfully and that you did not go sleigh-driving with him. . . . How many handkerchiefs will he not have used that day, weeping on your account. No doubt he will have previously taken an ounce of tartar, which will have purged his wretchedly dirty body."[5] Often Mozart sounds a salacious note, charging Marianne to ask a certain court baritone "whether he has again made the mistake of thinking that I was in bed instead of you"[6] and sternly insisting that she carry out her brother's orders: "Otherwise I shall give you a whipping. Quel plaisir!"[7] In her infrequent letters (mostly postscripts to her father's letters), Marianne responds in kind, evidently delighting in the sexual banter, calling him "my brother, that blackguard," and writing, "to you, you rascal! you villain! I give a juicy kiss."[8]

2. Anderson, *The Letters of Mozart,* I:117, March 3, 1770, Letter 82a.

3. Anderson, *The Letters of Mozart,* I:238, August 14, 1773, Letter 179a.

4. Anderson, *The Letters of Mozart,* I:143, from Naples, June 5, 1770, Letter 96a; Anderson, *The Letters of Mozart,* I:115, from Milan, February 17, 1770, Letter 80a. See also Anderson, *The Letters of Mozart,* I:221, December 18, 1772, Letter 166a.

5. Anderson, *The Letters of Mozart,* I:109–10, from Milan, January 26, 1770, Letter 77a.

6. Anderson, *The Letters of Mozart,* I:100, December 14, 1769, Letter 71b.

7. Anderson, *The Letters of Mozart,* I:143, from Naples, June 5, 1770, Letter 96a. Translation amended.

8. Anderson, *The Letters of Mozart,* I:258, Letter 195a; Anderson, *The Letters of Mozart,* I:283, September 29, 1777, Letter 211a.

Throughout, there is the sense of their mutual caring and love, magnified by the belief that their relationship, like the fabulous childhood in which it flowered, would endure forever. Mozart expresses his hope that "God will always grant you good health and will let you live another hundred years and will let you die when you have reached a thousand."[9] Repeatedly he assures her of his own love and asks her, in return, to "*aimez-moi toujours.*"[10] He addresses her as "*Carissima sorella mia*" or as "*allerliebste Schwester,*" and multiplies his kisses until they reach the millions and trillions.[11]

As they matured, the teasing tone was more often set aside to reveal their underlying, profound feelings. On July 20, 1778, following their mother's death, he belatedly greeted her from Paris on her name day: "Let us hope that the happy future is not far off when a brother and sister, so united and affectionate, will be able to talk to one another and tell one another all their most intimate thoughts and feelings. Meanwhile farewell—and love me, as I do you. I embrace you with all my heart, with all my soul, and ever remain your sincere—your true brother."[12] A few days later he wrote again, trying to console her on her sorrow: "Adieu, farewell. I will not awaken sad memories. Resign yourself to the will of God and trust in Him. Remember that you have a brother, who loves you with all his heart."[13]

Somewhere along the way they began to lose each other. At first it may have been the normal divergence of a brother and sister who continue to cherish memories of shared early experience despite the awkward sense that they have grown apart. By the end, however, there was a break between Mozart and his sister so total that, when Marianne furnished biographical data for Schlichtegroll's obituary in 1792, she claimed complete ignorance of the most basic information about her brother during his last years, including when it was that he "entered imperial service . . . , who his wife was, how many children they had of their union, how many of them are still alive, etc."[14] Com-

---

9. Anderson, *The Letters of Mozart*, I:149–50, from Bologna, July 21, 1770, Letter 103.

10. Anderson, *The Letters of Mozart*, I:106, January 7, 1770, Letter 75a.

11. Wilhelm A. Bauer, Otto Erich Deutsch, and Joseph Heinz Eibl, eds., *Wolfgang Amadeus Mozart: Briefe und Aufzeichnungen: Gesamtausgabe,* 7 vols. (Kassel: Bärenreiter, 1962–75), I:293, December 14, 1769, Letter 147, and I:301, January 7, 1770, Letter 153. See also Anderson, *The Letters of Mozart*, I:100, Letter 71b, and I:104, Letter 75a.

12. Anderson, *The Letters of Mozart*, I:575, Letter 315b.

13. Anderson, *The Letters of Mozart*, I:589–90, July 31, 1778, Letter 319a.

14. Marianne Mozart, "Data for a Biography of the Late Composer Wolfgang Mozart,"

munication between them had virtually ceased in the later 1780s, and she did not even personally notify him of their father's mortal illness or death. "I was not at all surprised," he wrote her, not without a hint of rancor, "as I could easily guess the reason, that you yourself did not inform me of the sad death of our most dear father, which to me was quite unexpected."[15] But even earlier, she had not attended his wedding, nor he hers, and neither of them ever saw the other's children. During the last three years of Mozart's life, a heavy curtain of silence had fallen between them, and, at his death, there was no word exchanged between his sister and his widow.

The correspondence sheds little light on the early sources of the bitter and hostile state into which their relationship eventually descended. One finds there no indication that Marianne resented his having come to absorb so much of their parents' attention or that she envied Mozart's success, fame, and adulation, which far overshadowed Marianne's own accomplishments. Although she was highly praised for the accuracy of her playing, she essentially ended her public career as a wunderkind in 1768, with very occasional performances as Mozart's collaborator in later years, and only a handful of appearances as a soloist and accompanist in Salzburg.[16] By the time Marianne passed her eighteenth birthday, she had come to be judged by a different standard than that applied to her as a child; thereafter, she stayed at home giving piano lessons from time to time while Mozart continued to make his mark in the capitals of Europe. And even after her own artistic career had ended, she remained uncomplaining. When Leopold and Mozart spent the better part of the next four years soaking up the splendors of Italy and hobnobbing with princes and popes, Marianne and her mother lan-

Spring 1792, in Otto Erich Deutsch, ed., *Mozart: A Documentary Biography* (London: A. & C. Black, 1966), 454–62 (at 461n) (cited henceforth as *Documentary Biography*). See also Nottebohm, *Mozartiana* (Leipzig: Breitkopf und Härtel, 1880), 95–111.

15. Anderson, *The Letters of Mozart*, II:909, June 16, 1787, Letter 548.

16. Many of Marianne Mozart's performances at Salzburg have left no trace. Among the documented performances are a joint appearance with Mozart on October 15, 1769; participation in Mozart's concert in the "Tanzmeistersaal" on August 15, 1777; performances for visitors Anton Janitsch and Joseph Reicha on January 25 and 26, 1778; continuo accompaniments in a concert by Count Czernin's amateur orchestra on April 12, 1778; accompanying Mozart at a concert at court in early September 1780. In a letter of March 24, 1781, Mozart suggested that his sister "*demand* two ducats" each time she performed at court, but the details of such performances have not survived. See Anderson, *The Letters of Mozart*, II:718, March 24, 1781, Letter 395. Her final joint appearance with Mozart took place in Augsburg in early March 1781.

guished in Salzburg, silently resenting though outwardly accepting Leopold's repeated explanations that he could not afford to let them travel, even for a short time. Perhaps there was no possibility of expressing rivalrous feelings so long as Mozart remained a faithful component of the family enterprise, an enterprise in which each member performed an assigned role without expectation of special favor. Or perhaps Marianne's natural resentments against her brother had been kept in check because of his centrality to the family's welfare.

Marianne Mozart had an apparently unlimited capacity for compliance: She was her father's daughter, obedient, subservient, self-sacrificing. Yet, if she could not express her feeling of despair when her mother and brother left Salzburg in September 1777 on an extended journey, her body spoke for her. "The day of their departure I spent mostly in bed, I vomited and had an extraordinary headache, that was the 23rd of September," she recorded laconically in her diary.[17] Leopold described her reaction in greater detail: "Nannerl wept bitterly and I had to use every effort to console her. She complained of a headache and a sick stomach and in the end she retched and vomited; and putting a cloth round her head she went off to bed and had the shutters closed."[18] Her fear of abandonment was quite on the surface: "I kiss Mamma's hands and I beg you not to forget me," she wrote on October 4.[19] And again, a few weeks later: "When things fare well or badly with you, think of us, who are obliged to live sadly here, separated from you both."[20] However, preoccupied with her son's affairs and her husband's anxieties, Anna Maria Mozart did not fully register her daughter's signals: during the last ten months of her life she never wrote a separate letter to Marianne, confining herself to wishing her well and sending her greetings.[21] On rare occasions only did she allude to Paris fashions that might interest her daughter.

And soon, Marianne maintained the pretense that all was indeed

17. Diary of Marianne Mozart, in Bauer, Deutsch, Eibl, *Wolfgang Amadeus Mozart*, II: 7, Letter 330. See also Anderson, *The Letters of Mozart*, I:296, October 4, 1777, Letter 215a.

18. Anderson, *The Letters of Mozart*, I:273, September 25, 1777, Letter 208.

19. Anderson, *The Letters of Mozart*, I:296, October 4, 1777, Letter 215a.

20. Anderson, *The Letters of Mozart*, I:336, October 23, 1777, Letter 227a.

21. Schwerin observed how few references there were to Marianne in her mother's letters, "despite the fact that her daughter's postscripts reflect the longing for her mother's presence. . . ." Erna Schwerin, "Anna Maria Mozart: A Profile of Mozart's Mother," *Friends of Mozart Newsletter* 16 (Spring 1984): 3.

well with her, reporting blandly and cheerily on the weekly archery contests and other miscellaneous Salzburg events. For it was her role to present an uncomplaining face to the world while she pursued her primary duty—to care for her father, an obligation that her mother made quite explicit when, for example, she wrote to her husband that Marianne's task was "to take care that you have no worries and to help you to pass the time so that you do not get melancholy."[22] For his part, despite abundant laments about himself, Leopold neither looked for nor perceived any signs that his daughter might be troubled: "I must tell you that in everything which has to do with the house Nannerl is extraordinarily industrious, hard-working and amazingly attentive; besides which she plays as much as she can and is an excellent accompanist. Every evening we practice for two or two and a half hours at least."[23] Obviously pleased at her talents as a housekeeper and companion, it was not in his interest to observe that his daughter, beneath her surface tractability, was discontented.

Mozart, however, was aware that Marianne was unhappy, for she confided to him things that she could not tell their parents. To him she revealed that she, too, wanted to leave what she called "this dull Salzburg."[24] She wrote: "I should like to have the pleasure of seeing you soon again, provided it is not in Salzburg."[25] A much more painful issue, however, was Leopold's reluctance to let her marry. Repeatedly, he turned away Marianne's suitors on transparent pretexts. Nothing seems to have come from her flirtation with young Franz von Mölk, whose name Mozart teasingly invoked as early as 1770. In 1778, when Marianne was already twenty-seven years old, she was courted by a widower named Johann Joseph Adam, who, to no avail, proclaimed his love for her from the housetops. Leopold described to Mozart how he had handled this effrontery: "The court valet *Adam,* now Lord High Steward, sought to make your sister's acquaintance. Once he took us by surprise but from that time on we were never any longer at home, and finally, since he often spoke about his love to our maid Tresel, I ordered her to tell him that we would be honored to receive him and his wife should he marry some day, but as long as he

22. Anderson, *The Letters of Mozart,* I:292, October 2, 1777, Letter 214a.
23. Anderson, *The Letters of Mozart,* I:343–44, October 27, 1777, Letter 230a.
24. Anderson, *The Letters of Mozart,* I:412, December 8, 1777, Letter 257a.
25. Anderson, *The Letters of Mozart,* I:438, December 29, 1777, Letter 268a.

is a widower we must prohibit him from visiting us, inasmuch as my daughter does not want to be the talk of the town."[26] (Even as he thus rejected an eligible suitor, Leopold lamented in the same letter that "your dear sister, who is already twenty-seven years of age . . . is not provided for, while I am growing old.")[27] It is not given whether Marianne returned Adam's affections or those of other suitors whose names may not have survived; but it seems sure that she was in love with Captain Franz Armand d'Ippold (ca. 1730–90), an older man of moderate means.[28] The love matter had progressed so far by the summer of 1781 that he and Marianne hoped to marry, if only they could be assured of supporting themselves and obtaining Leopold's consent. However, Leopold had by then apparently raised objections to the marriage, and Marianne had fallen ill—her frequent reaction to disappointment or inner conflict.

From afar, Mozart strongly supported the match and exchanged letters with both d'Ippold and his sister about it: "I should very much like to know how things are progressing between you and a certain good friend, you know whom I mean. Do write to me about this! Or have I lost your confidence in this matter?"[29] Things had reached a critical point in September, when Mozart wrote:

I am going to be quite frank with you about your constantly recurring indispositions. Believe me, dearest sister, that I am quite serious when I say that the best cure for you would be a husband— and if only because marriage would have such a profound influence on your health, I wish with all my heart that you could marry soon. . . . For you and d'Yppold there are scarcely any—indeed, I may say with certainty—no prospects in Salzburg. But could not d'Yppold manage to get something here? I suppose he is not *absolutely* pen-

26. Bauer, Deutsch, and Eibl, *Wolfgang Amadeus Mozart,* II:450, August 27, 1778, Letter 478.

27. Anderson, *The Letters of Mozart,* II:605, August 27, 1778, Letter 326.

28. D'Ippold had savings of 4,000 florins at his death. Jahn identified him as an Imperial Captain and a steward of the Court Pages. Otto Jahn, *W. A. Mozart,* 4th ed., ed. and enlarged Hermann Deiters, 2 vols. (Leipzig: Breitkopf und Härtel, 1905–7), II:734. Subsequent searches of the Salzburg archives, however, do not confirm this assumption. See Rudolph Genée, "Mozarts Schwester Nannerl," *Mitteilungen der Mozart-Gemeinde Berlin,* III (November 1896): 98–103 (at 102n). Despite his name, d'Ippold was not of aristocratic origin, having himself added the "de" to his name. The name is variously spelled d'Ippold, d'Yppold, and Diepold.

29. Anderson, *The Letters of Mozart,* II:751, July 4, 1781, Letter 415. Marianne Mozart's letters on this subject are not extant.

niless? Ask him about it—and if he thinks the project at all practicable, he has only to tell me what steps to take, and I will certainly do my utmost, for I take the greatest interest in this affair. If this were accomplished, you could certainly marry; for, believe me, you could earn a great deal of money in Vienna, for example, by playing at private concerts and by giving lessons. You would be very much in demand—and you would be well paid. In that case my father would have to resign his post and come too—and we could live very happily together again. I see no other solution—and even before I knew that your affair with d'Yppold was serious, I had something like this in mind for you. Our dear father was the only difficulty, for I wanted him to enjoy his rest and not to have to worry and torment himself. But I think that in this way it might be arranged. For with your husband's earnings, your own and mine, we can easily manage, and enable our father to live in peace and comfort.[30]

Whether or not Leopold learned of Mozart's attempt to help Marianne does not appear; what is known is that her possibly surreptitious correspondence with Mozart on this matter suddenly came to an end. Her illness worsened, so that within a few days after his fraternal proposal Mozart was writing to his father: "You gave me rather a fright about my sister, because it was so unexpected. I do hope that she is better now. I kiss her a thousand times and kiss your hands a hundred times and am ever your most obedient son."[31] Concern about her condition did not abate for several months, until, in mid-December, Mozart wrote her: "If you find a good opportunity of coming to Vienna for a time, just write and let me know beforehand."[32] But by then there was no further prospect of marriage; presumably, not yet ready to yield his daughter to another man, or desirous of a match with someone of higher social standing, Leopold had terminated the affair—at least, that is the consensus of Marianne's biographers.[33] Hum-

30. Anderson, *The Letters of Mozart*, I:766–77, September 19, 1781, Letter 425. Earlier the same year, Mozart had invited his father and sister to settle in Vienna: "There are many distinguished families here who hesitate to engage a male teacher, but would give handsome terms to a woman." Anderson, *The Letters of Mozart*, II:734–35, May 16, 1781, Letter 405.

31. Anderson, *The Letters of Mozart*, I:767, after September 19, 1781, Letter 425.

32. Anderson, *The Letters of Mozart*, I:785, December 15, 1781, Letter 437.

33. Walter Hummel, *Nannerl: Wolfgang Amadeus Mozarts Schwester* (Zurich, Leipzig, and Vienna: Amalthea Verlag, 1952), 58; also see Bauer, Deutsch, and Eibl, *Wolfgang Amadeus Mozart*, VI:74.

mel writes that she now showed "renewed courage in the fulfillment of the duty which she had undertaken, to fashion a peaceful, quiet existence for her aging father."[34]

Within the confines of that quiet existence, Marianne Mozart reflected upon the depth of her loss, considered what might have been, and, perhaps, measured her state against that of her brother, who had delivered himself from stultifying Salzburg and established a separate career in the glamorous capital; now he was about to marry a woman whom he loved, thereby putting a full stop to his family obligations. Her brother's emergence coincided with her own unhappy love affair. In a few years she would be married off to an elderly and ill-tempered widower with five young children, chosen by her father for his wealth and social standing, and shortly thereafter she would leave her first-born infant with her father—without caveat, blindly, automatically, either unaware of the depth of her sacrifice or wholly anesthetized to her own pain. Mozart alone had tried to save her, encouraged her to marry d'Ippold and to make her own living as a creative musician. In retrospect, of course, it seems inevitable that she would be unable to take these steps, which must have seemed so extreme to her. In the end, the risks were too great: she had neither the stomach nor the temperament to enter into a mortal contest with her father.

In some way, the manifest ideal of the Mozart family had always been that of self-sacrifice: each member of the family was enjoined to sacrifice himself or herself for the others, and sacrifice was seen both as an absolute good and as an absolute obligation. Of course, this ideal had overtones of Christian martyrdom, and Leopold Mozart more than once referred to his own crucifixion, as when he wrote of the "Salzburg cross, on which I am still hanging."[35] In the course of time Mozart came to renounce the sacrificial compulsion, but, because it played upon deep altruistic and familial currents within him, it nevertheless continued to exercise a powerful hold on him. What he could never fully grasp was that it is the logic of such fanaticism that those who will not conform to it are expelled from the kinship group, regarded as apostates and sinners against the sacred alliance; so that, by

34. Hummel, *Nannerl*, 58.
35. Anderson, *The Letters of Mozart*, I:496, February 25–26, 1778, Letter 291.

his resistance to Leopold's unremitting demands, Mozart had, in effect, become a culprit to his own family, one whose punishment was to be sent to Coventry. In contrast, Marianne, like a soldier of the Cross or a dedicated sister of mercy, could never consider placing her own interests above those of the family, and especially above those of her father, who represented the family incarnate.

Even as she was drawn ever closer to her father, Marianne was held up to Mozart as a paragon of filial piety—and even as her brother's replacement:

> Your sister alone is now my support, and I try to banish the cares which seem to overwhelm me by a very quiet form of entertainment, which is, to play through on the violin from six to eight every evening, arias, symphonies, masses, vespers, and so forth, while your sister plays the figured bass and gets practice in accompanying . . . [S]he extemporizes so successfully that you would be astounded. And do you know what has inspired her with this determination and terrific industry? *My death!* She realizes and foresees the misery into which she would be plunged, were I suddenly to breathe my last.[36]

And so, Marianne Mozart remained a dutiful daughter, agreeing with her father's every judgment and sharing his every prejudice. Her attitude toward her brother became indistinguishable from that of her father. Trembling with guilt and doubt over his defiance of his father, Mozart had waited vainly for any sign of encouragement, sympathy, or understanding from his older sister. Instead, she did not protest when Leopold, knowing Mozart's vulnerability on the issue, repeatedly invoked sister against brother, charging that Mozart's departure from Salzburg would lead to her impoverishment: "You will . . . make me and your sister into beggars," he wrote.[37] For example, in 1778, Leopold pictured her as distraught by Mozart's plan to tour Italy with the Webers: "Nannerl has wept her full share during these last two days," he wrote.[38] And when Mozart shot back, "Tell her she must not cry over every silly trifle, or I shall never go home again,"[39] he succeeded only in arousing Leopold's wrath. In response, he told how

36. Anderson, *The Letters of Mozart*, I:495, February 25–26, 1778, Letter 291.
37. Bauer, Deutsch, and Eibl, *Wolfgang Amadeus Mozart*, II:464, Letter 482.
38. Anderson, *The Letters of Mozart*, I:480, February 11–12, 1778, Letter 285.
39. Anderson, *The Letters of Mozart*, I:486, February 19, 1778, Letter 288.

Marianne had come to fear that, after his death, she would be forced into domestic service, despite which she was willing to sacrifice her own savings as security to help an unfeeling and profligate brother: "So your sister was not crying over a silly trifle, when she wept over your letter."[40]

Clearly, Mozart needed an ally, but during this period Marianne never disassociated herself from her father's views; instead, she reinforced the mythology that her brother was destined to be the instrument of the family's security and of her personal deliverance: "We are both longing for you to make your fortune, for that, I know for certain, will mean happiness to us all."[41]

Eventually, it became clear that Mozart would never again receive comfort from his sister. When, in 1782, he announced his intention to marry Constanze Weber, Marianne adopted her father's view that Mozart was forsaking his family obligations for an unworthy female interloper, and she joined her father in refusing to bless the marriage. Before the wedding, Constanze sent Marianne assurance of her love and asked for her friendship in return: "Without undue pride I may say that I partly deserve it and shall endeavor to do so wholly! May I in exchange offer you mine, which, indeed, has long been yours in the secrecy of my heart?"[42] The coolness of Marianne's responses to such sisterly overtures became a source of great pain to Mozart, and Constanze grew increasingly irate that she was not accepted by Mozart's family. On July 24, 1782, a week before the wedding, she sent Marianne greetings on her name day, and did not conceal her hurt feelings:

> Forgive me for . . . worrying you again with my scrawl. . . . And if my good wishes are a nuisance to you, as all congratulations are, my consolation must be that already I am not the only one who is bothering you in this way. All that I deserve is that for the love of God you should suffer me as you do all the others.[43]

During the years following Mozart's marriage, signs of affection continued to alternate with indications of the growing estrangement between the Mozart siblings. In later 1783, Mozart and his wife spent

---

40. Anderson, *The Letters of Mozart,* I:495, February 25–26, 1778, Letter 291.
41. Anderson, *The Letters of Mozart,* I:471, February 9, 1778, Letter 284a.
42. Anderson, *The Letters of Mozart,* II:802, April 20, 1782, Letter 447a.
43. Anderson, *The Letters of Mozart,* II:809, July 24, 1782, Letter 454a.

three months visiting Salzburg. But the atmosphere there had become so thoroughly contaminated that Leopold would not allow Constanze to have as a memento even one of the many gifts that Mozart had received on his early journeys.[44] Constanze recalled the constrained atmosphere there and related how "the behavior towards him and his wife gave [Mozart] the feeling that he had been wronged."[45] He was indeed deeply troubled, for he wanted nothing more than to bring about a loving reconciliation. More than forty years later, Constanze told Mary Novello, who, with her husband, the musician and publisher Vincent Novello, came to Salzburg in 1829 to interview Mozart's survivors, that as the family was singing the quartet "Andró ramingo e solo," from *Idomeneo,* with its rending depiction of a father, a son, and two women torn by conflicting desires, Mozart "was so overcome that he burst into tears and quitted the chamber and it was some time before she could console him."[46] Mozart refused to tolerate the grievous rejection of his bride: By signing most of his letters home "W. & C. Mozart" he pointedly reminded his father and sister that he and Constanze were inseparable. And, lest there be any misunderstanding, he once wrote explicitly: "Mann und Weib ist ein Leib" (Man and wife are one flesh).[47]

Having returned to Vienna after failing to gain acceptance for Constanze, Mozart continued to try to jolly his sister into showing the old affection, writing her, with perhaps a trace of hostility: "We both send Nannerl (1) a couple of boxes on the ear (2) a couple of slaps on the face (3) a couple of raps on the cheek (4) a couple of whacks on the jaw (5) a couple of smacks on the jowl (6) a couple of cuffs on the mug."[48] Similarly, in 1784, he warmly congratulated her on her marriage, expressed his regret at not attending the wedding, and offered instead a merry doggerel verse to warn his sister about her unaccustomed conjugal responsibilities.

44. Georg Nikolaus von Nissen, *Biographie W. A. Mozarts* (Leipzig: Breitkopf und Härtel, 1828), xviii.

45. Rudolf Lewicki, "Aus Nissens Kollektaneen," *Mozarteums Mitteilungen* 2:1 (November 1919): 28–30.

46. Nerina Medici di Marignano and Rosemary Hughes, eds., *A Mozart Pilgrimage: Being the Travel Diaries of Vincent and Mary Novello in the Year 1829* (London: 1955), 115; see also Jahn, *W. A. Mozart,* I:673.

47. Bauer, Deutsch, and Eibl, *Wolfgang Amadeus Mozart,* III:225, Letter 690; Anderson, *The Letters of Mozart,* II:817, August 24, 1782, Letter 461.

48. Anderson, *The Letters of Mozart,* II:863–64, December 10, 1783, Letter 501.

Wedlock will show you many things
Which still a mystery remain;
Experience soon will teach to you
What Eve herself once had to do
Before she could give birth to Cain.
But all these duties are so light
You will perform them with delight.[49]

But by this time their connection had been thoroughly undermined. Although Mozart wrote to her again in November (the letter
does not survive), their correspondence came to a virtual halt, to be
resumed briefly only in the aftermath of their father's death in 1787.
During those three years, Marianne relied on her father for news of
Mozart—births, concerts, journeys, compositions, publications, and
changes of lodgings—gleaned from his letters home. For although
their mutual bitterness was never far from the surface, Leopold and
Mozart kept the shreds of civility alive so that they could remain in
touch: neither of them could ever bring himself to break relations
altogether. Mozart and his sister, however, were no longer commu-
nicating. On one or two occasions she seems to have tried to initiate
a friendly exchange, but without success. In early November 1785,
Mozart failed to acknowledge her congratulations on his name day
(October 31) and instead sent his regrets and regards to her through
their father, who wrote to her: "He hasn't time to answer your letter
at once."[50] Marianne knew that her brother was expert at cloaking
chilly rejections in expressions of deep sentiment and concern, reinforced by regrets and excuses. Mozart and his sister had once been
one flesh, but that time was gone. In the aftermath of the Salzburg
reunion, with its rejection of his bride, he gave up his sister; in the
depths of her bitterness, she gave up her brother.

In some way that she could never specify, Mozart had spoiled Marianne's chances for happiness. Somehow, she felt she had been denied
the blessings of fortune because her brother had seized his own op-

49. Anderson, *The Letters of Mozart,* II:882, August 18, 1784, Letter 517.
50. Anderson, *The Letters of Mozart,* II:893, Leopold Mozart to his daughter, November 11, 1785, Letter 532. Occasionally Mozart sent greetings to Marianne through their
father; for example, in August of 1786: "Your brother sends his regards and writes that his
wife will soon come to childbed." Otto Erich Deutsch and Bernhard Paumgartner, eds.,
Leopold Mozarts Briefe an seine Tochter (Salzburg and Leipzig: Verlag Anton Pustet, 1936),
349, August 23, 1786.

portunity to make a life for himself. Clearly it was inconceivable that both of them could desert their father. And, of course, in showing Marianne the very possibility of fulfillment, Mozart could only cause her additional pain, for she was incapable of taking the step necessary to that fulfillment. Unfortunately, she never gave any indication that she felt her brother's pain, or that she understood the price he had paid for his "freedom." She had become the vessel into which overflowed Leopold's rancor and discontent; and once Mozart had irrevocably broken with the family enterprise, she was not only at last able to express pent-up hostilities toward him, but to do so with the encouragement and approval of her father. It was as her father's daughter that she refused to accept Constanze into the family, that she failed to bless Mozart's wedding, that she withheld from him a sister's comfort. What she could never understand was that her bitterness was discharged against the wrong object, for it was not Mozart who had crippled her life, conscripted her as a surrogate wife and servant, turned away her suitors, and married her to an unattractive widower.

She could not perceive these things because she was blinded by the family mythology that held Mozart to be forever a miraculous child who was ultimately responsible for the family's fortunes, who was the instrument of its salvation or downfall. That is why Marianne had pinned her hopes on Mozart's ability to rescue her; and in this he failed her. But in compensation for her misfortunes—not least of which was the loss of her brother—she gained her father's attention, gratitude, and love. Now it was she who became her father's consolation, his main correspondent, for whom he penned his epistolary chronicle of Salzburg daily life between 1784 and 1787. Now, father and daughter achieved a harmonious interchange and understanding, free of rancor or complaint, marked by deep mutual caring. "Deeds and not wishes are the indications of true friendship and tender fatherly love," he wrote her on her name day in July 1786. "Of this you are convinced, I know that; and that pleases me. I wish you continued health and—everything else you might wish for yourself."[51] On balance, she had not done too badly, and she had the deep satisfaction of knowing that she had been faithful to the principles of family solidarity to which the Mozarts were pledged and by which they had

51. Deutsch and Paumgartner, *Leopold Mozarts Briefe an seine Tochter*, 325, July 21, 1786.

made their lasting mark on eighteenth-century musical life. If, in the process, a brother and sister lost one another, that had to be accepted as the natural consequence of an unavoidable moral imperative.

The hostility and resentment, so long held in check, poured out of them when their father died in the spring of 1787. It was not that he was no longer there to mediate between two warring siblings, for he had not previously hesitated to set them against each other. Rather, by his disposition of his estate, Leopold now arranged things precisely so as to make their break inevitable and wounding. Mozart was informed of his father's death by Marianne's old suitor, Franz d'Ippold, in a letter of May 28, 1787. He revealed the fullness of his grief in two economical lines to his closest friend, Gottfried von Jacquin: "I inform you that on returning home today I received the sad news of my most beloved father's death. You can imagine the state I am in."[52] On June 2, Mozart wrote a guarded letter to his sister:

> You can easily imagine, as our loss is equally great, how pained I was by the sad news of the sudden death of our dearest father. Since at the moment it is impossible for me to leave Vienna . . . and since it would be hardly worth my while to do so for the sake of our late father's estate, I must confess that I too am entirely of your opinion about having a public auction. But before it takes place I should like to see the inventory so as to be able to choose some personal effects. But if, as Herr F. d'Yppold has written to tell me, there is a *dispositio paterna inter liberos,* then, of course, I must be informed of this *dispositio* beforehand so as to be able to make further arrangements:—hence I am now expecting an accurate copy of it and after a rapid perusal of its contents I shall let you have my opinion at once.[53]

Beneath Mozart's controlled words are sorrow, anger, and disappointment: He will not come to Salzburg because "it would be hardly worth my while"; he tenders very little sympathy to his sister before turning to matters of business. Clearly, he was not pleased with what he had learned from d'Ippold concerning Leopold's division of his estate. Neither the *dispositio paterna inter liberos,* a testamentary order that regulates the division of an estate among heirs, nor the full in-

---

52. Anderson, *The Letters of Mozart,* II:908, end of May 1787, Letter 547.
53. Anderson, *The Letters of Mozart,* II:909, June 2, 1787, Letter 547*.

ventory of the estate has survived, but there is sufficient documentary evidence available to conclude with a high degree of probability that Leopold Mozart's entire estate was left to his daughter except for his personal effects, which were to be auctioned and the proceeds divided between his children. Walter Senn concludes "that Leopold Mozart disposed of a portion of his possessions and thereby did not forget his daughter (even though the writings do not reflect this): that in the instructions concerning the effects (whether by testament or codicil) the individual possessions which were to be divided by the siblings, as legal heirs, were not named"; and he takes Mozart's failure subsequently to refer to a testament as "a sign that his father had provided only an unsatisfactory portion for him."[54]

To compound his sense that he had been treated unfairly, Mozart soon learned that Marianne refused to let him choose some personal effects for himself, and she even asked him through a third person[55]— she would not write him directly about this—to waive any proceeds from the sale. Only now, in his blunt letter of June 16, by which time he had received a copy of the testament and the inventory, did Mozart openly express his anger against her, chiding her for not personally informing him of their father's death and taking issue with her request for a waiver. He wrote:

> If you were still unprovided for, all this would be quite unnecessary, for as I have already said and thought a thousand times, I should leave everything to you with the greatest delight. But as the property would really be of no use to you, while, on the contrary, it would be a considerable help to me, I think it my duty to consider my wife and child.[56]

Negotiations now commenced between Mozart and his brother-in-law to permit Marianne to withhold from the auction whatever she wanted for herself in exchange for a flat payment to Mozart. On Au-

54. Walter Senn, "Zur Erbteilung nach Leopold Mozart," *Neues Augsburger Mozartbuch. Zeitschrift des historischen Vereins fur Schwaben,* vols. 62–63 (1962), 383–95 (at 385). Senn concludes that several references in the Minutes of the Princely Council dated September 21, 1787, to "the paternal inheritance apportioned to Mozart" admit of no other interpretation but that the testament actually existed (393–94). See also Erich Valentin, "Ein unbekannter Mozart-Brief," *Neues Mozart-Jahrbuch* 3 (1943): 87–94 (at 91–92).

55. Probably d'Ippold, who now turned down Mozart's request that he serve as his representative in the settlement of the estate.

56. Anderson, *The Letters of Mozart,* II:909, June 16, 1787, Letter 548.

gust 1, the deal was struck: Mozart was to get 1,000 florins in Viennese currency, and he was to regain possession of his manuscript scores, for these too had become a subject of contention inasmuch as Leopold had apparently bequeathed all musical scores to his daughter. "Please do not forget about my *scores*," Mozart underlined in his letter.[57] The original inventory of Leopold's goods numbered 579 items; [58]but when the auction took place between September 25 and 28, only 314 items were placed on sale, bringing 1,507 florins and 56 kreuzer. Included were "court dresses, hunting-gear, linen, kitchen utensils, furniture, jewellry, and musical instruments."[59] Mozart received more than half of the proceeds, but Marianne had retained many of the most valuable items, including musical instruments (several violins and a clavichord among them), paintings, fine clothing, luxury items, and most of the unique and expensive gifts to Mozart gathered during the early journeys.[60] After some delay, Mozart's original scores were returned to him toward the end of December 1787;[61] but, in keeping with the pettiness of spirit that surfaces in such conflicts, his sister withheld all duplicate copies and performance materials as her own property. Leopold's church music was sent to Holy Cross Monastery at Augsburg; Marianne kept the family letters for herself.[62]

Because the primary documents concerning Leopold Mozart's estate—including the testament, the inventory, and the records of negotiations between Mozart and his sister—are no longer extant, the amount of money he left to Marianne, except for 30 florins in loose coins, cannot be fixed (assuming, of course, that the money was formally bequeathed rather than handed to her sub rosa to avoid taxation). But the absence of documentation should not lead us to conclude that Leopold Mozart left no money. By my admittedly speculative estimate, Leopold's earnings from the first European journey

57. Anderson, *The Letters of Mozart,* II:910, August 1, 1787, Letter 549.

58. The auction list is transcribed in Rudolph Angermüller, "Leopold Mozarts Verlassenschaft," *Mitteilungen der Internationale Stiftung Mozarteum* 41, nos. 3–4 (1993): 1–32. The auction was announced in the *Salzburger Intelligenzblatt,* September 14, 1787. Deutsch, *Documentary Biography,* 296–97.

59. Deutsch, *Documentary Biography,* 298.

60. Senn, *Neues Augsburger Mozartbuch,* 389–90. Deutsch comments: "Nannerl had probably already helped herself to a number of things before the auction." Deutsch, *Documentary Biography,* 298.

61. Marianne Mozart to Breikopf and Härtel, August 4, 1799, in Bauer, Deutsch, and Eibl, *Wolfgang Amadeus Mozart,* IV:259, Letter 1251. In this letter, Marianne expressed her regret that she had not withheld some of the early scores.

62. Deutsch, *Documentary Biography,* 297.

(through the end of 1767) equaled more than 10,000 florins; even after allowing for certain losses during the trip to Vienna in 1768 and the Mannheim/Paris journeys in 1777–78, the bulk of this fortune remained intact thereafter. Indeed, it had doubtless increased substantially in later years from earnings on the Italian journeys, from interest and investments, and from Leopold's various business enterprises, all conducted while he continued to draw his full salary as deputy court kapellmeister. Whatever the margin for error in the estimates may be, when Leopold's frugality and modest expenses are taken into account, it is not reasonable to think that these savings could have evaporated.

Fortunately, we can partially reconstruct Leopold's ultimate cash position by considering some details of his daughter's financial situation, including the data from her own estate. Her marriage portion consisted of a dowry of 500 florins in cash, the interest on 1,000 florins, and 20 florins interest on a further 500 florins to be paid the day after the wedding night as a premium should she prove to be a virgin ("*Morgengabe seu in praemium virginitatis*").[63] When her husband died, on February 26, 1803, he left her a pension of 300 florins per annum (out of an estate of 28,000 florins), the capital of which was to revert to his children upon her death.[64] It was more than plausible that she was left so little by her husband because he knew she was already provided for by her father. At best, her dowry and legacy gave her a capital of 500 florins plus accumulated interest, totaling perhaps something less than 1,000 florins, a very modest pension sufficient for subsistence but not enough to generate further savings, even with her tiny income from giving piano lessons, which she resumed after her return to Salzburg. Nevertheless, when Marianne died on October 29, 1829, she left to her sole surviving child bonds in the amount of 6,775 florins, plus cash in the amount of 145 florins.[65] Factoring in the possibility that she used up some capital to cover a portion of her living expenses, I estimate that she had received from her father in cash somewhere between 6,000 and 10,000 florins. And if, in anticipation of death, she had already transferred further sums to her son in cash, the amount might be substantially higher.[66]

63. Bauer, Deutsch, and Eibl, *Wolfgang Amadeus Mozart*, II:460, August 31, 1778, Letter 480; Bauer, Deutsch, and Eibl, *Wolfgang Amadeus Mozart*, II:469, September 10, 1778, Letter 485.

64. Deutsch and Paumgartner, *Leopold Mozarts Briefe an seine Tochter*, xiii.

65. For details, see Hummel, *Nannerl*, 93.

66. See Johann Evangelist Engl, "Testament, Codicill, Nachtrag und Sperr-Relation der

In a letter of August 1, 1787, Mozart bade his sister "a thousand farewells," his subtle way of telling her that they would greet each other no longer. And in a letter of December 19 he advised her to expect that he would not answer her letters promptly in the future: "Well, good-bye, dear sister. Write to me frequently. If I don't always answer promptly, put it down not to any negligence on my part, but simply to stress of work."[67] There is one final letter, dated August 2, 1788, doubtless written because she had reproached him for neglecting to congratulate her on her name day (July 26): "Dearest sister," he wrote, with a mixture of nonchalance and cruelty, "with my whole heart and soul I wish you all that you believe is most advantageous to yourself. . . . You must realize that I have a great deal to do. Besides, you know very well that I am rather lazy about letter-writing. So do not take it amiss if I *seldom* write to you. But this must not prevent you from writing very often to *me*."[68] Whether to offset the harshness of these words or to underline them, Mozart sent Marianne some of his latest piano compositions and gave her news about his recent accomplishments—the Prague performances of *Don Giovanni;* his appointment as chamber composer to the emperor the previous December. Nevertheless, what he had once foretold as a remote possibility had now come to pass: "Please trust me absolutely and never think that I shall forget you," he had written in 1778 during an earlier crisis, "but remember that things do not always turn out, or at least not always exactly, as one wishes."[69]

By the unequal division of his estate, Leopold Mozart had laid the ground for conflict between his children, raising explosive issues of fairness and favoritism, and guaranteeing that a time that should have been devoted to mourning and healing would be fraught with bitterness and reproach. Clearly, he could not have acted otherwise, for he

Schwester W. A. Mozarts," in *17. Jahresbericht der ISM* (Salzburg, 1897), 29–34; this is now superseded by Rudolph Angermüller, "Testament, Codicill, Nachtrag und Sperrelation der Freifrau Maria Anna von Berchtold zu Sonnenburg, geb. Mozart (1751–1829)," *Mozart Jahrbuch 1986*, 97–132. See also Hummel, *Nannerl,* 94–95, and Deutsch and Paumgartner, *Leopold Mozarts Briefe an seine Tochter,* xiii.

    67. Anderson, *The Letters of Mozart,* II:910, August 1, 1787, Letter 549, and II:914, December 19, 1787, Letter 552.

    68. Anderson, *The Letters of Mozart,* II:918, August 2, 1788, Letter 557.

    69. Anderson, *The Letters of Mozart,* I:507, to Marianne Mozart, March 7, 1778, Letter 296a.

was in the grip of a compulsion to resurrect and reenact as literally as possible a scenario of disinheritance that had been played out in Augsburg earlier in the century between himself and his own mother. In the aftermath of her father's death, Marianne precipitated the final rupture with Mozart, perhaps in the knowledge that she was carrying out what she understood to be her father's wish, to disinherit his son, her brother.

Disinheriting him may itself have been felt as an act of piety, for, in her grief, Marianne may have believed that Mozart caused their father's death, or at least caused him to die in anguish. At the very least, it was self-evident to her that Mozart had blighted his father's last years by his egoistic elevation of his own interests above those of the family. Thus Mozart and Marianne's quarrel was not really about money, but about who would possess the father's surviving substance, which is to say, the memory of his love, his protection, his favor. By compelling Mozart to accept an unfair division of the estate, she was impressing upon him the idea that despite his brilliant career, his fame, his wife, and his fancy Viennese existence, it was she who had tangible proof of their father's love, definitive proof that she, rather than Mozart, was Leopold Mozart's favorite child and heir.

Nevertheless, she surely knew that Mozart's bond to his father was somehow more resonant than her own, that whatever his unending complaints against his son, Leopold Mozart never ceased to define his own life by his son's achievements. Even at the very end, when Leopold was railing against Mozart and always suspecting the worst, he was desperate for any word from him, even the briefest letter: "I do hope that I shall have a letter tomorrow, as I have written to him twice. Or perhaps he is going to come himself?"[70] "Perhaps one will come tomorrow," he would write,[71] indicative of a pathetic need that he did not succeed in concealing from his daughter, to whom it may have seemed that her father's letters were filled with a constant stream of reports about Mozart. Nor could he ever conceal his almost trembling excitement about his son's latest compositions, as, for example, when he wrote to her on September 16, 1786: "I forgot to write about the libretto for *Figaro*. Bring it along—I must have it."[72] Deep

70. Anderson, *The Letters of Mozart*, II:892, September 16, 1785, Letter 530.
71. Deutsch and Paumgartner, *Leopold Mozarts Briefe an seine Tochter*, 477.
72. Deutsch and Paumgartner, *Leopold Mozarts Briefe an seine Tochter*, 368.

as Leopold's affection for his daughter may have been, and limitless as was her capacity for compliance with his wishes, she knew that she was no match for her brother in the competition for paternal love, that Leopold Mozart's attachment to his son was the supreme passion of his life. Perhaps the saddest aspect of this sad story is that Marianne Mozart understood that she could never take her brother's place in her father's heart.

8

Mozart's piano concertos
and their audience

JOSEPH KERMAN

IN 1781, MOZART extricated himself from his quasi-feudal position with the archbishop of Salzburg and set himself up as an independent musician in Vienna. This was not easy to accomplish, and it was even harder to explain or rationalize to his father, Leopold. In one of his letters home, Mozart admits that he has been warned about the precariousness of life as a freelance. The Viennese are fickle, Count Arco, the archbishop's majordomo, told him. "At first you are overwhelmed with praises and make a great deal of money into the bargain—but how long does that last? After a few months the Viennese want something new." Mozart takes the point, but puts his own spin on it:

> It is perfectly true that the Viennese are apt to change their affections, but *only in the theater;* and my special line is too popular not to enable me to support myself. Vienna is certainly the land of the clavier! And, even granted that they do get tired of me, they will not do so for a few years, certainly not before then. In the meantime I shall have gained both honor and money.[1]

Months have grown into years. Leopold is not persuaded.

But in fact Mozart was right. His popularity in the land of the

1. Emily Anderson, ed., *The Letters of Mozart and His Family* (London: Macmillan, 1938), vol. 3, 1099–100. As Maynard Solomon reminds us, in 1781 Mozart also urged his sister, Marianne, to come to Vienna and set herself up as a pianist (Anderson, 1142).

clavier continued unabated for five years. In the early part of his decade
in Vienna, Mozart's career was essentially as a pianist—as a piano
teacher, as a performer at aristocratic soirees, and as a concert pianist;
for he was able to set up academies, or concerts for his own benefit,
centered around his performance of piano concertos. He composed
three or four new concertos for each of the four seasons from 1782–
83 to 1785–86. Add to these fourteen works three that were written
later, and several earlier concertos that he dusted off when he got to
Vienna, and we have a very impressive body of music—considerably
more extensive and certainly no poorer in quality than the symphonies,
string quartets, and other large-scale genres that he was working in at
the time.

At the end of the 1785–86 season, Mozart finally succeeded in
having an opera produced, only his second in Vienna. *Le nozze di
Figaro* premiered in May 1786. Thereafter, opera replaced the piano
concerto as Mozart's important public genre. After 1786 there were
many fewer academies—and fewer new concertos. Perhaps the reason
for this was that Mozart was just too busy and too preoccupied with
operas. Or perhaps fickle Vienna had finally tired of him, as Count
Arco prophesied. Or both. There has been speculation, too, about
some mysterious personality change that may have had the effect of
alienating his audience. I shall touch on this just lightly at the end of
the chapter.

Before Mozart's time, concertos seldom figured in Viennese public
concerts; regular concerts featuring concertos seem to have started
with him.[2] This seems worth pondering. As we do so, I think it is
more interesting to ask not why it happened but rather, when it *did*
happen, what it meant. At issue here is a situation that lasted only a
short while and that has left, as its trace, some beautiful music that
we still listen to today, in Civics and Celicas and supermarkets. What
is the meaning of the original situation, or structure, as some would
call it: the nexus of social occasions represented by Mozart's academies, involving just that audience and just this composer-performer,
and these musical texts, all at a certain particular time and place?

We can pursue one meaning, I think, by reading those texts not in
technical, strictly musical terms but metaphorically. The solo part and

2. H. C. Robbins Landon, *Mozart: The Golden Years, 1781–1791* (New York: Schirmer
Books, 1989), 52.

the orchestral part in a concerto and their relationship can be read as a composite metaphor for Mozart and his audience and *their* relationship. This view of the Mozartean concerto is not, I think, unique or original; it is basically similar, for example, to that offered a few years ago by the musicologist and social critic Susan McClary in a striking article.[3] To develop this view, I shall need to go back to first principles, at least briefly, and I shall also need to touch on some technical matters after all.

Just what goes on in a concerto? In a well-known statement, Tchaikovsky spoke of "a struggle [between] the powerful multicolored orchestra and its weak but high-spirited adversary," and his formulation is typical (even trite) in its dialectic character. Like everyone else, Tchaikovsky personified the solo instrument and the orchestra as human agents. The orchestra is strong and multicolored, he said, the solo is light but agile, and he saw them locked in an adversarial relationship.

More fundamentally yet, the concerto agents or actors differ in their participation in certain basic musical activities, for which my short terms are *discourse* and *display*. When musicians speak of "discourse"—or "logic," or even "music thinking" *tout court*—we are referring to the ongoing play of musical material and rhetoric, musical process, music's illusion of movement and import. Theme, tonality, and contrast are some of the carriers of traditional musical discourse, which takes place quintessentially in the symphony, the orchestral genre par excellence.

Display, on the other hand, is a primal quality of music-making that can exist at low levels of discourse. Display is playing loud and fast and singing sexy; display can be extemporaneous, unpredictable, out of control, refractory to analysis. In certain genres of Western music, solo display is repressed, but the concerto is not among them. A concerto without bravura would not be worth the name—would probably be called a sinfonia concertante, in fact. Virtuosity as well as discourse is required of the concerto soloist, who is both discussion leader and acrobat, rhetorician and jock.

Listen to a Vivaldi concerto, and much of the time you will hear

---

3. Susan McClary, "A Musical Dialogue from the Enlightenment: Mozart's Piano Concerto in G Major, K. 453, Movement 2," *Cultural Critique* 4 (1986): 129–68.

all this in a raw state. The orchestra discourses, the solo violin displays itself. You will not hear much "struggle"—a feature of the nineteenth-century concerto—in Vivaldi, and you will not hear much struggle in a Mozart concerto either. But Mozart added another element to the concerto that is of major aesthetic importance. The two concerto actors, so dissimilar in some respects, nonetheless enter into dialogue. The relationship established between them is not adversarial but something much richer and more interesting, and the art of the concerto now devolves upon that relationship.

No doubt there was dialogue of a sort in concertos before Mozart, just as there was dialogue of a sort in opera buffa; but Mozart is light years ahead of his predecessors and contemporaries in this regard. His dialogue technique in opera and concerto has been much studied and much admired. Without at all wishing to renounce the broader resonance of dialogue as a hermeneutic method, I also need to ground Mozart's practice in a mundane technical fact. Because dialogue transpires only when the principals speak the same language, in concerto dialogue the solo and the orchestra deal with one and the same musical material. In Mozart's concertos the solo and orchestra discuss with one another by, mainly, repeating each other's music. The art comes in the wonderful range of variation and nuance in the dialogic repetitions, repetitions that are experienced as responses.

Dialogue can take place on various levels. On the level of the immediate exchange of musical themes and other passages, we can speak of instantaneous response, rejoinder, repartee, and more generally of discursive *engagement*. But in other contexts—for example, in the Socratic context—it is possible to think of beginning a dialogue one day and coming back to finish it the next. Dialogue over an extended time period is, in musical terms, dialogue on the level of musical form. Involved here are concepts like delayed response, recapitulation, and what can be called discursive *reengagement*.

On the level of musical form, the global level, the subtlest and most powerful system of dialogic response was that codified for the first movements of classical concertos. Donald Tovey called this "ritornello" form; Charles Rosen's term is "concerto-sonata" form; other people call it "double exposition" form.[4] The first to hold the stage

4. The classic discussion is by Donald Francis Tovey, "The Classical Concerto" (1903),

in a Mozart concerto is the orchestra; the solo makes its appearance only some time later. The opening orchestral passage, or ritornello, has as its function the presentation or exhibition of the movement's basic musical material. Put another way, the orchestral ritornello lays down the basic conditions for the musical discourse.

Then the solo makes its formal entrance, to initiate the first of two long solo sections, which we can call the "solo spans." Here the orchestral material is re-presented in a genial transformation. The solo, in close cooperation with the orchestra, reengages with that material and edits it, subtracting some bits, adding new bits of its own, and so on. Both solo spans are terminated by emphatic but shorter orchestral ritornellos, of which the second also sets up the cadenza, the soloist's supreme moment of athletic glory. The movement ends with yet another ritornello, the final ritornello, ritornello No. 4.

The orchestral ritornellos serve among other things as a frame or container for the solo activity. The sequence goes: ritornello No. 1 (the long expository ritornello), first solo span, ritornello No. 2, second solo span, ritornello No. 3, solo cadenza, ritornello No. 4. The orchestra demarcates the various solo episodes, as well as offering the discursive material upon which the solo dilates. In an important sense, then, the orchestra can be said to control the form; and this was a situation that could not be maintained for long without challenge. We shall come back to this point later.

There is, however, also another level of activity in every classical concerto's first movement, apart from the level of engagement and reengagement with the orchestra—apart, indeed, from dialogue, even from discourse itself. Tovey and Rosen say less about this. In addition to joining the orchestra in a discursive drama, the solo conducts a private action of its own. What the solo does, twice, is to trace a progression away from dialogue toward virtuosity. It traces a broad trajectory from discourse to display.

This action is obvious, even garish, and probably also regressive. Let me illustrate it briefly from everyone's favorite Mozart concerto,

in *Essays in Musical Analysis* (London: Oxford University Press, 1936), vol. 3, 3–27, reprinted in Joseph Kerman, ed., *W. A. Mozart, Piano Concerto in C Major, K. 503* (New York: Norton Critical Score, 1970), 137–63. See also Charles Rosen, *The Classical Style: Haydn, Mozart, Beethoven*, 2d ed. (New York: Viking Press, 1971), 185–263, and *Sonata Forms*, rev. ed. (New York: Norton, 1988), ch. 5.

Example 8.1. Concerto in C Major, K. 467. A toy-soldier march in the string instruments is answered by a not very austere tattoo in the woodwinds.

the C Major Concerto, K. 467. First, here are the basic terms of operation as laid down by the orchestra in the first measure and following. A toy-soldier march in the string instruments is answered by a not very austere tattoo in the woodwinds (Example 8.1). The solo's dialogic response to this does not come until two and a half minutes later, at the beginning of its first solo span. After a somewhat comical preparation process, the solo plays an airy trill over the march music in the strings, simultaneously damping the orchestra's kind of energy and introducing its own kind. Then the solo melts the woodwind tattoos into gracious ornamentation (Example 8.2). The solo span has begun with witty discourse. More dialogue ensues—at closer quarters (Example 8.3)—but ultimately the solo span ends with display (Example 8.4). These solipsistic bravura passages end with a notorious concerto trademark, the climactic flashy cadential trill—a sort of "high five" or pirouette that invites an admiring response to the solo in its role not as dialogist but as athlete. When the orchestra cuts in at this point, we may hear the crowd roaring its approval; but we also hear the orchestra reasserting its hegemony over the formal process. That hegemony had been challenged by the passage of solo display.

Example 8.2. Concerto in C Major, K. 467. The solo melts the woodwind tattoos into gracious ornamentation.

Example 8.3. Concerto in C Major, K. 467. More dialogue ensues—at closer quarters.

In the second solo span, the trajectory from discourse to display is run through again in basically the same way, with this difference: that when the orchestra intervenes after the trill a second time, its task is less to cheer the soloist's bravura than to urge it on to more of the same, in the cadenza. This the orchestra does with an ostentatious formality that sometimes borders on the sardonic. The cadenza is occasion for increasingly uninhibited display, ending once again with a highly formal, flashy trill.

But after this, it is indicative that the movement's true cadence or ending is accomplished not by the solo but by the orchestra, playing

Example 8.4. Concerto in C Major, K. 467. The solo span ends with a long passage of display.

ritornello No. 4. After giving the solo its run in the cadenza, the orchestra briskly reasserts its authority. The orchestra opens the shop in the morning and closes it up at night.

On the global level, the subtlest mode of dialogic response in the classical concerto is that embodied in the first-movement form. The least subtle is that embodied in the concerto's last-movement form, the concerto rondo. Musicologists and music theorists have paid relatively little attention to this form. I need to make just one point about it that I think important.

In the concerto rondo, it is typically the solo that commences, with a tune or the beginnings of a tune. Then the orchestra at once repeats what the solo has played. But unlike a long-term reengagement, such as we have seen in the first movement of K. 467, the rondo repetition is without variation or nuance; it already feels less like a response or a rejoinder than an acknowledgment, confirmation, or echo. Later in the piece there will be two or even three other occasions when the orchestra hears the solo tune again, and echoes or parrots it again.

What is significant about these places is the *readiness* and the *blankness* with which the repetitions come. This much reiteration fixes and formalizes the relationship in a decisive way, whatever else happens between the various statements of the theme (Example 8.5). A good deal does happen, of course, between the statements. Nonetheless, the pervading sense in concerto rondos—from Bach's E Major Violin Concerto through Mozart all the way to the Gershwin Piano Concerto in F and Bartók—is consensus, a consensus in aid of play, and a consensus in aid of a happy ending.[5]

This relationship between solo and orchestra is very different from

---

5. A technical point: the "collusive" quality that I attribute to the repetitions in rondo themes seems to me to be independent of the syntactic function of the repeated phrases, which is largely determined by their cadences. Usually the repetitions are exact, as in themes that can be expressed diagrammatically as $a_1 A_1 b a_1$ ($A_1 A_1 B a_1$ in K. 467) or $a_1 A_1 b B$, etc.; other possibilities include binary structures such as $a_V A'_1$ in K. 450 and K. 456. (Lowercase and uppercase letters refer to solo and orchestral presentation respectively, subscript numbers denote cadences, and the prime mark in A' means a modified and/or expanded version of A.)

The finale of the Piano Concerto in D Minor, K. 466, feels entirely different from Mozart's other concerto rondos, for the opening solo theme is never repeated by the orchestra—though indeed the orchestra twice attempts, and egregiously fails, to accomplish this action. For a brief discussion of this very unusual rondo, see Joseph Kerman, "Mozart à la Mode," *New York Review of Books*, May 18, 1989, 51.

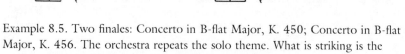

Example 8.5. Two finales: Concerto in B-flat Major, K. 450; Concerto in B-flat Major, K. 456. The orchestra repeats the solo theme. What is striking is the readiness and the blankness with which the repetitions come.

that in the first movement. To understand what may be behind this change, we shall need to return to the historical situation.

Mozart's piano concertos were not conceived in any spirit of abstract investigation of ideal relationship patterns. They were written for his academies, public concerts with which the young pianist-composer attempted to make the scene in music's capital city. The inner drama of concerto relationship can be viewed as the projection of an actual social dynamic. Here, too, one can interpret on different levels. Most generally, for example, one might try to identify the soloist with the post-Enlightenment artist and the orchestra with an evolving bour-geois or partly bourgeois audience. I am more comfortable consider-ing the concertos in their own particular situation—Mozart's situation vis-à-vis his patrons as he worked to establish himself in the musical life of Vienna from 1781 to 1786.[6]

Projected in the Mozart concertos, I suggest, is a single pervading myth. The concertos follow a standard three-movement plan. In the first movement, with its elegantly articulated strategy of engagement and reengagement, the concerto actors seem to enter into a collabo-rative test situation. The soloist presents himself to the orchestra and shows how he can cope with the conditions that they have laid down. These conditions are not inflexible; in the process of dialogue, they can change considerably, for the orchestra allows and even encourages criticism, initiative, even spontaneous display and acrobatics on the part of the soloist.

Then comes a quiet slow interlude of some kind (there are several kinds, all of them beautiful). Next comes a rondo (usually). Here there is less at stake than in the opening encounter. For the slow movement has solemnized a ritual of mutual acceptance between the principals, and the rondo finale feels less like a trial or a quest than a deal. It feels less like collaboration than complicity, even collusion.

The three movements of a concerto trace a sequence from inter-action to some sort of respite to complicity, from collaborative and

6. There exists a list of Mozart's concert subscribers in 1784, in a letter to Leopold. Though part of the letter is lost, the list includes 174 names. Landon, who prints and annotates the list as Appendix I of *The Golden Years*, compares it to the Almanach de Gotha: "an extraordinary testimony to [Mozart's] popularity" (107). Mozart himself remarked, "I have about 30 subscribers more than Richter and Fischer together" (Anderson, 1297–1300).

creative exchange to accommodation. I associate this sequence with the underlying theme of comedy, the "myth of spring," as Northrop Frye expounded it many years ago. In this myth, the individual is incorporated into society and society is transformed. In one Mozartean comedic fiction, Tamino sues and wins entrance to the social order by playing on a magic flute. In seventeen others, Amadeus plays the fortepiano.

True, the classical symphony could be said to trace a similar course, without reference to actors or social formation, artists or patrons, and the sequence there could perhaps be traced in strictly internal, non-metaphorical, technical terms. What is different in the concerto is the way the myth is personified. That is what is so striking, so winning. Joan Crawford said it best, in a movie few of us now remember: "I like some symphonies," said Joan, "but I like all concertos."

The sharpest test for my interpretation of the Mozart concertos is the Concerto in C Minor, K. 491, composed in March 1786. The first movement of this arresting work, as many have pointed out, breaks free from tradition in various ways. The freedom results, I think, from a protest by the solo against the hegemony of the band; the solo goes further than in any other concerto to wrest control of the discourse from the orchestra. In its equivocal effort to create or define the form, the solo is more assertive in this work—and also more vulnerable—than in any other Mozart concerto.

Several unusual features of K. 491 support this contention, I believe. For example, the solo does not begin its first solo span in the traditional way, with a version of the orchestra's main theme (as in K. 467), but with an expressive theme of its own invention. I take that as the solo's clear bid to establish its own agenda. That agenda includes a new policy for the discourse-to-display trajectory that I mentioned earlier. The trajectory is actually traced twice: In the first solo span, the solo gets (or takes) not one but two extensive bravura passages, each ending with formal trills, lasting eighty-four bars in all. Charles Rosen, who points out this innovation in *The Classical Style*, is not concerned there to attribute it to the solo or the orchestra; and if I am to be scrupulous, I must admit that there is no easy way to tell which of the two gets credit for its inception. But certainly the solo is the one who capitalizes on it.

Example 8.6. Concerto in C Minor, K. 491. Just when the confrontation is beginning to seem merciless, the orchestra relents and allows the piano to conclude its runs without further deflection. (*continues on next page*)

Judging from the sequel, one must also conclude that all this initiative on the part of the solo makes the orchestra restive, for the second solo span includes a rare example in Mozart of a real struggle between solo and orchestra. The passage in question begins with a series of familiar-sounding developmental modulations, after which the piano breaks free of the orchestra to make a vehement close, down in the low register. Too vehement, it seems, for the orchestra: The orchestra cuts in with a very aggressive new gesture; the piano is swept away—horrified—as this happens again and again. The fourth time it happens, just when the transaction is beginning to seem merciless, the orchestra relents and allows the piano to conclude its runs without further deflection (Example 8.6).

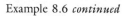

Example 8.6 *continued*

After this humbling episode, the solo loses its form-defining impulse. From now on, in the section of reengagement, the solo is distinctly subdued. When it is given a new theme to ornament, it does not do much of a job with it.[7] And it retains only a shadow of its two long bravura passages: To be precise, only 28 bars are left out of an original total of 84 (and only one trill).

There is therefore special importance and special pathos to the solo's performance in the cadenza. The solo has been muted, and a redress is needed. Although Mozart left no written-out cadenza for this concerto, which is actually an exceptional circumstance, he left an indication of one novel impulse that he had in mind. Even when he did commit his cadenza improvisations to paper, it was not Mozart's habit to enter them into the full autograph scores; but in these documents he did write the ending cadenza trill as a sort of cue. No such cue is present in the C minor autograph,[8] and this must indicate that Mozart meant the cadenza to run directly into the coda without a trill.[9] (To us, the novelty may not seem very extraordinary, but it is the only time Mozart is known to have abandoned this hallowed and conspicuous convention. Mozart's subscribers would have sat up and noticed.) And Mozart being Mozart, the abandoned trill is part of a larger purpose. The solo not having closed itself off with a cadenza trill, it can return with a wonderful effect to haunt the orchestra at the very end, in a famous passage, deeply influential upon Beethoven.[10] The smoky, glittery piano arpeggios that cloud the final ritornello—ritornello No. 4, which the orchestra should have for itself—challenge one more time the orchestra's authority. The issue of discourse versus display remains undecided. The power relations are in doubt.

7. Measures 444–62.

8. See the facsimile edition, *Mozart, Piano Concerto in C Minor, K. 491* (Washington, 1984), 33.

9. A cadenza for K. 491 without a trill, by Saint-Saëns, may be heard on the famous old recording by Robert Casadesus. Malcolm Bilson, in his fine DGG-Archiv recording with John Eliot Gardiner, plays a cadenza that ends without a trill, but instead of running directly into the coda, this cadenza ushers in the concerto's first theme played solo by the piano, prior to the coda. This, if I may echo Sidney's wonderfully uneasy criticism of Spenser, I dare not allow.

10. For a brief discussion of this, see Joseph Kerman, "Notes on Beethoven's Codas," in Alan Tyson, ed., *Beethoven Studies* (Cambridge: Cambridge University Press, 1982), vol. 3, 143–45.

As for the finale of the C Minor Concerto, that too breaks with tradition. It is, rather exceptionally for Mozart, not a rondo but a theme and variations, worked out in such a way that there is very little dialogue in it, whether collaborative-creative or complicitous-collusive. Emblematic is a passage at the very end, comprising the last portion of the last variation and the coda. Both segments are monopolized by the solo instrument. Instead of dialogue, Mozart is occupied with obsession here—with a single musical figure, which, when the orchestra tries to play it, the solo takes back (Example 8.7). That ostinato figure (D flat–C, in two different rhythms) comes no fewer than fourteen times: saturation of a most untraditional, unclassical, un-Mozartean sort. The piece is in fact uncanny, *unheimlich* in the best early Romantic sense.[11]

In this chapter I have developed a view of Mozart's concertos as adhering to a general myth of comedy, yet I have spent a good deal of time purporting to show how one concerto, the C Minor K. 491, does not follow the myth at all. K. 491 was the last piano concerto composed for the four-year run of academy concerts—in April 1786, at the end of Mozart's fourth season—and it was followed by *Figaro* just a few weeks later. Mozart's first concerto composition for Vienna was a shamelessly popular display piece, the Rondo in D Major, K. 383, of 1782. Four years later he offered Vienna the disturbed, disturbing Concerto in C Minor. The next season yielded only one group of concerts, in December 1786, and Mozart wrote only one new concerto for them, K. 503 in C Major. It is worth noting, too, that these concerts were the first for which he composed a special new symphony (this was the "Prague," K. 504). As Charles Rosen remarks, the C Major Concerto, K. 503, though never a favorite with the public, is "one that many musicians (historians and pianists alike) single out with special affection."[12] I myself once published a casebook on it. But as compared with the other C major concerto, K. 467, K. 503 is a monumental, rather forbiddingly magnificent work. It is not really much fun, and it is strangely cold: cold, despite the quality of melancholy that Rosen finely discerns in it. That Mozart did not write a

11. Also uncanny is the similarity of this figure to the orchestra's angry interrupting motif in the first movement (Example 8.6).
12. Rosen, *The Classical Style*, 251; see also McClary, "A Musical Dialogue."

Example 8.7. Concerto in C Minor, K. 491. Finale. Mozart is occupied with obsession here—with a single musical figure, which, when the orchestra tries to play it, the solo takes back. (*continues on next page*)

fresh theme for the rondo finale, instead borrowing from an old composition that was a nostalgic favorite of his, the opera *Idomeneo*—that too seems strange, even disquieting. Austere and abstracted, K. 503 registers a clear change in mood in the sequence of Mozart concertos. It could be said to register a loss of heart.

Perhaps the Viennese audience tired of Mozart by 1786; that is quite possible. It is also possible that Mozart tired of the Viennese audience. More precisely, he may have grown weary of the consoling myth that he and they had enacted together, in concerto after concerto, year after year. With his C Minor Concerto, he had put his tacit contract with them at risk; if any of his concert subscribers felt affronted and alienated by this deeply subversive work, we could hardly blame them. As Alfred Einstein remarked rather dryly, many years ago,

Example 8.7 *continued*

"It is hard to imagine the expression on the faces of the Viennese public when on 7 April 1786 Mozart played this work at one of his subscription concerts."[13] As I imagine it, the whole communal exercise had begun to strike Mozart as hollow, irrelevant to his developing needs as man and artist. It was first Mozart, not his audience, who had begun to experience alienation.

13. Alfred Einstein, *Mozart: His Character, His Work,* trans. Arthur Mendel and Nathan Broder (New York: Oxford University Press, 1945), 311.

9

Mozart's tunes and
the comedy of closure

WYE J. ALLANBROOK

ONE CANNOT HELP being aware of the significance of the Mozart bicentennial: After two hundred years, a day of death turns into a day of celebration. Of course, the desire on such an occasion is to avoid speaking trivially or partially—to attempt an all-embracing reading of the music that was preoccupying us throughout the bicentennial year. Certainly one does not need a bicentennial in order to offer such a reading; others preceded me in this activity over the past two centuries, and there have always been fads and fancies in Mozart interpretation. When I was first listening to music, Mozart was considered a delicate salon composer who must always yield to the heroic muscularity of Beethoven. But in general, taking Mozart seriously seems to have meant taking him tragically—the concept of the "gloomy Mozart," as Wolfgang Hildesheimer dubbed it in his 1977 biography.[1] In September 1990, on the eve of the bicentennial year, Richard Taruskin wrote a cautionary "kick-off" article in the *New York Times* entitled "Why Mozart Has Become an Icon for Today." Beginning with a sly reference to the "orgy of veneration in Lincoln Center" that suggested a prevailing attitude of un-critical sentimentality toward the composer—"our foundation stone, our icon, and our pedigree"—Taruskin reminded us of the nineteenth-

---

1. Wolfgang Hildesheimer, *Mozart,* trans. Marion Faber (New York: Farrar, Straus and Giroux, 1982), 47.

century literary cult of Mozart, which emphasized instead the composer's "violence, his sensuality, and his power to subvert." In a section
entitled "Deep Meaning?: Disintegration and Malaise?" he reviewed
the work of recent writers—notably, Rose Subotnik, Susan McClary,
and Neal Zaslaw—who had tried to combat our sentimentality with an
updated version of the nineteenth century's subversive Mozart—a reading that discerns in his music the signs of "stylistic, psychological, even
social" disintegration. Taruskin closed his article on readings of Mozart's music with a praise of melancholy quoted from the performer-
scholar Laurence Dreyfus: "The giant [performers] of our pantheon are
great to the extent that they learn to represent the depths of melancholy, and melancholy, as Kant recognized, was a kind of secret key to
the sublime."[2]

Certainly sentimental adoration has always been a strain in our responses to Mozart. But is it not equally naive and uncritical to exalt
the dark and the troubled, especially at the expense of the context in
which they reside? Melancholy is only one affect among many; when
late-eighteenth-century writers praised the effect of chiaroscuro they
did not see the "clear" as a mere foil for the "obscure," the light as
a setting for the shade. Furthermore, Kant speaks of music in connection with the beautiful, as an exemplar of purposive patterning; the
sublime, his second preoccupation in *The Critique of Judgement,* seems
to be primarily a moral, and not an aesthetic, category, concerned with
the philosophical implications of our confrontation with the imposing
in nature.[3] One must take care when citing Kant in urging the interpretation of the Gloomy Mozart.

---

2. Richard Taruskin, "Why Mozart Has Become an Icon for Today," *New York Times,*
September 9, 1990, H35–H40. The studies to which Taruskin refers are: Rose Rosengaard
Subotnik, "Evidence of a Critical World View in Mozart's Last Three Symphonies," in
Developing Variations: Style and Ideology in Western Music (Minneapolis: University of Min-
nesota Press, 1991), 98–111; Susan McClary, "A Musical Dialectic from the Enlightenment:
Mozart's *Piano Concerto in G Major, K. 453,* Movement 2," *Cultural Critique* 5 (1986),
129–69; and Neal Zaslaw, *Mozart's Symphonies: Context, Performance Practice, Reception*
(Oxford: Clarendon Press, 1989); Laurence Dreyfus, "Early-Music and the Suppression of
the Sublime," *Journal of Musicology* 10 (Winter 1992): 117.

3. The following passage from the *Critique of Judgement* states succinctly Kant's view
of the difference between the beautiful and the sublime in this regard: "A feeling for the
sublime in nature cannot well be thought without combining therewith a mental disposition
which is akin to the moral. And although the immediate pleasure in the beautiful of nature
likewise presupposes and cultivates a certain *liberality* in our mental attitude, . . . yet freedom

It is a curious quirk of the psychology of our fallen nature that when we hear that a reading of a text or art work enshrines that fallen nature, we feel better. A flippant remark to be sure, but it admits of translation into deeper terms; for instance, George Steiner, in his study of the centrality of Sophocles' tragedy *Antigone* to the history of modern consciousness, writes of the nature of philosophizing since the nineteenth century:

> The major philosophical systems since the French Revolution have been tragic systems. They have metaphorized the theological premiss of the fall of man. . . . To philosophize after Rousseau and Kant, to find a normative, conceptual phrasing for the psychic, social, and historical condition of man, is to think "tragically."[4]

As in philosophy, so in aesthetics, but not always with the profundity of Kant or Heidegger. Our uncritical exaltation of storm and stress from a topos to a life-style is perhaps one result of this profound shift in outlook that occurred in the transition to the nineteenth century. The "heavenly city" of the eighteenth-century philosophers stressed not the fall of man but the possibility of redemption, and hence was essentially a comic notion. Early discussions of *commedia* as a genre were not concerned with the anatomy of humor; they spelled out the vision of the human estate that comedy by its nature represented. Dante defined a *commedia* as a work that "begins in adversity of a certain sort," but issues in a happy ending; tragedy, on the other hand, is "admirable and placid" at the start, but its end is "foul and horrible."[5] Looking back to Dante for a gloss on an eighteenth-century composer is not an entirely arbitrary critical activity; as the historian Carl Becker once observed in a series of lectures on the Enlightenment:

is thus represented as in *play* rather than in that law-directed *occupation* which is the genuine characteristic of human morality, in which reason must exercise dominion over sensibility. But in aesthetical judgments upon the sublime this dominion is represented as exercised by the imagination, regarded as an instrument of reason" (Immanuel Kant, *Critique of Judgement,* trans. J. H. Bernard [New York: Macmillan, 1951], 109).

4. George Steiner, *Antigones: How the Antigone Legend Has Endured in Western Literature, Art, and Thought* (Oxford: Clarendon Press, 1986), 2–3.

5. Dante, Epistola X, to Can Grande della Scala (trans. mine). "For this reason," Dante continues, "certain writers in their salutations are accustomed to say in the place of a greeting, 'May you have a tragic beginning and a comic ending.' "

> There were . . . many differences between Voltaire and St. Thomas,
> but . . . they had in common . . . the profound conviction that their
> beliefs could be reasonably demonstrated. . . . It may be said of the
> eighteenth century that it was an age of faith as well as of reason,
> and of the thirteenth century that it was an age of reason as well as
> of faith.[6]

The Enlightenment faith was, of course, a faith in universal reason
and human perfectibility, a faith in the possibility of discovering for
society a model of the divine harmony of nature. It is with this faith
that our modern impatience lies. The tragic outlook we acquired from
the Romantics leads us to admire the loss of this faith as a sign of
personal growth; the only politically correct position seems to be Fal-
staff's "Tutto declina"—"everything always gets worse." Now I am
not a political Pollyanna; certainly in this century we are constantly
assaulted with evidence supporting that motto. But I do think we are
wrong to impose this attitude indiscriminately on previous eras. Becker
observed trenchantly of our relation to the *philosophes:* "We agree with
them more readily when they are witty and cynical than when they
are wholly serious. Their negations rather than their affirmations enable us to treat them as kindred spirits."[7] In what follows, I propose
to see what happens if we try to take Enlightenment affirmations as
seriously as its negations, no matter how alien to our current sensibilities the endeavor may seem.

The musical result of the pursuit of the Gloomy Mozart is an agenda
that shapes a dangerous misconception of the conventions of the Classic style—a presumption that these conventions have somehow been
imposed from without, by the Enlightenment's musical thought po-
lice, and that it is intellectual progress to grow away from them, even
if in the process the individual becomes divided against himself. This
division is forced by critics' convictions that they must distinguish
between Mozart's true voice and his conventional mask, that the authentic Mozart is to be discovered buried under a mound of sedi-
mented conventions. In the nineteenth and early twentieth centuries,
this search was motivated by psychological or aesthetic rather than

---

6. Carl Becker, *The Heavenly City of the Eighteenth-Century Philosophers* (New Haven:
Yale University Press, 1932), 8.
7. Becker, *Heavenly City*, 30.

social concerns—the Romantic preference for self-expression over the shared communications of a common musical language. The Romantics exalted the pairing of "original and dark" over that of "conventional and sunny." They ignored the other piano concertos in their admiration for K. 466 in D Minor, and lopped the D major epilogue off *Don Giovanni* so that the opera could end in D minor tragedy. Otto Jahn, the great nineteenth-century biographer of Mozart, stated baldly in connection with the D minor concerto that "Mozart's compositions in the minor keys are his deepest and most important."[8] Hildesheimer tries to be more evenhanded in his discussions of tonality: He speaks of his distrust of the conventional German fascination with Mozart's *Molleintrübung* ("darkening into the minor"), and criticizes Abert for his notion of Mozart's pessimism.[9] But Hildesheimer twice admits that he too "automatically prick[s] up [his] ears at Mozart's use of the minor"[10] and finds the String Quintet in C Major, K. 515, profound because, though composed in the major mode, it mysteriously shares the tragic affect cast by its companion, the Quintet in G Minor, K. 516.[11] It is only recently that a political or cultural critique of the Enlightenment has become part of the search for Mozart's "true voice." But whether this voice is seen as transcendent, in the Romantic perspective, or undermining, as in that recent speculation, the elements presumed to mask it remain the same—tonality (notably, the "stranglehold" of the major mode), the impulse to strong closure, and a value that I shall advance in what follows as the *comic variety of the surface*.

Let us look briefly at the contents of the recent critique. Its advocates see the tonal and formal procedures of the Classical style as rigid conventions imposed by a general "cultural viewpoint," one that in enshrining the values of rationality and progress stifled individual autonomy.[12] For example, as Susan McClary puts it: "If Mozart was to communicate effectively. . . , his music had to shape itself in keeping

---

8. Otto Jahn, *Life of Mozart* [1891], trans. Pauline D. Townsend (New York: Cooper Square, 1970), vol. 2, 476.

9. Hildesheimer, *Mozart*, 45, 47, 200–201.

10. Hildesheimer, *Mozart*, 84, 163.

11. Hildesheimer, *Mozart*, 201–2.

12. See note 2 for the three representative works cited by Taruskin. To this list I would add at least one other: Marshall Brown, "Mozart and After: The Revolution in Musical Consciousness," *Critical Inquiry* (Summer 1986), 689–706.

with those premises. . . . His harmonic strategies ally him with beliefs in rationality, progress, and ceaseless, obsessive striving for goals."[13] Occasionally, so the argument goes, in works like the three late symphonies or the "Dissonant" Quartet,[14] Mozart managed to speak authentically despite the dead weight of this convention; he seeded those works with covert suggestions that undermine the illusions of his repressively optimistic society. So-called sonata form, with its powerful tonal order, is presumed to be the vehicle of this repression; these supposed conflicts and rebellions seethe beneath its archetypal and controlling surface. Subotnick, for example, sees sonata form as a kind of "empty logic," almost nonmusical in its representation of rationality; astonishingly, in her opinion it can be "adequately described with scarcely any reference to specific examples."[15] As she sees it, the musical content resides beneath the surface of the form, in sensuous conflicts and discords that are Romantic rather than Classical in their nature.

Their vision of the individual's secret struggle for autonomy leads some proponents of this critique to revivify another Romantic shibboleth, one we had just begun to work free of—the notion that every great work of art possesses a deep-seated, underground unity. Early apostles of unity, such as Hans Keller, spoke of unity in the philosophical terms of the nineteenth century:

> The oneness, the simultaneity is the inner reality, the Kantian thing-in-itself, the Schopenhauerian will, the Freudian unconscious (which is essentially timeless), while the temporal succession is its necessary appearance, the Schopenhauerian idea, the Freudian conscious. . . . *Variety is the necessary means of expressing a unity.*[16]

To Subotnik, the sensuous Romantic elements in Mozart's last three symphonies create a subliminal web of reference across the movements that unites each work in a way that the "rational principles of connection as function" are powerless to achieve.[17] In this they approach as a limit the "romantic stress on the single identity of a whole struc-

13. McClary, "A Musical Dialectic," 135.

14. This is the piece Marshall Brown uses as his exemplar.

15. Subotnik, "Evidence of a Critical World View," 103.

16. Hans Keller, "The Chamber Music," in H. C. Robbins Landon and Donald Mitchell, eds., *The Mozart Companion* (New York: W. W. Norton, 1969), 116.

17. Subotnik, "Evidence of a Critical World View," 107.

ture," something unattainable "through the agency of nothing more than a cultural homogeneity of style" (read, the dead weight of late-eighteenth-century convention).

But this strange bifurcation of the composer into cultural conformist and closet rebel[18] stems from a fallacious assumption. To represent as mere convention the ubiquity of the major mode in Mozart's works and the importance in them of the "sonata principle" is historically inaccurate. In the musical language that Mozart inherited from his Baroque predecessors, the prevalence of major keys and the so-called sonata principle appeared as two striking new tropes. For instance, a glance at Neal Zaslaw's recent book on Mozart's symphonies reveals that of the ninety-eight symphonies attributed to Mozart only five are set in a minor tonality and two of those are not actually Mozart's compositions![19] Compare this startling statistic to the look of any list of works by a Baroque composer, where major and minor keys are distributed with relative indifference.

As for "sonata form," I would prefer to characterize it as a gradually emerging compositional process, a new mode of taking tonality that reinforces dramatic continuity while admitting the new delight in contrast and counterstatement—in chiaroscuro, light and shadow. No longer should we devalue the brilliant surface variety of Mozart's instrumental works—the foreground play of musical style and topic across the background of harmonic process—the shifting lights of various kinds.[20] I hesitate to suggest a source for these new tropes, though comic opera and popular dance music come to mind. But their relative novelty argues that they evolved not to repress a new musical impulse but to empower it, not to stifle this pleasure in expressive

18. For example, Subotnik sees Mozart's nature as split into Classicist and Individual: "Mozart the Classicist crystallized the general stylistic language of eighteenth-century music into a conception of an encompassing, yet particular, universal structure, only to dissolve that structure simultaneously into an expression of (merely?) individual style" ("Evidence of a Critical World View," 104).

19. Zaslaw, *Mozart's Symphonies*, 545–49.

20. This would seem to be an appropriate moment to give proper credit to the work of Leonard G. Ratner, whose account of modes of expression in Classic music has irrevocably altered our hearing of it, and who is responsible for reintroducing the word "topos," or "topic," into the discourse about musical rhetoric (Leonard G. Ratner, *Classic Music: Expression, Form, and Style* [New York: Schirmer, 1980]). Mention should also be made of another important study of this subject, from an overtly semiotic point of view, that has recently appeared: V. Kofi Agawu, *Playing with Signs: A Semiotic Interpretation of Classic Music* (Princeton: Princeton University Press, 1991).

contrasts but to guarantee it. Hence the new emphasis on the variety of the comic surface. Unity, says Charles Rosen—in a discussion, significantly enough, of the D Minor Piano Concerto—is a quality that is characteristic of the tragic.[21] The *commedia*, on the other hand, is a *speculum mundi*, a cosmic mirror that presents all species of things in their compelling diversity, and affirms their integration, however provisional at times, not into an organic oneness, but into an overarching communal hierarchy. It is this model, I would argue—the model of the *commedia*—that Mozart's compositional choices suggest.

I should like to celebrate this secular "divine comedy" of Mozart's by bringing to light a compositional habit of his that, while seemingly casual, exemplifies the dominance in his music of the comic mode. I do not offer this analysis in final refutation of the Gloomy Mozart; it would take far more than this chapter to root out the ingrained assumption that profundity and melancholia always go hand in hand. And because I do not believe that a fleeting moment of counterpoint or a quirky modulation can be translated into a "life-style" or a "worldview," I am uncomfortable with reading musical structures symbolically as political or philosophical positions.[22] Hence I do not propose to offer a global counter-reading that views his compositional habits as evidence of Mozart the counterrevolutionary, or Mozart the *philosophe*. But I hope this modest illustration of the composer's ways of working may remind us of the vigor and significance of habits too easily spurned as mere convention, and that it may suggest the possibility of reintegrating the Gloomy Mozart with the other parts of his soul.

21. Charles Rosen, *The Classical Style: Haydn, Mozart, Beethoven* (New York: W. W. Norton, 1971), 235.

22. Subotnik does not hesitate to read musical detail as directly symbolic of ideology: she asserts as her central hypothesis that Mozart's last three symphonies "give musical articulation to an incipient shift in philosophical outlook" ("Evidence of a Critical World View," 99). McClary sees in particular dispositions of soloist versus tutti in K. 435, II, "nothing less . . . at stake than the foundations of social order" ("A Musical Dialectic," 147), and entertains one reading of the concerto movement as promoting "the kind of argument that leads to politically motivated psychiatric treatment" ("A Musical Dialectic," 151). Zaslaw (*Mozart's Symphonies*, 543–44) ventures a symbolic reading of the coda to the finale of the *Jupiter* Symphony: he suggests that the absence from the "final synthesis" of a brief scrap of a galant theme perhaps reminiscent of Salzburg and Leopold's domination could be a metaphor for "Mozart's dreaming of escaping his oppressive past and giving utterance to his fondest hopes and highest aspirations for the future."

My subject is a topos that Mozart used from time to time at moments of closure. It is a humble topos, and appropriately so: Remember, Dante considered the vernacular—the famous *dolce stile nuovo* he appropriated for the *Commedia*—to be the proper language of comedy.[23] I call this topos the "tune." In my private slang I dub it "the tune that sprouts from the top," but this is admittedly not a technical designation. It does, however, suggest one of the striking features of Mozart's tunes—their frequent descantlike quality: They often appear unexpectedly atop what had seemed to be the leading voice, like those lovely ornamental parts that suddenly soar over the melodic line of a familiar hymn. They also often "emerge from the top" rhythmically: They rise above the previous level of the beat, to mark out a more spacious temporal arch. The tune always consists of new material, not previously exposed; it seems to arise out of a sufficiency, to be an embarrassment of riches. But it always has a function—that of a closural sign.

A few words must be said here about what I mean by a "tune." If I were forthrightly to open the lid of this Pandora's box, a host of words would fly out, demanding to be distinguished from one another—tune, melody, figure, motive, subject, theme. . . . Significantly, *Grove's Dictionary* has no entry for "tune," and the *Harvard Dictionary of Music* says simply, "*See* Melody." Perhaps it will help if I state that I do not consider Mozart as generally a composer of tunes, nor indeed of melodies, except in the most generic sense of the word—"a coherent succession of pitches," as the *Harvard Dictionary* offers it.[24] In common parlance the word "melody" and even more the word "tune" suggest something singable, with sustained tones, simple, smooth motions, and a sense of shapeliness and closure; when we hear a tune in this ordinary sense in Mozart, we know it. For like most late-eighteenth-century composers, Mozart tended to construct his eloquent "successions of pitches" from melodic fragments—motives or figures, to capture a few of those words that I just let escape from the box. These fragments, "configurations that are clearly rec-

---

23. Dante, Epistola X: "Tragedy and comedy differ likewise in their way of speaking: for tragedy is uplifted and sublime, while comedy is unstudied and humble." And later, on the style of the *Commedia* itself: "It is unstudied and humble, as it is in the diction of the vulgar tongue, in which even women communicate."

24. Harold S. Powers, "Melody," *The New Harvard Dictionary of Music* (Cambridge, Mass.: Harvard University Press, 1986).

Example 9.1. K. 465, IV, measures 1–8.

ognizable in their own right . . . in another context,"[25] are not in themselves particularly tuneful or melodic. They create a double level of action that causes us to look beneath the surface "melody" to find a line with the sustained tones and simple motions we generally expect of a melody; we sometimes call this the "structural melody."

An example will help. The last movement of Mozart's "Dissonant" Quartet, K. 465 in C Major, begins with an exuberant country-dance melody—melody in the generic sense, that is, in that it is a well-shaped collection of figures or motives (Example 9.1). It can be broken down into a number of disparate little pieces, each with a recognizable nature of its own. For instance, the repeated notes of the opening upbeat are taken up as a "motive" even within the melody itself, when they are developed into a chromatically rising scale of repeated notes in measures 5–6; this fragment recurs as a countersubject later (measures 55–58), and in a descending version incorporating the appoggiatura, or "sigh motive," that was also part of the opening melody (measures 111–14). From this opening period the movement proceeds, as the first movement of a sonata allegro or "key-area" piece will do, to stake out a new harmonic place that provides a sense of motion away *from* and a counterstatement *to* the opening key area. It develops the first melody, and then arouses interest in a close in the new key by some frenetic "country fiddling" (measures 69–87). The inevitable close is then postponed—we are teased—by a feint to a plateau that is a harmonic overreaching of the target key, a harmonic "mistake" that is stabilized fleetingly and falsely by what I would call a "tune" (measures 89–102): sustained notes that one could sing rather than the quick detachable motives of the opening melody, and with a strong sense of "finitude and closure" (the *Harvard Dictionary* again) (Example 9.2). This simple phrase is repeated four times, the third time with a few small alterations that bring it to crisis, and the fourth time as a cadence in the proper key. In its extreme simplicity, this is a self-

25. Powers, "Melody," *The New Harvard Dictionary of Music.*

Example 9.2. K. 465, IV, measures 89–101.

conscious tune; it makes book on its very "tunefulness." It seems to spring from nowhere, and is not plundered to be developed later (although it is *repeated,* intact, at an analogous structural place later in the movement). With its sustained notes and its emphasis on the downbeat of the measure, the tune rises above the level of the previous rhythmic action; it puts the brakes on the rapid sixteenth notes of the country fiddling. As I pointed out before, we are actually being teased by this particular tune, which is staking out a false plateau, beyond the ultimate goal of the section. The other tunes I will discuss are very like this one, but they will not be used to tease; they will all in some penultimate or antepenultimate way be working toward closure for a section, a movement, or, in a finale, for an entire work.

I should say something about Mozart's usual modes of closure—how he customarily puts the period to a movement. In the music of the Classic style the sense of a just end—of a close that completes a dynamically balanced process—was important as it had not been in music before and has not been since. The repetitive closing formulas at the ends of Beethoven's more grandly arched movements are sometimes the butt of knowing jokes, but, harmonic conservative that he was, he knew they were necessary to balance the radical upheavals he had engineered earlier on. Full closure in a Classic sonata movement comes in two or three waves; if we use closure as a measure, sonata form has two clear sections, a binary whole often followed by a brief coda, or "tailpiece." After establishing a tonal home base, the piece moves to a new harmonic plateau, and closes with a firm cadence, convincing enough that if you did not remember you had just left home, you might think you could stop here. The task of the rest of the movement is to recast the new material in the old key, to reach a point where it will seem rhetorically convincing to close with this same cadential material, but in the old harmonic place—a musical "end rhyme."

Thus, gestures of closure occur twice in this process, initially in the

Example 9.3. K. 465, I, measures 209–17.

wrong key and ultimately in the right. The materials of these cadential zones have their own habits. Two types are particularly familiar: one the solid, primarily harmonic closing formula, not elaborating particular thematic material, but exuding rhythmic and harmonic conviction; the other a reflective, valedictory close, usually involving previous motivic fragments made end-oriented, often over a drone bass. (The drone, used as a closing gesture for its stabilizing effect, often bears with it a pastoral affect; a suggestion of Arcadia at the cadence is certainly appropriate to the comedic close.) Either of these types can provide closure by itself; the first movement of the "Dissonant" Quartet strings them together one after the other. (In Example 9.3, measures 209–12, the closing formula, are elided with measures 212–20, the valedictory close over the drone.)

But this close was not the final one; in this movement Mozart felt the need for a coda. Perhaps he felt that end rhyme alone would not suffice to bring to a close a movement that begins with a famously perplexing slow introduction (its confusions are the cause of at least

Example 9.4. K. 465, I, measures 236–42.

Example 9.5. K. 387, IV, measures 92–99.

one of those articles on Mozart's undermining of Enlightenment values—in fact, rather the best one).[26] The coda evens the balance on the other end of the movement, and provides my first example of a closural "tune that sprouts from the top." The cadence in Example 9.3 is undermined by a little bridge that leads into an intense rhythmic and harmonic play on the opening theme (measures 221–36). Rising up out of this imbroglio comes a brief new tune, exuberant, articulate, and precise (Example 9.4). It adds the culminating comedic touch to a movement that began in purposeful rhythmic amorphousness and harmonic mystification.

Sometimes the "tune" plays a more considerable role, providing not just a snatch of articulate melody, but a celebration of arrival that serves as the matter for the end rhyme itself. Examples of this occur both in the last movement of the String Quartet in G Major, K. 387, and in the trio of the String Quintet in C Major, K. 515. The tune in K. 387 (measures 92–107, 235–50; see Example 9.5) provides a welcome release from the tension generated at the outset by the opposition of a dense and labored fugal exposition with a frenetic contredanse—school counterpoint versus country fiddling. Entirely new material, it emerges on a different rhythmic level that is a mean between the two previous styles, and provides a spirited close, one so successful that it is repeated, with ornaments. It is penultimate; a little valedictory phrase develops out of it to pat the period home.

In the second movement of the C Major Quintet (the minuet and trio), the moment of greatest articulation—and the comic celebra-

---

26. Brown, "Mozart and After."

Example 9.6. K. 515, II, measures 1–10.

Example 9.7. K. 515, II, measures 64–72.

tion—occurs just off the center of the movement, at the end of the trio. The minuet itself is subdued and reflective. It seems to begin *in medias res* on its way to a cadence, with a sinuous, low-profile line. A tiny fragment of a waltz is grafted onto the second member of the phrase (measures 7–10) to provide closure for a line that might otherwise have ended in anticlimax (Example 9.6). The Trio also seems to begin *in medias res,* with a gesture that could appropriately be styled a "bridge passage," a gesture of pure expectation. Articulateness builds slowly. First comes another little waltz phrase, of a piece with that in the minuet (measures 57–64); and then finally out bursts the exuberant, regular, and high-pitched tune (Example 9.7, measures 64–72). It is utterly new and broadly arched—the measure becomes the beat. The first violin reaches up to the high E achieved only once previously in the movement. This tune closes both the first and second sections of the trio.

Other tunes emerge like the one in the coda of the "Dissonant" Quartet, out of the blue in the final close; these are tunes that give the greatest sense of comic superfluidity, of the overflow of celebration. One of my favorites occurs in the last movement of the difficult E-flat Major String Quartet, K. 428, with its somber opening unison. The last movement is, as is customary, a celebratory contredanse, but a sense of rhythmic tentativeness, of breathiness, marks the opening material. At the close a tune emerges over a repetition of the theme, a true descant that smoothes out the theme's uncertainties, thus re-

Example 9.8. K. 428, IV, measures 305–12.

Example 9.9. K. 515, IV, measures 393–421.

moving the last source of topical tension (Example 9.8; for the theme, see the second violin part). The tune, a brief eight measures, occurs only once—antepenultimately—but afterward the main theme returns over a drum bass, its restlessness now pinned to the ground, so to speak. The last movement of the C Major Quintet, K. 515, sprouts the same sort of tune (Example 9.9); again it is penultimate, new, and comically exuberant—and here, to our satisfaction, it is repeated.

Finally—my last example from the chamber music—a brilliant tune occurs at the close of the Quintet in E-flat Major, K. 614, a quintet with its first movement in hunt style. The second section of this movement ends inconclusively, with a half cadence that sets the stage for the tune's bold peroration (measure 214). Bagpipe grace notes on a higher rhythmic level strike a dense dissonance with the upper parts, one resolved by the first violin's upward flight and then exuberant descent to a cadence (Example 9.10). Again the material is new and unexpected, descant-like, and penultimate. The movement closes with a valedictory comment on the hunt motif.

With my next example I move to the piano concertos, where I shall make an ending. There is a nice descant tune at the end of the last movement of the nineteenth concerto, K. 459 in F Major; it takes off at the close of the cadenza, rising up over the complex of nervous rhythms that constitutes the rondo's main theme (Example 9.11). Again just a scrap of tune, its unexpected arrival is *ante*penulti-

Example 9.10. K. 614, I, measures 215–20.

Example 9.11. K. 459, III, measures 462–70.

mate (measure 462). It stabilizes the situation for a *pen*ultimate pedal (measures 470–86), and an ultimate chattering cadential dialogue between soloist and orchestra that momentarily seems to be acting out Zeno's paradox: If you keep halving the unit, can you cross the distance to your goal? Of course, just as in the paradox, the end has to be willed, and it is a masterful close.

My final example is one to which I returned several times in talks during the Mozart year. It has come to represent to me the crux of the issues I have been discussing in this chapter, and no wonder, for it has been an iconic piece for Mozarteans since the nineteenth century. This is, unsurprisingly, the Piano Concerto in D Minor; its presence has already been felt in this chapter. As I said, this concerto was beloved of the Romantics, who had little traffic with the others; presumably its tragic mode expressed the "voice of the true Mozart." Perhaps with this sort of talk in mind, Charles Rosen called it "as much myth as work of art."[27] The first movement of the concerto is

27. Rosen, *The Classical Style*, 228.

Example 9.12. K. 466, III, measures 396–403.

gripping in the monolithic force of its tragic stance. The finale opens with a turbulent D minor theme, but its close has always disappointed: It ends in D *major*, with a gay penultimate tune and a sassy trumpet call (Example 9.12).[28] To proponents of the Gloomy Mozart, this ending is a puzzlement; they reject it out of hand or strain to justify it. It will be clear by now, I hope, why to me this ending is not problematical. A good many of Mozart's darkest works in minor tonalities end in the major; the tragic close—the "dying fall"—is not the rule.[29] This is not, however, mere convention; the problem is ours for having such a difficult time accepting the comic as a meaningful premise. The happy endings of Mozart's operas are clearly a celebra-

28. The treatment of this tune in the Rondo is more complex than a simple reference to it can suggest. It actually serves twice, both as the cadential tune to close major sections of the movement, like the tune in K. 387, IV, and as the coda tune, as in the majority of the other examples. It occurs first in F major (measure 140), to close the first run-through of the Rondo themes, and recurs in D minor in a second major cadential section just before the cadenza (measure 303). In the coda, however, it is significantly changed. The opening theme, for piano alone just as the movement began, introduces the tune—in fact, is turned into its antecedent phrase, so that the tune seems to enter as its "answer" (measure 355). On its final repetition (measure 396), the tune itself is made more concisely complementary and cadential, its two four-measure lengths with half-cadence transformed into three two-measure units of dominant-tonic alternation. These three units pave the way for the introduction of a new fourth unit, the last word in periodicity—the sassy trumpet call:

Original tune (measures 140ff.)								Coda tune (measures 396ff.)							
mm. nos. x:	1	2	3	4	5	6	7	8	1	2	3	4	5	6	7	8
phrases:	1	2	3	4	1	2	3	4	1	2	1	2	1	2	1	2
figures:	a	b	b	c	a	b	b'	d	a	b	a	c	a	b	x!	...
harmony:	V	I	ii	V	V	I	V	I	V	I	V	I	V	I	V	I

The trumpet call is then detached (the Zeno's paradox effect again) to lead up to the final touch—an unexpected six-measure terraced buildup over the subdominant that provides an extraordinarily powerful "whiplash" effect to the final tonic chords. This brilliantly planned coda orchestrates the comic close in full serenity of purpose; it is difficult to see it, as many have, as an aberration or a torturous compromise.

29. Some minor-key works with finales that close in *minor* are the Piano Sonata in A Minor, K. 310/300d, and the Piano Sonata in C Minor, K. 457, the Piano Concerto in C Minor, K. 491, and the two G minor symphonies, the "Little," K. 183, and the "Great,"

tion of the social man, of reconciliation, and of accommodation to the way things are—witness the D major epilogue of *Don Giovanni*. I submit that Mozart's instrumental music maintains the same confidence in the social equilibrium; in almost every work, it mirrors in the chiaroscuro of its surface the diverse modes of human existence, adopting as its dynamic model that motion out of adversity toward the happy ending that graces the universal comic narrative. These cadential tunes may seem marginal, but when they occur they are so unmistakably joyous in their comic spontaneity that they cannot fail to persuade us—if only momentarily—of the validity of the comic close. Two hundred years after Mozart's death, we still celebrate the enduring affirmation of his *commedia per musica*.

K. 550. Among minor-key works that end in *major* are the Serenade for Wind Instruments in C Minor, K. 388 (rearranged as the String Quintet in C Minor, K. 406), the String Quartet in D Minor, K. 421 (which ends with a *tierce de picardie*), the Piano Quartet in G Minor, K. 478, and the String Quintet in G Minor, K. 516. Note that, with the addition of the D Minor Piano Concerto, this list of Mozart's important minor-key instrumental works is nearly complete.

10

Don Giovanni against the baroque; or, The culture punished

MICHAEL P. STEINBERG

"IN THE AUTUMN of the year 1787, accompanied by his wife, Mozart undertook a journey to Prague for the premiere of *Don Giovanni.*" This well-known statement of fact comes not at the beginning of a standard Mozart biography or monograph but from the opening of one of the nineteenth century's most lyrical German novellas: Eduard Mörike's *Mozart auf der Reise nach Prag* (Mozart on the Journey to Prague), published on the centennial of Mozart's birth. For Mörike, Mozart's journey represented a journey to *Don Giovanni,* and therein to a new level of aesthetic and existential understanding. In *Don Giovanni,* according to Mörike, Mozart confronted death, musically and existentially. The imaginary plot of Mörike's story duplicates the same passage from courtly elegance to metaphysical mystery that Mörike saw in Mozart's lifelong musical journey. Thirty hours by carriage northwest of Vienna, Mörike imagines, the Mozart entourage stops to rest at the manor house of Moravian landowners. Gathered in the parlor, the family persuades the composer to play excerpts from his new opera at the piano. He agrees, and in his thunderous rendition of the conflict between Don Giovanni and the statue of the Commendatore—for Mörike, the energy of life and the energy of death—he astounds his audience, exhausts himself, and transmits the force of death. When asked by his listeners what had gone through his mind the night he composed these passages, Mozart replies that he had thought of his own death.

Mörike's agenda for the Mozart centennial was broadly revisionist. Nineteenth-century Romantic musical taste, he seemed to argue through his novella, needed to reevaluate Mozart's work as a music of power rather than a music of manners. The fight between life and death for which he read *Don Giovanni* confirmed Mozart's status as a visionary, and as a precursor of high Romantic sensibility. For Mörike, as for Kierkegaard before him, Mozart's power lay in his musical confrontation with universals. Here, as generally in this idealist strain of philosophical aesthetics that grants music a special status as a human discourse capable of touching the absolute, *Don Giovanni* has a place of honor for its internal insistence that dramatic and philosophical content is internal to the music. In Kierkegaard's words:

> Don Juan can only be expressed musically. I have learned this myself essentially through music, and I ought therefore to guard in every way against giving the impression that the music arrives on the scene as an import from without. If you propose to treat the matter in this way, then you may, for all of me, admire the music in this opera as much as you wish, you will not have grasped its absolute significance.[1]

A century later, this Kierkegaardian, Mörikean view has become a commonplace, at least among those who understand the greatness of the late operas. Many Mozarteans have chosen to extend this evaluation back to all of Mozart's work, to hear visionary profundity in even the jottings of the child prodigy. *Il re pastore* thus becomes a musical setting of Plato's *Republic*. For the majority, however, the argument of Mörike's "journey" holds: The courtly Mozart of the *ancien régime*, who sat on Maria Theresa's lap and delighted the princes of Europe, developed into a political commentator in *Le nozze di Figaro*, a sexual commentator in *Così fan tutte*, and an erotic-existentialist commentator in *Don Giovanni*.

Sex and death, according to this view, are eternal; politics are ephemeral, at least in their specific representations. The sexual politics of *Figaro* are therefore eternal, but the class politics are of the mo-

---

1. Soren Kierkegaard, *Either/Or*, trans. David Swenson and Lillian Swenson (Princeton: Princeton University Press, 1943), vol. I, 115.

ment, of 1789 in particular. It took Peter Sellars to show us how to apply the intricate class differentiations of *Figaro* to contemporary New York, but the success of this move lay precisely in the specificity of the contemporary applications. Dr. Bartolo became a professor of Italian at Columbia University—a job that Lorenzo da Ponte had also filled—and that made his rumpled west-side presence supremely inappropriate in the East 56th Street Trump Tower. He became the lowest-class figure who could possibly be allowed to proceed past the lobby security. Profundity in *Don Giovanni* has been found in its universality, in its presentation of cosmic energies. Thus, in the recent Salzburg Festival production, the entrance of the avenging statue was accompanied by the disappearance of the temporal world; the Don's demise was played against a backdrop of dark emptiness, stars, and planets.

But does profundity lie only in universal statements (sex and death) and universalizable ones (the competing powers of the cosmos)? Say yes, and you will make historians uncomfortable. Historians are attracted to the specific and often to the unique. We are usually suspicious of universals and, therefore, rarely interested in them. As a result, universalists (many political philosophers, for example) have tended to be angry with us. Historical scholars in nineteenth-century Germany made the further distinction between the historian and the antiquarian. The antiquarian, according to this distinction, is interested only in the unique and nontransferable in the past. The historian is interested in the specific, but in the specific with transferable significance.

For the modern cultural historians from whom I have learned most, a historical phenomenon must be understood for its specificity, intricacy, and richness of character, but that specificity may be transferable to other epochs. Epochs can speak with each other if their mutual references are precise. Peter Sellars's *Figaro* shows how this principle can work; his *Don Giovanni*—like his *Figaro,* a parable of 1980s New York, but of Harlem's mean streets rather than Fifth Avenue's lofty co-ops—shows how it can fail. Sellars's *Don Giovanni* renounced the universal, and it also renounced, obviously, the antiquarian. It found, however, only a fragment of the specific: violence and death. It neglected life, which meant, musically and dramatically, that it neglected the erotic.

But just as important—and here is the surprise in my argument—the Sellars *Don Giovanni* neglected the political. I want to argue here that the greatness of *Don Giovanni* lies not only at the level of the universal and the existential, but at the level of the specific, the historical, and the political. First of all, it presents a world of strict social hierarchy, enforced through intricate behavioral codes. Second, and more specifically, it is itself a work of concentrated political power and critique, wrestling in contestatory fury with the politics and the political culture of the Habsburg Empire. Mozart's journey to Prague was a journey to a theater free of imperial control, to a place where he could look back on Habsburg culture and, with the opening chords of *Don Giovanni,* hurl modernist thunder at Habsburg society. In *Figaro,* he teased ("If you want to dance . . ."); in *Don Giovanni,* he accused, claiming for himself the last laugh, even if the last laugh were to come from hell.

Don Giovanni was a hit in Prague in a way that it was not, a season later, in Vienna. The reasons for this discrepancy are intricate and have a great deal to do with Viennese political circumstance in the aftermath of the Turkish war and the ensuing illness and unpopularity of Emperor Joseph II, Mozart's patron. But there is also the question of what might be called macro-circumstantial evidence, having to do with long-term Bohemian-Austrian tension and the consequential differentials in ideology and cultural taste between Prague and Vienna. Prague, the Bohemian capital, had been the seat of the Holy Roman Empire until 1612. Its religious and linguistic duality had done much to launch the conflict, in 1618, that became the Thirty Years' War. In defeat, Bohemia was systematically reduced to the status of a marginal Habsburg province, controlled by imperial power, German language, and Jesuit educational policy. This situation still held in the late eighteenth century. The Josephinian reforms were considered foreign impositions by many Bohemians, as Napoleonic reform would be several decades later by many Germans. When the Prague musical public praised Mozart as a "German Apollo," they clearly had in mind a spirit who could foster German culture in Prague in a non-Viennese manner, perhaps in an anti-Viennese manner.[2] The most interesting mystery—and it remains, I think, a mystery—is the extent to which Mozart and da Ponte complied with the spirit of Prague. That Mozart had suffered, in Andrew Steptoe's words, "a catastrophic decline in

2. See the discussion in Volkmar Braunbehrens, *Mozart in Vienna, 1781–1791,* trans. Timothy Bell (New York: HarperPerennial, 1991), 293–316.

popularity" among the Viennese in 1786 is relevant but not sufficient as an explanation.[3]

The result is the principle of "*Don Giovanni* against the baroque," or "the culture punished." In arguing the significance of the work's cultural politics, I want in no way to appropriate the work's meaning or its mystery, or to displace other readings. I do want to restore a dimension and, if possible, add to its power and to its mystery. In my discussion I will make frequent references to Joseph Losey's 1979 film of the opera. More than any other reading of the work, Losey's has restored the dialogue between *Don Giovanni* and history. In the austerity of Ruggero Raimondi's disposition in the title role, and in the aesthetic claims of the surrounding Palladian baroque splendor, the full tension between *Don Giovanni* and the ideology of the baroque seemed to be fully refracted—and for the first time, at least for me.

Contrary to the morality play that Mozart and da Ponte inherited from their sources, and into which latter-day Austrian audiences have at times tried to redefine the opera *Don Giovanni,* the hero of Mozart's and da Ponte's work is not so much the punished *("il dissoluto punito")* as he is the punisher. His powers—sensuous energy and affective manipulation—are musical powers as well. Contrary to the often repeated comment that Don Giovanni scores no sexual victories during the course of the opera, and that the opera is therefore the story only of his demise, he exerts power from beginning to end over the world around him. He is too smart to think that he can control that world. Although he is not identical to musical energy in the opera's cosmos—Joseph Kerman and others have argued convincingly that his own music is the opera's least innovative—he is at least *simultaneous* to the opera's musical and emotional energy. After his demise, the surviving characters sag and droop, like Wagner's gods in the absence of Holda's apples. They regain life only in their memory of Don Giovanni, even if they censor their memory into a moralizing posture.

3. Andrew Steptoe, *The Mozart-Da Ponte Operas* (Oxford: Clarendon Press, 1988), 59. In his discussion of "Opera in Context: Vienna, Prague, and *Don Giovanni,*" 115–20, Steptoe suggests that the success of *Don Giovanni* in Prague but not in Vienna resulted from the relative lack of sophistication of the "backwater" audiences in Prague, who could still be entertained by the pre-rationalist hocus-pocus of the plot. I am not convinced by this view.

Don Giovanni's challengers and victims are the representations of cultural authority. First, the representation of paternalism: the Commendatore, the father, perhaps *(perhaps)* the emperor. His second series of challengers, the three women under his spell, embody in different ways the collaboration, or compromise formation, of sexual desire with social, cultural, and religious order. Because of their own desire and their resulting inner conflict, at least two of the three women (Anna and Elvira) become intricate characterizations and figures of considerable dramatic power and agency. In their public personae, nevertheless, they represent the culture of the baroque, which is the culture of Catholic power, sacred and secular, of cosmic control through the authority of its static and totalizing representation. Don Giovanni confronts this authority with the energies of dissolution and movement, with those qualities of transitoriness, flux, and contingency that were the defining principles of modernity for Baudelaire and other nineteenth-century critics. In his 1859 essay "The Painter of Modern Life," Baudelaire defined modernity in terms of "the transitory, the contingent, and the fugitive," and stated that these qualities form one side of art, the other side being that of the absolute and the immutable. In my language, this is the opposition between the modern and the baroque.[4]

But first, why define baroque culture in terms of stasis and totality? Because I have recently spent some time on this definition, I will resort here, with apologies, to the irritating practice of self-quotation:

> In this context the term *baroque* emerges not as a periodizing label and not only as an artistic or architectural style but as a cosmological claim representing theological, cultural, and political principles of the Counter-Reformation. The very claim that the hierarchic chain of being uniting the Catholic world and God could be represented was itself a Catholic principle rejected by Protestantism (and in turn

---

4. I am aware that my association of the character of Don Giovanni with the energies of modernity, and those of the women with the energies of the baroque, may tend to heroize the Don and vilify the women in ways that may, in turn, obscure the true patterns of victimization in the opera. The drama begins, as many critics have reminded us, with Don Giovanni's attempted rape of Donna Anna—attempted, that is, if we believe her later account to Ottavio. This situation is clearly fundamental to the moral topography of the opera. The reading I offer here, which sees the historical and also moral topography in ways favorable to Don Giovanni, does not attempt to displace readings with a morally different focus. It does, however, necessarily argue for the overdetermined quality of the moral topography of *Don Giovanni* as a whole.

reaffirmed in the rejection of the Reformation). The baroque thus combines a system of representation with the confidence in the very possibility of such an act of representation. It is thus a cultural style that conjoins Catholic Europe with Habsburg Austria, (formerly) Habsburg Spain, France, and Italy as principal coordinates. . . . The baroque claimed to represent an entire cosmos from the vantage point of a Catholic center that controlled the principles and the process of representation.[5]

Totality is thus the first principle of the baroque; theatricality is the second, the means to the representational and political end. As Hermann Broch argued, national theaters emerged out of Catholic courts, and "there were no Protestant theater cities."[6] Protestant theater, when tolerated, did not represent official culture; the Globe Theatre was hardly the agent of official Elizabethan self-representation. When Emperor Joseph II offered Mozart his patronage, he licensed him as an agent of imperial representation. For obvious reasons, *Figaro* came as a shock.

In *Don Giovanni*, Mozart moved his cultural critique of baroque ideology into the music, and he made music into a critique of the ideology of representation. The music of *Don Giovanni* is the voice of negation, with Habsburg culture as its specific referent and target. The character of the Don cannot, of course, be said to possess the critical and cultural self-awareness that inhabits his music and the voice of the orchestra. The music seems to me to have a mind of its own. Don Giovanni carries a negativity of his own, but it is not a highly self-conscious one; it resembles the diabolical spirit that Goethe invested in the figure of Mephistopheles, who describes himself (*Faust*, Part I, lines 1337–38) as "the spirit that always desires evil and always creates goodness" ("Der Geist, der stets das Böse will, und stets das Gute schafft").

How do these opposing energies play themselves out through the course of the drama? The overture, where the interpretation of drama and the aesthetic of absolute music converge, has been the predictable locus of philosophically oriented interpretation of the work, with Kier-

5. Michael P. Steinberg, *The Meaning of the Salzburg Festival: Austria as Theater and Ideology, 1890–1938* (Ithaca: Cornell University Press, 1990), 3.

6. Hermann Broch, *Hugo von Hofmannsthal and His Time*, trans. Michael P. Steinberg (Chicago: University of Chicago Press, 1984), 63.

kegaard and Wagner providing early and powerful readings. Wagner wrote on the *Don Giovanni* overture briefly in 1841; Kierkegaard's *Either/Or,* published in 1843, treats the overture and the work itself at length.

For the young and angry Wagner, writing in Paris, the allegro of the *Don Giovanni* overture represented "the struggle between inexorably opposing forces."[7] But what about the overall duality between the overture's opening andante and the allegro section? As post-Wagnerian listeners, we have grown accustomed to hearing the opening of the overture according to a Wagnerian musical aesthetic, which I would argue is both anachronistic and wrong. We assume that the opening chords represent the Commendatore, the statue, and the punishment he metes out to Don Giovanni. After all, the entrance of the statue into the Don's dining room recapitulates these opening chords. But in this way we give these chords the status of a leitmotiv. I would argue for a much more primitive musical definition of these chords and the sequences of ascending and descending chromatic runs that follow them. They establish the opera's principal musical language as one of austerity, fury, negation, and extrahuman power. In the description of Géza Fodor:

> This wholly musically-conceived beginning is at the same time one of the most fantastic visions of musical literature: a true apparition. The mass of dominant chords, developed with inherent asymmetry, voiced in the tonality of D-minor by the entire orchestra, evokes inarticulate monumentality. The intonation is chilling: it is not without justification that Abert likens it to the concept of Medusa's head.[8]

The avenging statue is allowed, in his second appearance, to inhabit this external fury, but he is not identical to it.

Like a true apparition, the meaning of the overture's opening chords can never fully be known. But I am going to make a more dire assertion: Their power lies in the fact that they can never truly be *heard.* They assert themselves first as a foreign force, in the way that divine law is both absolute and absolutely foreign. What we have here

7. The phrase is from Daniel Heartz's summary in *Mozart's Operas* (Berkeley: University of California Press, 1990), 176. The original essay is "De l'ouverture" of 1841.

8. Géza Fodor, "Don Giovanni," in Agnes Heller and Ferenz Feher, eds., *Reconstructing Aesthetics* (Oxford: Blackwell, 1986), 150.

is an instantiation of a Reformation and Old Testament idea of divine authority, musically prefiguring and opposing a Catholic representational world. The chords have the status of divine force, which is foreign and inappropriable, as opposed to mythic force, which is, dangerously, appropriable by human agency. (This distinction between the divine and the mythical is Walter Benjamin's, from the 1921 essay "Toward a Critique of Violence.") At the opera's end, this force is personified, and at the same time depersonified, in the figure of the avenging statue. Retroactively, we can say, lamely, that the music represents the statue. But we are not so informed at the first hearing of the overture, and that is the significant experience of its dramatic force. In this sense of the listener's time-bound consciousness, there is no such thing as repetition in music.

The second section of the overture, in contrast, embodies worldly energies, with suggestions of pomp and ceremony provided by its instrumentation. These are the energies of everyday social life, compatible with the empire's official representational content and style, from the Catholic aristocracy (Anna and Ottavio) to the productive, and reproductive, peasantry (Zerlina and Masetto). In Fodor's words again, "As the apparition disappears, the world-stage is occupied by the realm of sensuality, in complete ignorance of the forewarning."[9] The two parts of the overture thus inscribe, for Fodor, Kierkegaard's opposition between the spiritual and the sensual—the sensual defined as a realm "created by Christianity through its exclusion by the spirit."[10]

Compatible with Fodor's and Kierkegaard's descriptions of spirit versus sensuality is the more conventional program given to the two sections of the overture, positing the contrast between death and life, the Commendatore's claim and Don Giovanni's prior exploits. But I would place the Commendatore and Don Giovanni together in the overture's opening D minor andante, and the social world in the D major allegro, which abruptly follows. I hear, therefore, a dramatic and musical alliance between the Commendatore and Don Giovanni as negative forces.

Joseph Losey felt, I think, the same alliance, as manifest in the dire disposition of Ruggero Raimondi's Don, the most convincing physical incarnation of the character I have seen. Don Giovanni is possessed of an essential negativity (some might call it a death wish), of a force that is not seen again on the operatic stage until Carmen. Don Giovanni and Carmen alike are possessed of a sexuality that is extrasocial and antisocial, and only generations of sedate opera audiences have been able to redefine their sexual danger as lyrical charm. (The prelude to *Carmen* is sequentially different from the *Don Giovanni* overture— the worldly allegro comes first, the ominous adagio second—but it juxtaposes similarly opposing representations of negativity and the social world.) Raimondi got it right: The opposition that inhabits the drama from the opening bars of the overture is not so much that between spirit and sensuality as that between otherworldly negativity and worldly affirmation.

If Don Giovanni and the Commendatore are immediately allied in the opening energy of the overture, a third musical spirit must be added to them, and that is the voice of the composer. Once again, we must reject the received clichés. If the andante embodies austerity and negation and the allegro embodies worldliness and sensuality, then two centuries of popular Mozart reception will place the Mozartean spirit comfortably in the second mold. But this is the result of inattentive listening. Mozart is able to compose, as in the allegro, within the paradigm of worldly entertainment, but his truest voice stands in the critical austerity and remove of the opening andante. How can we be sure of this? Perhaps through the realization that the andante is built on a generative exploration of a single D minor tonality. What unfolds is the birth of consciousness through the spirit of music, in a Kantian dynamic where the critical subject stands apart from and prior to the experience of the world. Richard Wagner will begin *Das Rheingold* with a similarly fundamental elaboration of a tonality, E-flat major, but his universe is a Hegelian one, in which consciousness and world germinate simultaneously.

What I want to insist on at this point is the specific historical, cultural definition given by Mozart to the worldly, sensual realm inhabited by the overture's second half and the entire stage action up to the statue's arrival at dinner. It is clear that the historical Austrian association with Spain gives an internal, Habsburg, and even Austrian guise to the literal Spanish locale of the drama. Although the action is entirely secular, the secular culture is deeply inhabited by Catholic ritual practice and behavioral stricture. Religious example is set by the aristocracy, and Donna Anna is the prime carrier of the Catholic aura, its power as well as its fissures. On the social scale, Anna and Ottavio stand opposite Zerlina and Masetto.

On the issue of class, as well as on issues of emotional and musical focus, the most difficult and most persistent question about the characters seems to remain "Who is Elvira?"—the character invented by Molière. She is the energy of ambivalence, the messenger between the worlds polarized in the opera. She admits to her own internal conflict between religiosity and sensuality with more honesty than Anna will ever have. Her musical style is the most wide-ranging in the opera. When, in her warning to Zerlina ("Ah! fuggi il traditor!"), she defends the strictures of the spirit against the temptations of the flesh, she sings an accomplished baroque opera seria aria, a parody of Handel.[11] The rhetorical move seems to be hers even more than Mozart's; she seems to understand the expressive as well as the cultural style she is quoting. On the other side, the aria in which she gives in to her desire, "Mi tradì quell'alma ingrata" (added for the Vienna premiere), is musically and vocally as self-destructive as Don Giovanni's final cadences. As for her social position, I would argue that her independence points to a proto-bourgeois identity, even if she is formally identified as a noblewoman. Her autonomy, mobility, and stylistic eclecticism make her the proto-bourgeois foil to the patriarchally dominated Anna. In Elvira, we have the makings of the decisively bourgeois Fiordiligi and Dorabella.

It is Elvira's temporary alliance with Anna and Ottavio that gives the forces of the baroque world their strongest moment in the reaction against Don Giovanni's negativity. Again, Losey's instincts are to be given credit: The three masked figures arriving by gondola from a dock on the Brenta and approaching Don Giovanni's villa provide the true mystery and terror that their collective apparition demands. (Palladians will know, furthermore, that the Villa Rotunda is, in fact, not on the Brenta at all and that Losey's moment has therefore an aura of surreality about it.) Don Giovanni must be understood to be genuinely afraid of this avenging trinity, as this first-act finale prefigures the second-act finale, and this trinity prefigures the avenging statue. The musical moment that embodies the trinity's collective identity is

11. This last point is an issue of considerable debate, as recounted by Daniel Heartz, *Mozart's Operas*, 208–9.

the trio, marked "adagio," in which they call on the heavens to protect them in their mission. Musically, we have the return here of the realm of the spirit, a music purged of all sensuality. But this is the spirit of the baroque in its fullest union of sacredness and political power; it is not the critical spirit of the Mozartean voice.

There is another element at work here. Purged along with the sensual are the attending formal qualities of temporality and movement. The senses, time, and motion are all arrested in this prayerlike utterance. The sudden suspension of action is all the more striking in its separation from the movemented party music that surrounds it. The musical and dramatic effect of the interrupting trio corresponds to what Joseph Frank called "spatial form in modern literature."[12] The modernist writers whom Frank examined in his essay of that name "ideally intend the reader to apprehend their work spatially, in a moment of time, rather than as a sequence."[13] But where Frank's concern was to identify spatial form as a modernist technique, my purpose is to identify it here, precisely because of its limited and strictly demarcated appearance, as the injection into the music and drama of austere, conservative ideological power—specifically, the ideology of the baroque, the energy of the Counter-Reformation, rationalized in Habsburg imperial politics, which wants to hold still the world against the modernizing and dissipating momentum of the Reformation.

Ottavio, Anna, and Elvira are under the masks. Don Ottavio does not seem to be interesting to Mozart at this point; if we remember that the aria "Dalla sua pace" was added for the Vienna premiere, we realize that he has not yet had an aria; he has been given no individual attention. In the trio, his voice serves as an obbligato, a grounding principle. The two women weave together their melodic lines in a shared determination to suppress their own desire. An ascending, chromatic run is answered, perhaps annulled, by a corresponding descent. The cumulative effect is the construction of musical arches that accumulate structurally to form a perfect, enclosed musical space: to form—stretching my image a bit, but not irresponsibly—a baroque cupola out of music. For an instant, pious terror displaces sensuality,

12. Joseph Frank, "Spatial Form in Modern Literature," *Sewanee Review* (1945), reprinted most recently in Frank, *The Idea of Spatial Form* (New Brunswick: Rutgers University Press, 1991), 5–66.
13. Frank, "Spatial Form," 10.

and a cathedral seems to displace Don Giovanni's palace, his party, and the opera house itself. With great understanding of this moment's musical architecture, Joseph Losey's camera tracks the ceiling of the Villa Rotunda as the trio unfolds. Baroque architecture, certainly in Austria and Italy, as every visitor to Vienna's Karlskirche will know, integrates sensuality into its overall scheme. *This* baroque (perhaps Mozart's and Da Ponte's idea of the Spanish baroque) is unable to do so. The sensuality of Don Giovanni is too blunt for social integration.

Let us relate this last point to a specific production decision. In the Franco Zeffirelli staging of *Don Giovanni* lately usurping the Metropolitan Opera stage, the opera's entire action proceeds under the protective form of baroque arches, which define the proscenium space. Zeffirelli, who includes in his curriculum vitae the choreography of large-scale Vatican ceremonies, understands well the theatrical power of Catholic baroque spectacle. In its relation to the opera as a whole, this particular representation is a serious mistake, for it claims, through baroque gesture, to impose form and theatrical coherence on a music drama that shreds and negates all such ideological pretenses. The previous Metropolitan production, set within Eugene Berman's constantly moving and changing drops, showed a far superior understanding of the drama's character. But the moment of the Anna-Elvira-Ottavio trio is the one moment where the baroque enclosure fits. The moment provides, to use Géza Fodor's term, an apparition, and thus the enemy of the senses, of time, and of movement.

Don Giovanni was originally conceived in four acts, and the ending of the third act was to come with the sextet following the unmasking of Leporello, who has wooed Donna Elvira while disguised as his master. Daniel Heartz describes the music of the sextet and its effect on contemporary audiences as follows:

> It relies for its music on several characteristic turns of phrase of rhythms that Mozart has used earlier in connection with the same personalities. Moreover, it relies heavily on the recurrent use of a single motif, the descending chromatic fourth.
>
> To Mozart's audience, the motif meant pain, suffering, and death—it could not be otherwise, since they and their forebears had for several generations heard similar chromatic descents in mass settings to convey the words "Crucifixus, passus et sepultus est," cor-

roborating their experience in the opera house on the demise of heroes and heroines (e.g., Dido).[14]

Elvira begins the sextet in flirtatious conversation with the man she thinks is Don Giovanni. Daniel Heartz ferrets out of Mozart's chromaticisms the double nature of Elvira's passion: the sensual censored by the sacred. When she talks of the terror that makes her feel like dying ("un tal spavento, che mi sembra di morire"), an ascending chromatic run in the violins suggests the sexual subtext of the verb "to die." "The perceptive listeners among Mozart's audience," adds Heartz, with high expectations of the late-eighteenth-century ear, "must have relished this point."[15]

Elvira's passion shifts from desire to suffering with an attendant refocusing of the dynamics of theatricality. At first, she and Leporello are pursued by Anna and Ottavio, Zerlina and Masetto, but as Leporello reveals his identity, Elvira is of course driven away from him to join the other four in a new condemnation, first of Leporello but then again of the now-absent Don Giovanni. In other words, the five become an audience, watching in horror and anger as Leporello plays out his, and Don Giovanni's, little costume play. In becoming an audience, the five characters are as manipulated by the drama as the actual opera audience, watching from the other side of the footlights.

At this moment again, Joseph Losey exhibits a stroke of genius. He sets the scene not in a Vicenza street, in a villa, or on the Brenta, but on the stage of the Teatro Olympico, Palladio's last structure and the architectural apotheosis of the baroque theater. The stage is actually inhabited by a permanent set duplicating, in fact, the streets of Vicenza that lie outside it and using carefully angled ramps and *trompe l'oeil* murals to create an illusion of size and depth—and, in effect, to parody Renaissance perspective. At the sextet's opening, Losey uses the space as if it were the real space of the city streets, having the three pairs converge from the side ramps. But as the unmasking of Leporello proceeds at the footlights, the characters are represented as if *performing* the work for an invited, aristocratic, possibly even clerical, audience. As the five victims of Don Giovanni condemn him, first believing him to be at their mercy and then knowing that he has once again escaped, the rage of the baroque is thus revealed to be not only the-

14. Heartz, *Mozart's Operas,* 210.
15. Heartz, *Mozart's Operas,* 212–15.

atrical, inhabiting the world stage, but self-consciously so. The plot moment, like the stage of the Teatro Olympico, comments on the phenomenon of the vanishing point—in this case, Don Giovanni himself.

Time, temporality, movement, and sensuality inform the musical side of *Don Giovanni* that carries the Mozartean energy of modernity. It is a dangerous energy, which targets baroque authority as its specific, political, and ideological enemy. The modernist spirit moves; the baroque spirit holds still and claims authority over the world theater. Indeed, the baroque spirit defines the world as a world theater, as a delimited space, as a way of claiming totality. So it is neither an accident nor a trivial occurrence that the dialectics of modernity and baroque, world and spirit, motion and stillness, and time and space finally converge in a last battle between the two sides, and that the personification of a petrified culture appears onstage as a statue, the stone guest. The grasp of the baroque is the staying hand of death. In a fascinating study, Malcolm Baker has suggested that the conceit of the speaking statue spoke itself to the profusion of lifelike imagery on eighteenth-century tomb sculpture. Styles of mediation between life and death reflected the changes in, and challenges to, Christian belief. An audience at *Don Giovanni* could still be expected to take very seriously an appearance onstage "of tomb sculpture which for so long had been the static intermediary between the earthly and the eternal."[16]

When, clairvoyantly, Don Giovanni agrees to accompany the statue, he does so in formal tones that have recently prompted musicological comment:

> Ho fermo il core in petto.
> Non ho timor. Verro.
>
> [Stout-hearted,
> Unafraid: I'll come.]

Joseph Kerman comments as follows: "These four bars could never have been predicted. Their unexpected features—stiff, pompous dotted rhythms and baroque-sounding counterpoint, provided by the

---

16. Malcolm Baker, "Odzooks! A Man of Stone!" in Jonathan Miller, ed., *Don Giovanni: Myths of Seduction and Betrayal* (New York: Schocken Books, 1990), 68.

strings alone—are also features of Donna Elvira's Act I aria 'Ah, fuggi il traditor.' "[17] What do we make of the Don's late-baroque gesture? Is he assuming the rhetoric of the culture that punishes him for his punishment of it? He says he will never repent: Does this baroque gesture belie his claim or, with final parodic scorn for his worldly surroundings, reinforce it?

In homage to the power of *Don Giovanni* the opera, I want to conclude with the observation that we must consider the work, as an opera, to be a failure, just as *Hamlet* must be considered a failure as a play. Both are too great and too dangerous to be successes when measured against the formal paradigms in which they emerge—and which they transcend. What I really mean, therefore, is that the genres of opera and drama become inadequate when measured against *Don Giovanni* and *Hamlet,* as the critical imperatives that *Hamlet* defines through words and *Don Giovanni* defines through music amount to an attack on the very claims to representation on which the genres depend. Such an attack necessarily includes in its range the formal discourses—tragedy and opera—within which they themselves reside as dramatic works. The works are self-destructive in a way that exceeds the kind of formal self-consciousness and self-transcendence that we associate with all innovative or modernist moments in the history of creative art. In this sense, *Don Giovanni* and *Hamlet* are already modernist works. Their creative energy resides at least partially in their unbridled negativity, through which the works, like their leading characters, consume themselves.

   Thus, the endings of the works, the final sextet in *Don Giovanni* and Fortinbras's speech in *Hamlet,* are sapped of the dramatic energy that has driven the works up until the moment of their protagonists' disappearance. Not that these endings are devoid of dramatic integrity; on the contrary, nineteenth-century operatic taste preferred that both works end with the deaths of their heroes, and both works were often performed with these alternative, hyperoperatic endings. Such nineteenth-century operatic conventions, like many of the opera houses that were built to serve them, bespeak the neo-baroque in action. (In

17. Joseph Kerman, "Reading *Don Giovanni*," in Miller, ed., *Don Giovanni,* 124. The translation of the four lines is uncredited and, I assume, Kerman's own.

fairness, it must be introduced into the record that Gustav Mahler, as conductor at the Vienna Court Opera, also cut the final sextet from *Giovanni*. But the coordinates were different. He thought it smug, and felt that his audiences were too eager to see the libertine punished and social order reestablished.) I would argue that the sextet, by showing us six people's aimless futures, undoes any pretense to closure or symmetry.

Contrary to baroque ideology, then, *Hamlet* and *Don Giovanni* have, one might say, messy endings, making manifest the continuity of life beyond and outside the representations of art—political life in *Hamlet*, social life in *Don Giovanni*. By their own conviction, the plays themselves are ultimately *not* the thing. They, and the strengths of their leading characterizations, ethically point the way beyond the limits of human consciousness and representation, but cannot lead us there.

11

Nineteenth-century Mozart: the fin de siècle Mozart revival

LEON BOTSTEIN

Back to Mozart? Why back? Why to Mozart? . . . If we observe the major works of music that have been written since the death of Wagner, we find that there is much to be praised . . . but neverthe-less one cannot suppress the feeling, however unclear, that in gen-eral terms, something is wrong and somewhere things are rotten in the development of music today. . . . None of the great masters is as far removed from us as Mozart. . . . The public . . . closes its eyes in wonderment when one speaks of him but remains distant when his works are played. It would behoove us first to find Mozart again before debating whether one can return to him. . . .

The deep satisfaction for which we yearn is denied us by the newest music of today. . . . We are aroused, not satisfied; fired up but not warmed; entranced but not elevated. . . . Music has become hysterical, like an unhappy woman who has been wrongly impris-oned for a long time. Music must become healthy again. . . .

With our modern means of expression we must create once more in the spirit of Mozart: That would most likely be the right answer. If we truly look deeply into the wondrously translucent childlike eyes of Mozart's art, can we still speak of a "return"? I think the more truthful answer should be "Forward to Mozart!"[1]

1. Felix Weingartner, "Zurück zu Mozart?" in *Akkorde: Gesammelte Aufsätze* (Leipzig: Breitkopf und Härtel, 1912), 108–12.

THE WORDS JUST QUOTED were written around 1910 by Felix Weingartner, the eminent Austrian conductor and composer. Although Weingartner began his career under the spell of Liszt and Wagner, by the time he was called to succeed Gustav Mahler at the Imperial Opera in Vienna in 1907 he had established a reputation as both a reformer and a reactionary. His seminal 1895 essay on the art of conducting had attacked the Wagnerian performance tradition and advocated in its place a cleaner (i.e., less influenced by the musical aesthetics of the day) and more historically sensitive (from today's perspective) style of performance of the eighteenth- and nineteenth-century orchestral repertoire. This challenge to the Wagnerian performance tradition, particularly of Beethoven, was but one symptom of a deep mistrust within the music world at the fin de siècle of the aesthetic direction being taken by living composers, especially those who continued to draw their inspiration from Wagner.[2]

Weingartner was responding to a fin de siècle "back to Mozart" movement that was not only a reflection of this mistrust but also the culmination of more than a century of struggle over the soul and meaning of Mozart. As Weingartner's argument made plain, German musicians (or those for whom German music was the essence of high-art music) were using the battle cry "Back to Mozart!" to signal a deep dissatisfaction with the state of musical culture. For them a new model and source of inspiration was needed as an antidote to the musical aesthetics associated with Wagner and his followers—Max von Schillings, Engelbert Humperdinck, Friedrich Klose, Hans Pfitzner, and Richard Strauss among them.[3] For all its attractions, the *verismo* movement of the Italians Mascagni, Leoncavallo, and Puccini could not provide this remedy, since it was seen as a debasement of the "higher" qualities of musical culture.[4] Furthermore, when Weingartner published his essay in 1912, a form of modernism even newer than neo-Wagnerism—one that cultivated the apparently banal, ugly,

2. Weingartner's views are contemporary with those of the theorist Heinrich Schenker (1868–1935), who advocated a seemingly more historically faithful performance practice located in the establishment of an authentic text, which eliminated the printed overlay of interpretive habits accumulated over time.

3. See the excellent contemporary assessment of the fin de siècle malaise, together with a thorough review of contemporary composition, in Rudolf Louis, *Die deutsche Musik der Neuzeit* (Munich: Georg Müller, 1912).

4. On this point, see, for example, the comments in Walter Niemann, *Die Musik seit Richard Wagner* (Berlin: Schuster und Loeffler, 1913), 98.

and arbitrary (the music of Gustav Mahler and Arnold Schoenberg)—
had made an appearance during the first decade of this century.[5]

Neo-Wagnerism seemed to dominate not only composers but the
tastes of the audience. The challenge seemed to be to find a way to
render the "classical" tradition "forward-looking" and not merely "in
retrospect." From the perspective of adherents to the idea of "absolute" music, the possibilities and limits of music qua music remained
unheeded in a vulgar and philistine aesthetic environment.[6] From the
perspective of those calling for a Mozart revival, the writing of new
music had become an undisciplined forum for the extravagant illustration of emotion and subjectivism. A composer himself, Weingartner
believed that one could neither retreat by surrounding oneself with
music from the past—even Mozart—nor use self-consciously a musical
vocabulary rooted in the past. Although Mendelssohn had sparked the
revival of interest in Bach in 1829 (which, in turn, nourished the
development of historicist aesthetics), by the end of the nineteenth
century Bach, despite a flourishing interest in his music, remained too
austere a figure, too distant from modern life to be the standard-bearer
of an alternative to neo-Wagnerism. Bach commanded awe but
seemed excessively serious, religious, academic, and humorless. He
had become an indispensable part of music education in the late nineteenth century, but the interest in him was as a historical figure. He
offered little potential as a real alternative to the seductive lure of
Wagnerism. It was the spirit of Mozart that the new century required.[7]

Why did Mozart emerge as the ideal candidate for aesthetic renewal? Of the four canonic figures of Viennese musical classicism—
Gluck, Haydn, Mozart, and Beethoven—Beethoven was easily the
most significant figure from the perspective of nineteenth-century
composers and audiences. Although Beethoven dominated the classical repertoire in the concert hall and at home, among Wagnerian and
anti-Wagnerian circles the image of Beethoven that had triumphed by
1900 was the one fashioned initially by Robert Schumann but augmented decisively by Wagner himself. Beethoven's music, particularly
the chamber music, may have remained common ground for all

5. The modifiers in this sentence mirror the vocabulary and views of Weingartner in his
essay "Originalität" in *Akkorde*, 173–83.

6. See Niemann, *Die Musik seit Richard Wagner*, 41, 62, 65, and particularly 287–88.

7. Louis, *Die deutsche Musik der Neuzeit*, 262–65.

camps. But the late-Romantic characterization of Beethoven as inno-
vator, creator, and rebel—in terms of his aesthetics, personality, and
ambitions (all presumably audible in the orchestral music)—predom-
inated over the characterization of Beethoven as the symbol of musical
classicism.[8] The Beethoven of the late nineteenth century fit all too
neatly into the Wagnerian claim that Wagner's conception of music
and its relation to drama had been the logical, progressive, and historically valid consequence of Beethoven's art.

Gluck, meanwhile, seemed too identified with the issues of opera,
and Haydn too removed from any impulse associated with nineteenth-
century Romanticism. Furthermore, unlike Bach, Mozart had not ever
been forgotten. Although only a fraction of Mozart's nonoperatic repertoire was in active use, all musicians, Wagnerian and non-Wagnerian
alike, paid ritual homage to his greatness.[9] To all, including the general
public, Mozart was a name to be revered, on a par with Shakespeare,
Goethe, and, as Otto Jahn suggested in 1858, even Sophocles. *Don
Giovanni, Figaro,* and *Die Zauberflöte* were standard repertory items,
and excerpts from them were widely known. Therefore, if a true revival
of classical aesthetics—defined as the logical alternative to Wagnerian
ideas—could be effected by invoking Mozart, the conceits of Wagner
and his followers would not remain undisturbed. Such were the hopes
of the advocates of a "back to Mozart" movement.

From the standpoint of the composers, critics, performers, and teachers at the end of the nineteenth century who sought to encourage a
rediscovery and reappraisal of Mozart, the elevation of public taste was
at stake; the defeat of a superficial and decadent modernism in new
music would be a natural by-product of the revival of the refined
"classicism" that Mozart embodied. The problem was that, as Max
Bruch put it in 1891, "in these days there are many who cherish

---

8. Beyond Wagner's famous Beethoven essay from 1870, see Klaus Kropfinger, *Wagner
and Beethoven: Richard Wagner's Reception of Beethoven,* trans. Peter Palmer (Cambridge:
Cambridge University Press, 1991), which describes the character and significance of Wagner's view of Beethoven. For a less subtle but nevertheless useful book in which the impact
of Wagner's view of Beethoven on the fin de siècle can be gleaned, see Alessandra Comini,
The Changing Image of Beethoven: A Study in Mythmaking (New York: Rizzoli, 1987), 252–
305.

9. In Rudolf Louis's book, for example, Haydn is mentioned once, in passing, whereas
Mozart is discussed extensively. Furthermore, in the concert and stage repertory, Mozart
held a more prominent place than Haydn circa 1900 in German-speaking urban centers.

Mozart in speech, but in their hearts remain completely distant from him and have lost all understanding for true musical beauty and organic form."[10]

Even among the neo-Wagnerians, the revival of Mozart was not necessarily unwelcome. Wagner's warm praise of Mozart in his polemical writings was placed against any fin de siècle use of Mozart as a defense of a reactionary historicist canon of classicism. As with Beethoven, Wagner himself had provided an alternate historical interpretation of Mozart consistent with the aesthetics of neo-Wagnerianism. However, further complicating the fin de siècle Mozart debate that Weingartner entered in 1910 was the explicit if infuriating embrace of Mozart by avowed modernist composers such as Max Reger, Arnold Schoenberg, and Ferruccio Busoni. "I pray every day: God almighty, grant us a Mozart; we have such need of him," wrote Max Reger to Karl Straube in 1904.[11] Composers were turning to Mozart to find ways to free themselves from the restrictive terms of a late-nineteenth-century, neo-Romantic aesthetic debate that had pitted the innovations of Wagner and his followers against the so-called traditionalism of Brahms and other conservative nineteenth-century opponents of Wagner.[12]

Much like the role that the rediscovery of Biedermeier aesthetics played in the evolution of Viennese modernism in design and architecture at the beginning of the twentieth century, the reevaluation of Mozart that began at the end of the nineteenth century was to be crucial to the "new" musical modernism of Reger, Busoni, and Schoenberg (especially after 1913, when Schoenberg's expressionist period came to a close). The return to Mozart became the musical analogue of a fin de siècle credo of stylistic integrity that favored visual simplicity, directness, and a respect for ideas of structure and function, rather than the late-nineteenth-century penchant for decoration and aesthetic camouflage (i.e., the visual analogue of Wagnerism).[13] Adolf

10. Letter, November 29, 1891, from Bruch to Joseph Joachim in *Briefe von und an Joseph Joachim* (Berlin: Julius Bard, 1913), vol. 3, 404.

11. Max Reger, *Briefe eines deutschen Meisters,* ed. Else von Hase-Hoehler (Leipzig: Koehler, 1938), 123.

12. See Busoni's "Mozart Aphorismen" from 1906 in Ferruccio Busoni, *Wesen und Einheit der Musik* (Berlin: Max Hesse, 1956), 143–45; his references to Mozart in letters dated June 1, 1908, and October 12, 1910, in Ferruccio Busoni, *Selected Letters,* ed. Anthony Beaumont (New York: Columbia University Press, 1987), 89 and 114; and also the references to Mozart in Arnold Schoenberg's 1911 *Harmonielehre.*

13. See Mara Reissberger and Peter Haiko, " 'Alles ist einfach und glatt.' Zür Dialektik

Loos's 1908 critique of ornament and decoration in modern life—as corrupt and analogous to crime (vis-à-vis ethics and law) in relation to aesthetic and ethical truths—can be compared to Reger's and Busoni's turn to Mozart and other pre–nineteenth century models of classicism. Predictably, the example of Mozart continued to exert a powerful influence on the direction taken by twentieth-century musical neoclassicism in the 1920s in France and Germany, during the era of the Bauhaus and *Neue Sachlichkeit.*

An example of how centrally Mozart figured in the aesthetic debates of the early twentieth century can be found in a leading Viennese textbook on music history. In the last edition (1915) of his widely used "compendium" of music history, Adolf Prosnitz (who had taught elementary piano and the obligatory courses in music history at the conservatory in Vienna from 1869 to 1900) wrote:

> There came an era of musical romanticism when Mozart's art was in retreat. His music was considered harmless and old fashioned against romanticism's raving, subjective musical language and its passionate life of sentiment. In our day, in which a tumultuous movement rages through our musical world—one of the poeticizing and the painterly push towards the superficial and the perverse (even including the celebration of real bacchanalias)—owing to the fatigue of nervous overstimulation, there is now a countermovement among circles of music lovers. It reflects the longing for the ennobling and pleasure-giving enjoyment of pure and beautiful music; for the classical calm of the true work of art. Therefore many voices have let themselves be heard with the slogan: Back to Mozart.[14]

At the other end of the aesthetic divide from this reactionary characterization of Mozart stood two types of modern Romanticism, that of Strauss, Mahler, and Debussy, and that of a younger and less established generation, including Schoenberg and Franz Schreker.[15] Ironically, by 1915 both Strauss and Schoenberg were breaking new ground in their music, drawing considerable, although contrasting, inspiration from Mozart. For Schoenberg, Mozart's formal procedures

der Ornamentlosigkeit," in *Moderne Vergangenheit: 1800–1900* (Vienna: Das Kunstlerhaus, 1981), 13–19.

14. Adolf Prosnitz, *Compendium der Musikgeschichte 1750–1830. Für Schulen und Konservatorien* (Vienna: Alfred Hölder, 1915), 157.

15. In 1908 Schreker, influenced in part by the back-to-Mozart discussion, composed a ballet for orchestra entitled "Rokoko," which ignored the visual and dramatic elements of the stage. See R. S. Hoffmann, *Franz Schreker* (Vienna: Universal, 1921), 99–102.

in the chamber music and symphonies (later expanded by Brahms)—
the use of variation and the techniques of transformation of melodic
material—were exemplary for his own effort to design a contemporary
grammar of music that could empower new music to communicate
sensibilities and experiences that were uniquely and purely musical.
Despite the decisive differences between Schoenberg's cultural politics
and those of Prosnitz, the redemption of the aesthetic power of purely
musical means was at the core of their divergent critiques of contemporary musical life.[16]

In the case of Richard Strauss, Germany's most celebrated composer at the fin de siècle, the operatic Mozart became crucial as a
model. As he prepared for a new production of *Così fan tutte* in Munich in 1910, Strauss encountered the comic subtlety, the humor, and
the lightness of Mozart—in other words, an alternative to the Wagnerian definition of the dramatic. As Strauss recalled in 1944, for him
Mozart had "solved all problems before they were even raised; . . . in
his work all phases ('the whole scale of expression of human sentiment') of the emotional life of human beings become transfigured,
spiritualized, and freed of all the limits of realism."[17] Here Strauss
implicitly contrasted the elaborate, nearly literary representational
musical strategy of Wagner (i.e., "realist") with the clearly artificial
aesthetic character of Mozart's music—which, ironically, better
approached the profundity of human experience. Although one thinks
first of *Der Rosenkavalier* (completed in 1910) when considering
Strauss's turn to Mozart, the two versions of *Ariadne auf Naxos* (1912
and 1916) and the explicit effort in *Die Frau ohne Schatten* (1917) to
write a sequel to *Die Zauberflöte* are the clearest examples of Strauss's
midcareer appropriation of Mozart as a guide to a new aesthetic strategy.

Among the less reactionary fin de siècle proponents of a Mozart
revival were scholars and critics such as Guido Adler, Mahler's childhood friend and a seminal figure in the development of modern musicology. For Adler, a return to Mozart was justified by more than any
need for a renewal of healthy musical aesthetics. Through an appre-

16. For a comparison, see Schoenberg's polemical articles, written between 1909 and
1911, collected in Arnold Schoenberg, *Stil und Gedanke. Aufsaetze zur Musik,* ed. Ivan
Vojyech (Reutlingen: S. Fischer Verlag, 1976), 157–73.
17. Richard Strauss, *Betrachtungen und Erinnerungen* (Zürich: Atlantis Verlag, 1949),
91.

ciation of Mozart's music, a set of crucial cultural and political ideas could be communicated. In a speech to secondary-school students held in the Musikverein of Vienna in honor of the 150th anniversary of Mozart's birth in 1906, Adler stressed four reasons why a new generation might well seek inspiration in Mozart:

1. Mozart's music rested on a love of all mankind, on an ethical universalism. Although Mozart had been a great German artist, his music transcended all national and religious barriers.

2. Mozart succeeded in reaching the hearts and minds of experts—those schooled in music—as well as the broader popular audience. He was, in a word, an artist who realized the democratic and egalitarian potentials of art.

3. Mozart used dissonance only out of necessity. The perfect integration of form and content made the modern habit of using the superficial and shocking aspects of chromaticism and extended tonality for their own sake superfluous.

4. Mozart realized the "only true manner" of rendering drama into music: He mirrored the human soul in sound.[18]

For Adler (as for Prosnitz and Weingartner), there was also an aesthetic component to his position: at stake were the relation of so-called extramusical content to form in music and the idea that ultimately—despite Wagner—the only true content for music was music alone. The unique properties of music as opposed to those of words and images (to which music seemed, in modern times, to be subordinated) had to be reasserted against the use of music as illustrative of the extramusical, as in the famous tone poems of Richard Strauss or even the early symphonic narratives of Gustav Mahler. Mozart, particularly in the operatic repertoire, displayed with uncanny virtuosity the seemingly unique autonomous power of music to speak to humanity on its own independent terms.

Precisely because Mozart stood for an aesthetically independent, nonrepresentational aesthetic divorced from mundane everyday reality, his music seemed the ideal antidote to the stress, complexity, harshness, and emotional exaggeration of modern life. Mozart was a welcome alternative in a world where music—presumably a universal language of art—had become merely another mirror of a fragmented

18. Guido Adler, "Mozart: Festrede bei der Mozart-Feier für die Mittelschulen Wiens," April 18, 1906, in the Adler Archive, The University of Georgia Library, Athens, Georgia.

modernity. Art could therefore assist in rescuing the human soul from the inhuman and ugly facts of contemporary existence, which included the specter of decadence, excessive materialism, overconfidence in the notion of historical progress, and heightened naturalism, tending toward the desire for extreme effects.[19]

The assertion of a dichotomy between the ideal, true nature of musical art (Mozart) and a fashionable and distinctly modern but ultimately deceptive technique of musical naturalism (Wagner) emerged in Vienna in the 1880s. The critic Theodor Helm (a passionate Bruckner enthusiast) described how the opponents of Wagner sought to exploit the fact that the applause at the performance of a Mozart work far exceeded that for Wagner's *Faust Overture* at a concert in Vienna in February 1883, twelve days after Wagner's death. Was it really a triumphant vote by the public for "nature" as opposed to "the unnatural" in music?[20] Or was it philistine antimodern conservatism? Hugo Wolf, aware of a new tendency for the anti-Wagnerians to appropriate Mozart, devoted most of his 1886 review of the debut of a new production of *Le nozze di Figaro,* organized to celebrate the hundredth anniversary of the first performance, to quoting Wagner's lavish praise of Mozart.[21]

Not surprisingly, Eduard Hanslick, the distinguished anti-Wagnerian partisan, took the occasion of the 1891 celebrations of Mozart's death to make the paradoxical and pessimistic observation that the performance of more of Mozart's music than had been heard for years in Vienna did not seem tedious. Yet although it had been a welcome balm—"a temporary return to a lost paradise" (by which Hanslick meant an era without Wagner and his followers)—an inevitable gap between Mozart and modernity would always remain. For Hanslick, music and life had evolved, perhaps unfortunately, beyond any "return" to Mozart. Hanslick, despite his conservative tastes, recognized that the nostalgic embrace of an excessively historicist aes-

19. One among the many sources for this view of modernity and the need to use musical classicism and Mozart as antidotes is found in the eleventh edition of Bernhard Kothe's *Abriss der allgemeinen Musikgeschichte,* ed. Rudolph Procházka (Leipzig: F. E. C. Lückart, 1919), 365; and Karl Storck's *Geschichte der Musik* (Stuttgart: Muth'sche Verlagshandlung, 1910), 782–84.

20. Theodor Helm, *Fünfzig Jahre Wiener Musikleben* I (Vienna: IIIm Verlages der Herausgebers, 1977), 169–70.

21. Hugo Wolf, *Musikalische Kritiken* (Leipzig: Breitkopf und Härtel, 1911/1983), 274–76.

thetic on the part of the audience would ultimately doom the future of any new music.[22]

During the 1891 celebrations commemorating the hundredth anniversary of Mozart's death, a generation younger than Hanslick sought both to avoid a conservative Mozart-Wagner dichotomy and to counter Hanslick's view of Mozart as ultimately stylistically dated and emotionally foreign to a modern audience that was capable, however, of responding to greatness in Wagner. In the 1891 Salzburg ceremonies, the Viennese critic Robert Hirschfeld was careful to cite Wagner repeatedly in his *Festrede*. Hirschfeld attempted to win over the Wagnerians to a reconsideration of Mozart by using Wagner as a basis for correcting Wagner's own limited view of Mozart; he suggested delicately that Wagner's view of Mozart as having been historically superseded had been premature. Mozart, as Wagner knew so well, was the master of light in music. Hirschfeld extended the image of enlightenment beyond its use as a metaphor to describe the character of Mozart's music. Mozart's mission had been "a harmonic one—to bind and unite." Mozart was to the history of music what Plato had been to the history of philosophy. The ethos of Mozart's art was the ideal synthesis of "wisdom, beauty, and strength." Despite the passage of time, the task for the modern age was to be able both to intuit and to understand Mozart in this manner. His music was akin to a metaphysical ideal, which, despite surface dissimilarities, Wagner's work itself mirrored in a thoroughly contemporary manner.

Hirschfeld argued further that, as a result of Wagner's considerable success in raising the public's standard of taste, it was now (circa 1891) possible to popularize Mozart's music and make it relevant without compromising it. By stressing Mozart's "German" character (by which Hirschfeld meant those qualities that Joseph Joachim described in 1898 as "the gift to assimilate, so that the material becomes universal ideal thought, intelligible to all nations"), Hirschfeld sought to amalgamate into one unified ethos Mozartean classicism, the idea of absolute music, the early Romantic tradition of instrumental music, and Wagner. What eluded Hirschfeld was the ability to connect a return to Mozart with any constructive agenda for new music. In Hirschfeld's celebration of Mozart (in contrast to Hanslick's), one

22. Eduard Hanslick, "Die Mozart Feier" in *Fünf Jahre Musik* (Berlin: Allgemeiner Verein für deutsche Litteratur, 1896), 149–60.

encounters an early example of how the cult of Mozart would be used later in the twentieth century as the basis for a regressive generalized critique of innovative musical modernism after Brahms, Wagner, and Bruckner.[23]

By the early twentieth century, a reconciliation between popular musical taste, Wagnerism, and the capacity to appreciate the classical tradition exemplified by Mozart had become at best a remote possibility. Too much of the fin de siècle Mozart revival had been explicitly targeted against the Wagnerian heritage. Furthermore, even Schoenberg (not to speak of Stravinsky) doubted that Wagner's popularity had enhanced the public's capacity actually to understand Mozart's musical genius. The generation of performing artists born after 1870 (which included pianist Artur Schnabel and violinist Carl Flesch, two key advocates of Mozart) knew that there had too long been a great gap between the "official" praise given Mozart in the standard narratives of music history and his actual place in the repertoire.[24] The task of commemorating Mozart as more than a historical artifact required an alliance with twentieth-century modernism in new music.

The demand for Mozart on the part of the audience in the mid and late nineteenth century had been weak indeed. During his entire career Gustav Mahler conducted (apart from the operas) only the last two symphonies and the *Requiem*. Between 1848 and 1910, only seven symphonies were in the repertoire of the Vienna Philharmonic, which also included three serenades, two overtures, five piano concertos, two violin concertos, and a host of operatic excerpts. Mozart was no more evident in the concerts of the other major Viennese sponsor of concerts in the nineteenth century, the Society of the Friends of Music. In Vienna the only exceptions were 1891 and 1906, the anniversary years.[25]

23. Robert Hirschfeld, *Festrede zur Mozart-Centenarfeier 1891 zu Salzburg* (Salzburg: H. Kerber, 1891); for the Joachim quote, see his letter to his nephew (in English) from 1898 in Joseph Joachim, *Briefe*, vol. 3, 482.

24. See Artur Schnabel, *My Life and Music* (New York: Dover, 1988), 27; and Carl Flesch, *Memoirs*, trans. and ed. Hans Keller and C. F. Flesch (New York: Da Capo, 1979), 27–59 and 174.

25. See Knud Martner, *Gustav Mahler im Konzertsaal: Eine Dokumentation seiner Konzerttätigkeit, 1870–1911* (Copenhagen: K. Martner, 1985); Richard von Perger, *Denkschrift zur Feier des 50 jaehrigen Bestandes der philharmonischen Konzerte in Wien 1849–1910* (Vienna: C. Fromme, 1910); and Robert Hirschfeld and Richard von Perger, *Geschichte der k. k. Gesellschaft der Musikfreunde in Wien* (Vienna: Druck von A. Holzhausen, 1912).

From the perspective of an almost unbearable excess of "Mostly Mozart" in the late twentieth century, Bruch and Weingartner were perhaps accurate in their view that the essential greatness of Mozart seemed lost on the musical public. Concert performances of Mozart were comparatively limited, even though amateur readings of his music at home persisted. There was more extensive praise of Mozart spoken and taught than music heard. The accepted notion during the second half of the nineteenth century was that Mozart had been brilliant, elegant, and divine. But his music appeared mannered and dated. If Bach was seen primarily as the canonic composer of sacred music, Mozart remained certainly an indispensable icon of secular classicism within late-nineteenth-century musical education. But Beethoven, not Mozart, was (as Hanslick's views implied) the nineteenth century's pivotal source of emotional and aesthetic inspiration. Even Hirschfeld felt compelled to debunk the widespread idea that Mozart's music was neither deep nor reflective of sorrow and tragedy. In a startling concession to a primitive association of music and emotion, he countered by citing as evidence all the great Mozartean works written in a minor key.[26]

The nineteenth century's sense of its distance from Mozart is evident in the following remark from Frederick Delius, who recalled, "As a child I had only heard the music of Handel, Bach, Haydn, Mozart, and Beethoven, and shall never forget the thrill I got when I first heard someone play the posthumous waltz of Chopin, which seemed as if an entirely new world had opened up to me."[27] This happened in the late 1860s. Delius vindicated Franz Liszt's lament, written in 1841, that in music, the achievement of great figures, particularly Mozart, in contrast to those in art (Michelangelo, Rubens, and Raphael), would be "ephemeral and fleeting."[28]

The estrangement from the power of Mozart among most audiences in the nineteenth century did not escape a select group of mu-

---

26. As the narrative in Storck suggested, it was Beethoven's work that truly divided the past from the present; it was the "most powerful boundary stone in the whole history of music." Mozart, by contrast, represented, apart from pure genius, the essentially "immortal . . . most sunfilled beauty and . . . eternal youthfulness." *Geschichte der Musik*, 552–55.

27. Lionel Carley, *Delius: A Life in Letters, 1862–1908* (Cambridge, Mass.: Harvard University Press, 1983), 379.

28. Franz Liszt, *An Artist's Journey*, ed. Charles Suttoni (Chicago: University of Chicago Press, 1989), 195.

sicians who saw in the alienation from Mozart a telling and dangerous limitation. In 1861, a year before Delius's birth, Clara Schumann, writing from Detmold, recounted the following experience to Joseph Joachim:

> One reason will make my stay unforgettable. I used the opportunity of having an orchestra around and learned the concertos by Mozart in G and A major. As I did so I both rejoiced and wept. For music to bring me to tears means that it must certainly be heavenly—the Adagio in the G major, which is heavenly pleasure, and both first movements, and in the A major, the last. What fresh life in all the instruments; what a wealth of feeling and humor! Had I only one individual around who would have rejoiced with me. To share such joy alone is quite difficult. How tragic it is that the public remains essentially unengaged faced with such music, and yet it needs nothing more than a natural capacity for feeling.[29]

This striking lack of popularity and receptivity for Mozart's instrumental music in the late nineteenth century was clearly bound up with the cultural politics of new music. Despite Wagner's praise of Mozart (which was restricted primarily to his operas), the progressive movement associated with the "New German School" and Liszt and Wagner paid little more than lip service to Mozart. The circle emanating from Mendelssohn's Leipzig—particularly Carl Reinecke—and those around Clara Schumann, Joachim, and Brahms (who edited the Mozart *Requiem* for the Breitkopf and Härtel edition of the complete works begun in 1877) provided the main source of support for keeping Mozart's works in active concert use. In 1891 Reinecke was moved by the failure of the Mozart piano concertos ever to be played to write a book advocating their "reawakening."[30]

For Brahms and Schumann, Mozart served as the guiding figure for an alternative Romanticism from the one advocated by Liszt. The notion that Mozart had been a key figure in Romanticism was fashioned first by Ludwig Tieck and E. T. A. Hoffmann. In Hoffmann's view, Mozart's Romanticism offered a unique exit from the limits of musical classicism (Haydn and Gluck). Mozart distilled classicism and

29. Letter of February 10, 1861, in Joseph Joachim, *Briefe*, vol. 2, 129. The reference is most likely to K. 453 and K. 488.

30. See Carl Reinecke, *Zur Wiederbelebung der Mozartschen Clavier-Concerte* (Leipzig: Gebrüder Reinecke, 1891). Busoni also pursued this point.

integrated the need for a contemporary means of expression of the boundless, thereby setting the stage for Beethoven.[31] As the divisions within musical Romanticism deepened in the 1850s and 1860s, the Romantic dimension of Mozart became identified exclusively with his operas, particularly *Don Giovanni.*

Used as a contrast to Liszt and Wagner, Mozart came to represent moderation, restraint, economy, subtlety, purity, and elegance of a so-called purely musical sort. To Brahms and his allies, the Romanticism of the New German School was decidedly anti-Mozartean: formless, excessive, dependent on effects created through color and not form, tied to emotionalism and appeals to the extramusical. Later in the century, composers such as Tchaikovsky found themselves caught in a nearly schizophrenic web between the Mozartean model and contemporary late-Romantic expressive sensibilities. In his explicitly "Mozartean" works (opera 33 and 61), Tchaikovsky often resorted to a coy but distinctly affectionate historicist veneer to give voice to his Mozartean side.

In the midcentury, Mozart remained a limited presence among composers and amateurs in those genres rejected by Wagner and his followers, particularly chamber music and solo piano music. For much of the musical public, Mozart became almost exclusively a dimension of *Hausmusik.* It was in the arenas of concert hall orchestral music and symphonic form, as well as even in opera, that Mozart suffered most during the mid and late nineteenth century. Only *Don Giovanni, Figaro,* and *Die Zauberflöte* remained in the regular repertoire. *Don Giovanni* became regarded as the greatest and most "modern" Mozart, along with the three last symphonies, the *Requiem,* the late string quartets and quintets, and the D Minor Piano Concerto.[32]

The fin de siècle call for a Mozart revival mirrored, however, social and cultural development that went beyond the mere neglect of Mozart during the midcentury. With the expansion of the audience for music during the second half of the nineteenth century, a new pattern of tension between the audience and contemporary composers

---

31. David Charlton, ed., *E. T. A. Hoffmann's Musical Writings* (Cambridge: Cambridge University Press, 1989), 261.

32. The best sources for this general assessment are the collections of reviews by Theodor Helm and Eduard Hanslick, the collection of the reviews of Wilhelm Kienzl (*Im Konzert* [Berlin: Allgemeiner Verlag für deutsche Literatur, 1908]), and the program listings for the musical calendars of Vienna and Berlin.

emerged, particularly after the death of Wagner. The evolution of conservative historicist aesthetic taste in music developed rapidly after Wagner. The fin de siècle slogan "Back to Mozart!" among amateurs and concertgoers, as distinct from composers, became less a cry on behalf of one or another school of contemporary composition than a harbinger of how the taste for a canon of classicism and the repertoire of the past would be employed as a weapon against the seemingly radical surface of new music per se.

The audience and critical community of the later nineteenth century were the products of a new piano-based pattern of musical instruction that would redefine musical literacy in ways that made the assimilation of new music increasingly difficult. If the Bach revival before 1848 and the growing interest in music history influenced composers such as Mendelssohn and Brahms, the fin de siècle rediscovery of Mozart represented the use of the past by the audience not on behalf of the present but against it.[33]

The fin de siècle Mozart revival marked the beginning of a twentieth-century process of domination of the concert repertoire by the past to the exclusion of contemporary music. The intense cultivation of Mozart after 1900 coincided with the gradual marginalization of twentieth-century music first from the home, then from the concert stage, and finally from the radio and gramophone. In contrast to the worlds of art and literature, in music the near-fanatical enthusiasm for past masters became the ground and justification for the avoidance or rejection of music written in one's own time—even by composers who explicitly invoked the example of Mozart.[34]

The debate surrounding the fin de siècle "return to Mozart" movement mirrored the divisions that had evolved within the reception of Mozart during the nineteenth century. It also set the stage for the

33. See Leon Botstein, "Listening through Reading: Musical Literacy and the Concert Audience," *Nineteenth Century Music* 16 (Fall 1992): 129–45.

34. This is a simplified distillation of the critical position articulated by Theodor W. Adorno—itself a subject of needed scrutiny, but polemically appropriate in this context. See the essays "Anmerkungen zum deutschen Musikleben" (1967) in *Impromptus* (Frankfurt: Suhrkamp, 1968), 9–28; and "Über die musikalische Verwendung des Radios" from "Der getreute Korrepetitor" (1963) in *Gesammelte Schriften* XV (Frankfurt: Suhrkamp, 1976), 369–402, both of which extend the argument Adorno put forth in his 1938 essay, "Über den Fetischcharakter in der Musik und die Regression des Hoerens" (reprinted in *Gesammelte Schriften* XIV), whose arguments apply more closely to the fin de siècle habits of listening.

direction that twentieth-century Mozart reception would take. The Mozart we hear today—and to whom we respond—has been irrevocably mediated by the first 150 years of interpretation and categorization that followed his death.[35]

During the turn-of-the-century Mozart debate, one of the most common clichés about Mozart's personality was the idea that he had been a "naive" composer. As Richard Batka, the eminent Prague music critic, put it in 1909: "Mozart was a naive composer insofar as a great deal streamed into his creations directly from the unconscious."[36] This use of the concept "naive" derived from two interrelated sources: (1) the legend (and fact) that Mozart had been a "natural" genius whose achievement seemed effortless and (2) the consistent application of Schiller's distinction (from 1796) between the naive and the sentimental in aesthetics to the case of Mozart. A late nineteenth-century psychological fascination with the artist and the process of artistic creation—the links among intellect, imagination, and emotion—merged with a tradition of early nineteenth-century aesthetic discourse.

Mozart's stature as a "classical" master in fact owed a great deal to the Schillerian framework. For Schiller, the "naive" artist was "natural." He experienced the unmediated harmony of nature, morality, and humanity in an inspired way that combined reason and imagination with moral and aesthetic perfection. This made the contemporary "naive" artist the modern equivalent of the luminaries of antiquity in his achievement of the exemplary, flawless, finite balance between nature and art that was characteristic of classical antiquity. In the nineteenth century, Viennese classicism became for music the moral equivalent of antiquity in art and architecture.

The "sentimental" artist, however, was forced in the making of art to engage in the consequences of irrevocable historical change. Although the sentimental artist sustains a longing for a bygone era, of necessity he must develop skills of reflection and idealization. Because of historical progress, these abilities have become indispensable to the task of realizing through art the infinite aesthetic possibilities sug-

35. See Thomas Seedorf, *Studien zur kompositorischen Mozart-Rezeption im fruehen 20. Jahrhundert* (Laaber: Laaber Verlag, 1990), 1–36.

36. Richard Batka, *Geschichte der Musik* (Stuttgart: Ernst Klett, 1909), 177.

gested by modern existence. In modern times, only Shakespeare and Goethe, Schiller argued, could be considered as possessing elements of the "naive" gift.[37]

This distinction was used in music during the nineteenth century to characterize the difference between Mozart and Beethoven. Beethoven seemed to engage modernity, to employ reflection, idealization, and a moral impetus concerning modernity in a manner that appealed to one's sense of the infinite, the imaginary, and the unknown. Beethoven was to classicism what Michelangelo had been to the Renaissance. In contrast, Mozart was compared repeatedly to Raphael and Plato.[38]

In 1857, in a leading music lexicon, Mozart was described as the most perfect embodiment of "musical beauty and musical-artistic completeness. If one wants to speak of a classical artistic ideal (in the sense of antiquity), and if one wants to contemplate its realization in a total unity including the reciprocal integration of form and content, then Mozart stands in the first place before all other composers."[39] Likewise, in Saphir's famous *Konversations-Lexikon* from the midcentury, the by then tiresome cliché that Mozart had been uniquely endowed with "genius of heavenly harmony"—and that he had been the "Olympian" recipient of the ideal ethereal spirit of the Promethean flame of "genius"—was subject to satire filled with reminders of Mozart's "earthly" pursuits, such as billiards and women.[40] Crucial to this view of Mozart as a unique classical model—as the naive, pure, and exceptional artist—was of course the widespread awareness of Mozart's unrivaled precocity and talent.

It was as if the facile labeling of Mozart as the "naive" modern analogue in the early nineteenth century to antique classicism functioned as a way of setting Mozart apart from contemporary music in order to avoid an invidious comparison. One might say that a sort of revenge on Mozart's greatness was taken by composers and critics in the several generations after the death of Beethoven. Realizing that

37. See Friedrich von Schiller, "Über naive und sentimenalische Dichtung" (1796) in *Gesammelte Werke* IV (Frankfurt: Insel Verlag, 1966).

38. See, for example, Antonin Dvorak's views of Mozart as "sunshine" and his comparison of Mozart to Raphael in Otakar Sourek, ed., *Antonin Dvorak: Letters and Reminiscences* (New York: DaCapo Press, 1985), 129–41.

39. Eduard Bernsdorf, *Neues Universal-Lexikon der Tonkunst* (Dresden: Schaefers Verlag, 1855–56), vol. II, 1039.

40. M. G. Saphir, *Konversations-Lexikon für Geist, Witz und Humor*, 2d ed. (Berlin: Gnadenfeld u. Comp., 1889), vol. II, 94–107.

they lacked the incomparable facility and divine gift of Mozart, they enshrined him in a remote temple, all by himself, as an object apart.

Robert Schumann repeatedly resorted to this rhetorical ploy. He distanced himself from Mozart by praising Mozart's "tranquility, grace, ideality, and objectivity." Schumann utilized a familiar linkage between Mozart's unique childhood achievement and his presumably lifelong naive, natural, and childlike character to enhance Mozart's status as the symbol of ideal (immortal as opposed to concrete mortal) classicism; as an almost deracinated, ethereal, and pure superhuman figure beyond comparison with ordinary humans. Schumann believed that Mozart somehow had developed into an "ideal" artist independent of sensual reality, unlike Beethoven or Haydn (or anyone else).[41] Schumann wrote in an epigram: "What a genius, what a child: O truly I tell you, if you don't become like him, you will never enter the heavenly sphere of art."[42] As Leon Plantinga noted, Schumann applied Winckelmann's categories about the greatness of ancient art to Mozart.[43]

By midcentury, Mozart had come to symbolize pure music, naively created, heavenly in nature, perfect in form—the moral equivalent of Platonic philosophy. One music historian at the end of the century summarized this line of Mozart interpretation by calling Mozart's music a kind of "natural philosophy" bordering on the transcendence of subjectivity. It rendered into music a Platonic ideal of beauty. The notion that music was essentially abstract—and, in the nonpejorative sense, "artificial" in relation to nature—made logical the notion that the Platonic ideal of beauty would be essentially musical. In 1898 Heinrich Köstlin summarized Mozart's achievement as residing in the fact that "his pathos was none other than beauty itself, as the classic master in the strictest sense of the word; as the embodied genius of music—of the beautiful in music in all its separateness from any ancillary purpose and meaning."[44]

41. Robert Schumann, *Gesammelte Schriften*, 5th ed. (Leipzig: Breitkopf und Härtel, 1914), vol. II, 213.

42. Schumann, *Gesammelte Schriften*, 278. For a closer examination of the childlike attributes of Mozart, see Maynard Solomon, "Mozart: The Myth of the Eternal Child," *Nineteenth Century Music* (Berkeley: University of California Press, 1991), vol. 15, 95–106.

43. Leon Plantinga, *Schumann as Critic* (New Haven: Yale University Press, 1967), 92, 105.

44. Heinrich Köstlin, *Die Geschichte der Musik im Umriss*, 6th ed. (Leipzig: Breitkopf und Härtel, 1910), 433. It is ironic that the two major nineteenth-century biographies—

Mozart emerged from this post-Beethovenian discourse as quite sui generis, that is, apart from all subsequent composers. His music (particularly his instrumental music) readily became regarded as disconnected from everyday life. The nearly philosophical status of his music set it apart from the emotional and sensual experience of music per se. Mozart was the perfect realization of the pure spirit of beauty.

Not surprisingly, he easily became the symbol of the aesthetics of absolute music in the mid-nineteenth century, despite his operatic output. Although Brahms (who had played the D Minor Concerto at the Hamburg centennial festival in 1856) was frequently associated with this ideology, the emotional power of Mozart did not appear distant. To him the power of Mozart's instrumental and vocal music was so direct and so powerful that listening to it became nearly unbearable.[45] As Ludwig Wittgenstein noted with some irony, commenting on Franz Grillparzer's assertion that Mozart wrote only "beautiful" music, there was something "ungrateful" and "mischievous" about the way posterity in the mid-nineteenth century treated Mozart in the name of the concept of the beautiful. Wittgenstein reacted against the mid-nineteenth-century extraction of the word "beautiful" from its associations with the kind of emotional "distortion" we associate with grief and pathos, from the nineteenth-century pseudorealist musical representational language of emotional states. Not only was the "extension" of the "range" of musical language after Mozart poorly construed, but Mozart was too neatly and inadequately understood.[46]

In contrast to this process of aesthetic distancing and idealization on the part of composers of the 1809–10 generation—Chopin, Mendelssohn, Schumann—was the early-Romantic line of interpretation of Mozart as the first Romantic, as the acute observer and representer of emotion and the infinite character of human imagination. In this view (derived from E. T. A. Hoffmann), only a romantic and profound spirit rooted in modernity could genuinely appreciate Mo-

by G. N. von Nissen (who married Mozart's widow) from 1828 and by Otto Jahn from 1856—contained a far more differentiated picture of the composer, despite a veneer of idealization. Jahn even questioned the quality of the early work and posited stages of development in Mozart's style. Nissen managed to integrate the Romantic view of Mozart's human character with the usual rhetoric of genius and normative aesthetics.

45. See Max Kalbeck, *Johannes Brahms* (Berlin: Deutsche Brahms-Gesellschaft, 1921), I/i, 239 and 255, III/1, 87.

46. Ludwig Wittgenstein, *Culture and Value* (Chicago: University of Chicago Press, 1980), 55.

zart. In the 1830s, Joseph Eichendorff regarded the music of Mozart as quintessentially Romantic, as evocative of the mysterious and mystical in the human spirit that could transform, through art, the finite into the infinite.[47]

Richard Wagner did the most to enhance this alternative nineteenth-century anticlassical image of Mozart as a figure of Romanticism. Using the precise language and rhetoric of the classicizing school, Wagner, in *The Art Work of the Future* (1849) and *Opera and Drama* (1850), accepted the premises of Mozart's "naive" genius and the unique clarity and classical beauty of his work. But Wagner detected a Romantic "unending sea of yearning." Mozart breathed into music not an idealized spirit of form but for the first time "the passionate breath of the human voice." Mozart had been guided by human love. The "endless" desire of the human heart was translated into the singing power of Mozart's melodic line.[48]

Wagner could deal more easily than Schumann or even Brahms with the formidable legacy of Mozart because he had abandoned the instrumental genres of Mozart. Liberated from any possible direct comparison except in the arena of opera, Wagner argued that Mozart remained trapped by the literary operatic conventions of his time. Mozart lacked musically adequate poetic and dramatic texts, since he started to use music in a truly dramatic manner only in his operatic overtures. The true dramatic power of music had been left unexploited, even though Mozart showed, through his use of music alone, the power of music to express the essence within drama and poetry. By focusing on the operatic work, Wagner stressed the gestural and emotional rhetoric in Mozart's music rather than its abstract and formal attributes. His observations on Mozart's magical transformation of classical melodic practice into an individualized instrument of emotional expression implied the aesthetic and historical links between the continuous linear melodic strategy of his own writing and the legacy of Mozart.

Wagner's analysis and praise of Mozart also picked up on a third strand of argument within nineteenth-century Mozart criticism. This strand emphasized the political dimensions of Mozart's achievement.

47. Gernot Gruber, *Mozart und die Nachwelt* (Munich: Piper, 1987), 97.

48. Richard Wagner, *Prose Works*, trans. W. A. Ellis (New York: Broude, 1966), vol. I, 121, vol. II, 34–41, 81–82.

Particularly after the publication of Otto Jahn's massive Mozart biography, the image of Mozart as the first composer to fight the feudal system of aristocratic privilege became widespread. Jahn's four-volume biography and the growing familiarity with Mozart's letters helped to deepen the late-nineteenth-century portrait of Mozart. Jahn stressed Mozart's independence, his refusal in Paris and Salzburg to submit to authority. Mozart the Freemason came to the fore, as did Mozart's sympathy for egalitarian ideas and the popular audience (as opposed to aristocratic patrons). *Die Zauberflöte* became the locus classicus of this line of argument from the mid-nineteenth century until the writings of Adorno.[49]

Coincident with these claims was added the later-nineteenth-century appropriation of Mozart as a particularly German composer. Even Jahn took pains to point this out.[50] The most vociferous claimants were, of course, the Wagnerians. Houston Stewart Chamberlain was explicit on this score.[51] Mozart's apparent concern for the general public, as well as the accessibility of his music and his independence of clerical and aristocratic power, became important to polemicists who wished to use Mozart to counter the idea of concert music as primarily an esoteric high art, the exclusive province of aristocrats and middle-class parvenus (who sought to achieve social standing through the display of refinement in aesthetic judgment). To these fin de siècle nationalists, Mozart's music mirrored not merely the social privilege of a few but a national popular imagination later fully realized by Wagner. In Wagner, the German ideal of the spiritual audience-composer relationship, first hinted at by Mozart's operas, triumphed.

The nineteenth-century struggle over the political soul of Mozart continued into the early twentieth century. The two warring parties were the one claiming Mozart for a distinctly German sensibility and the other (exemplified by Adler, Hirschfeld, and Joachim, all, ironically, born as Jews) regarding Mozart as the apostle of a cosmopolitan universalism. The political intersected with the aesthetic. The view of Mozart as an early Romantic and the Germanocentric interpretation ran together. Likewise, the image of Mozart as the embodiment of

49. T. W. Adorno, *Einleitung in die Musiksoziologie* (Frankfurt: Suhrkamp, 1968), 31.

50. See, for example, Otto Jahn, *W. A. Mozart* (Leipzig: Breitkopf und Härtel, 1858), vol. III, 300, 405.

51. H. S. Chamberlain, *Die Grundlagen des 19. Jahrhunderts* (Munich: Bruckmann, 1909), vol. I, 557.

absolute music fit neatly into the claim that his work mirrored the principles of universalism.[52] The final irony rests, of course, in the historical realization that the "cosmopolitan" view of Mozart's art among individuals such as Adler and Hirschfeld was itself a form of Germanocentrism. To these men (and to Arnold Schoenberg, Heinrich Schenker, and Paul Hindemith as well), the so-called purely musical and formal achievements of Mozart were concrete evidence of a transcendent universalism inherent in German culture. That unique universalism lent credibility to the idea that the musical creations of Bach, Handel, Haydn, Mozart, Beethoven, and Brahms formed the proper objective measures against which all compositional technique, in the strictest sense, might properly be judged.

This antinomy would reach its macabre apotheosis in the Mozart Jubilee celebrated in Vienna by the Nazis in 1941, graced by the enthusiastic participation of Strauss, Furtwängler, and the German musicological community.[53] The 1941 portrait painted in Vienna of the great German Aryan Mozart should be placed side by side with the claims of Kurt Weill and Arnold Schoenberg dating from the 1940s in America. In 1941, both emigré composers were writing music in the full conviction that they were the legitimate heirs of Mozart.[54]

Looking back at the late-nineteenth-century debate about Mozart, one can argue that the linkage between Mozart and the aesthetics of cultural reaction triumphed over the connection between Mozart and aesthetic modernism in the twentieth century. The success of postmodernism in the late twentieth century has coincided with the most radical popularization of Mozart in history, a rage for Mozart that has developed in tandem with the decline in audiences for new music. The connection between contemporary music and the example of Mozart sought by Reger, Busoni, Schoenberg, and Strauss in the early twentieth century has resulted in a vacuum in the late twentieth century. Mozart has now fully become part of a musical museum, separate from

52. See, for example, Emil Naumann, *Illustrierte Musikgeschichte* (Berlin and Stuttgart: Spemann, 1885), vol. II, 726–95.

53. See Gert Kerschbaumer, "Mozart schweigt," in *Die Zeit* 43 (October 18, 1991).

54. See Kurt Weill's 1925 commentaries on Mozart's *Die Zauberflöte* and *Die Entführung aus dem Serail* in Kurt Weill, *Ausgewählte Schriften* (Frankfurt: Suhrkamp, 1975), 141–44, and the references to Mozart in Schoenberg's great essay "Brahms the Progressive" from 1947, in *Style and Idea*, ed. Leonard Stein (London: Faber and Faber, 1975).

contemporary musical and cultural life. We argue less about the political significance of Mozart's art perhaps because it no longer seems
to matter.

What remains from the fin de siècle Mozart revival is, of course, its
aesthetic influence on twentieth-century neoclassicism and modernism, particularly within the tradition of the Second Viennese School.
Despite the fantastic commercial popularity that Mozart's music now
enjoys, from the historian's perspective the turn to Mozart in the early
twentieth century constituted an effort to revive the claims among
many musicians on behalf of a model of purely musical hearing and
listening. A premium on form and procedures of musical development
within works of music—on structural devices overtly detached from
the sort of extramusical illustration associated with Wagner—became
a hallmark of much twentieth-century concert music. The turn away
from the associative musical strategies of late Romanticism helped
make much of twentieth-century music less accessible and therefore
less popular. Wagnerism held the key to the mass audience. Therefore,
from the vantage point of the late twentieth century, the rediscovery
of Mozart during the early 1900s helped lead, on the one hand, to
the most extreme deification and dissemination of Mozart and his
music within the museum of music, and, on the other (albeit indi-
rectly, through the medium of modernist advocates of theories of absolute music), to the relative marginalization of contemporary music
and musical modernism in our own time.

12

The abduction from the theater: Mozart opera on film

STANLEY KAUFFMANN

"WHENEVER I GO to an opera," said Lord Chesterfield, "I leave
my sense and reason at the door with my half-guinea, and deliver
myself up to my eyes and ears." What would he have said about opera
on film? Would his eyes and ears have insisted on some recourse to
sense? Obviously opera is a hybrid, a marriage of theater and music,
but can a marriage accommodate a third partner with a third set of
conventions? Would Lord Chesterfield have thought the triad more
aesthetically scandalous than sensorily engaging?

Many modern observers do so consider it, and, in my view, they
are essentially right. The only occasions when the combination succeeds are, to be tautological about it, when it succeeds. From the start,
film hungered after opera, even in the days of silent pictures. The
opera star Geraldine Farrar made a film of *Carmen* in 1915; *Der Rosenkavalier* was filmed silently in 1926 (under the supervision of Richard Strauss and his librettist, Hugo von Hofmannsthal). These are only
two instances of the continual attraction that opera has had for film,
an attraction based on the belief that if the theater itself could nourish
film, so could this hybrid form of theater. With the advent of sound,
operas on film have become, if not numberless, so plentiful that they
are not worth trying to count. The film world is ravenous, even for
this improbable fare.

The opera house itself relies on a centuries-old set of conventions between stage and audience. We know that people in the world around us do not sing their conversations, and we also know that if we accept these conventions, we profit in beauties. But the film art has its conventions, too: Whatever its stylistic variations, film asks its viewers to accept lights and shadows on a screen as manifests of realism—that is the mode toward which film consistently tends. Accepting that contract, the film audience, too, is rewarded with beauty. But nothing in opera, nothing whatsoever, tends consistently toward realism. (*Verismo* at its most intense is still a long way from realism.) To transfer opera to film is to obfuscate the fundamental contracts of both arts. One fights the other.

It's worse. When we go to an opera or a film, we know the contract of conventions in advance. But a viable contract that covers all films of operas has yet to be drawn up. Almost every director who films an opera has to find, or try to find, his or her own solution to the problem by creating the contract between this particular film and its audience. This is so generally true that it might as well be stated as a fact: Every film of an opera needs to write its own contract with the audience. Therefore the audience, as it prepares to watch an opera on film, must ask itself, whether consciously or not: What is the contract this time? What conventions are we expected to observe here? In large measure, the success of the enterprise depends on the viability of that contract.

Mozart has, inevitably, proved irresistible to filmmakers, and they have operated under a variety of audience contracts. Here I will examine three films of Mozart operas. My purpose is not to draw overall conclusions—I doubt that any such will ever be drawn—but to determine how each director conceived his contract.

The Magic Flute, directed by Ingmar Bergman

The first point to be noted here, for it is the source and genesis of this film, is the curious imbalance of Bergman's career. Here is an artist who is securely established as one of the greatest directors in film history, yet he has spent only about a quarter of his professional life in film. He has done most of his directing in the theater, where he has put on plays from Athens to Broadway, as well as operas and operettas. Twice he had hoped to do productions of *The Magic*

Flute, and he even used an excerpt from the opera in his film *Hour of the Wolf.*

In 1972, when Swedish television asked Bergman to make a film of the opera, he was at the height of his theater and film careers. We can infer from the result that he determined to use both aspects of his experience. He could have had no interest in merely photographing a theater performance; on the other hand, he also wanted to avoid the desperate pretense that what we are seeing is not an opera at all but a "real" drama—despite the fact that, in this stubbornly realistic medium, actors have to sing their feelings and thoughts.

Bergman, genius that he is, devised a quite new contract with his audience. He provides a vicar for the audience itself, an on-screen audience that watches the performance he is filming. He goes further by taking us backstage from time to time, allowing us to see both sides of the stage. Thus the performance of Mozart that we see is held in two beams of vision, one from behind and one in front. The camera consequently creates a fourth dimension, in which the other three dimensions—stage, backstage, and audience—come together to underscore both the conventions that underlie cinematic art and the supervening beauty to which this coalescence can lead. In this way, Bergman creates a unique arrangement with his viewers that is at once intimate and lofty.

He began by devising a theater production of *The Magic Flute* solely for use in this film (it has never been put on elsewhere). Then, almost as an ironic touch in this late-twentieth-century venture, he put that production in an eighteenth-century theater located in the palace of Drottningholm outside Stockholm. (The grounds and the auditorium that we see are at Drottningholm. For technical reasons, the stage was replicated in a Stockholm film studio.)

After a brief prelude in which we see the palace woods and hear a few twilight bird calls, we move into the opera house, where we see the audience listening to the overture. Soon after the performance starts, we are briskly introduced to backstage life when Papageno, lounging in his dressing room, almost misses his first entrance. Thus, before long, the four elements are fused: the audience in the theater, the opera performance, the world of the performers, and the film that encompasses all these. Now must be added a fifth element, ourselves, the audience for whom it has all been done. We are given a godlike vantage point, and our overview completes a work that is larger than either a theater performance or an orthodox film.

We come then to Bergman's view of *The Magic Flute* and his complex approach to it. Obviously, he knows the opera's history; its use of Masonic symbols; its susceptibility to charges of antifeminism today; its mixture of German opera and singspiel; and, in the Queen of the Night's two great arias, its Italianate flavor. His comprehension of all these elements is reflected in his production, but he attends this approach with another—what can be called, with the dignity it deserves, a child's view of *The Magic Flute*.

Bergman has told us that he fell in love with the opera when he was twelve years old and that it has haunted him all his life. When he first saw it, he assumed, though it is not in fact the case, that Sarastro was the father of Pamina and that he stole her from her wicked mother for her own good; and this early assumption Bergman retains in the film, adding some rearrangements in the second act that are consonant with his boyhood vision. Thus this sophisticated film, without being coy, is the realization of a youthful point of view.

Bergman underscores this view in several ways. During the overture we see many members of the audience; we are given several glimpses of the film's cinematographer, Sven Nykvist, and, during the coda, a very swift look at Bergman himself; but the image that recurs most often, both during the overture and during the performance itself, is that of a child. She is Bergman's daughter, Linn, and she quite clearly serves as a deputy for the boy Bergman seeing *The Magic Flute* for the first time.

Other evidence abounds of the child's-eye view. The libretto of the opera contains a number of maxims for human behavior that, despite the celestial music to which they are set, can strike the listener as a bit didactic. Bergman has these maxims inscribed on banners, and this display has a double effect: It renders them, with gentle humor, as Aesopian morals fitting a cautionary tale, and it shows Bergman's awareness that he is dealing with consciously crystallized innocence. And then there are the animals. When Tamino first plays his flute, animals appear, enchanted as they once were by Orpheus. But these are animals from the Peaceable Kingdom—large, funny, friendly creatures from the nearest marvelous toy shop. When Sarastro appears, he is in a chariot drawn by two toy lions; when he descends from the chariot, his first action is to kiss a child. Throughout the film, we are reminded that there are children in the Drottningholm audience and that within each member of the audience everywhere there is a child. One of the triumphs of this film is the way that Bergman merges a full rendition of the work's profundities with his still-persisting childhood view of it.

One more point to be noted: light. In Bergman's work generally, light is almost choric; it not only fits the moment but underscores it without straining to do so. In *The Magic Flute*, however, he uses light quite differently. The world outside the theater, the audience, and the backstage areas are all lighted in a relatively realistic manner; but in the performance of the opera onstage, Bergman uses theatrical light changes of intensity and shade within a scene, different faces seen in different ways. (In one sequence, for example, the Queen of the Night changes from her usual self into an older, fiercer woman—presumably her hidden self—and back again.) All through the film Bergman seems to exult in doing precisely what he could not do when making realistic films: using light in the same sheerly instrumental way that he had employed in the theater.

This film, then, is the fruit of Bergman's double career. Out of all the elements described above, including his particularized view of this opera, he creates a new form that is impressively complex yet utterly lucid. The contract that Bergman offers his viewers is at once an invitation to the making of an opera performance, to the making of a film of that performance, and to a vantage point that acknowledges the ridiculousness of the project while lavishing gratification on us. We are swept away by delight and cozy conspiracy. This is Bergman's mastery, simultaneously cunning and straightforward.

Don Giovanni, directed by Joseph Losey

Losey's approach is diametrically opposed to Bergman's. Losey wants the audience to forget, if possible, that it is watching an opera performance; his intent is to make his *Don Giovanni* just another film among films, except that in this case the actors sing.

To put his approach in perspective, let us first look at the work itself, a treatment of one of the basic myths of the Western world. So rooted is this myth in our culture that it comes as a surprise to note that Don Juan made his first appearance in a Spanish play published as recently as 1630. Some elements in his character and adventures caused him to be taken up immediately—one can say immediately— in other countries. The Italians wrote plays about him, as did the French. Molière's *Don Juan,* in my opinion his best play, was written in 1665, only thirty-five years after the Don's first appearance. Other plays followed, continuing to, though not concluding with, Bernard Shaw's *Man and Superman.* But Wolfgang Hildesheimer writes, "Without Mozart, without the proportions and dimensions he brought to the figure, Don Giovanni would scarcely be the archetype he is now, with a history so well explored."[1] Shaw would have agreed.

Mozart was not the first to write an opera about the Don. In fact, he and his librettist, Lorenzo da Ponte, were discussing possibilities for a new collaboration when they learned of an opera about Don Juan that had been produced in Venice only a few months before, with music by Giuseppe Gazzaniga and a libretto by Giovanni Bertati. Mozart and da Ponte decided to write a Don of their own. Da Ponte leaned on Bertati's libretto; Mozart, we may assume, had no need of help from Gazzaniga.

Why were they so interested? Why has the Don Juan myth persisted? Is it only that men get an empathic thrill out of a man who is arithmetically stupefying in his success with women, or that women cannot help feeling, perhaps against their will, that there is something diabolically appealing in such a man? If so, why Don Giovanni? Stories about libertines are not hard to find. For instance, there are several operas about Casanova, but Casanova is not exactly a fixture in Western mythology. Surely there must be something more to Don Giovanni than his libertinism.

Losey, although otherwise he falls short, has some sense of a theme deeper than amorous athleticism. In the first scene of the opera itself, there is a murder; and in the last, divine retribution. But Losey frames both scenes by showing us a blazing fire in the first and in the last moments of his film. Losey also adds to his cast a new, silent character: a servant dressed in black, who is seen frequently throughout the film, apparently to remind us that although the Don may frivol, fate has not forgotten him. This story of a man of the world is enclosed in the embrace of an unseen world.

1. Wolfgang Hildesheimer, *Mozart,* trans. Marion Faber (New York: Vintage, 1983), 156.

But there is even more to the Don's story—an element that is not only nonreligious but antireligious. Molière's Don Juan is a man who knows of that larger, unseen world and deliberately chooses to challenge it. Shaw said of Mozart's work, "Don Juan is a tragic hero or he is nothing: his destiny is announced by Mozart from the very first chord of the overture."[2] All three of these great artists have seen in the Don a good deal more than a philanderer. My favorite passage in da Ponte's libretto comes near the end, at the appearance of the stone guest, the statue of the Commendatore. The statue says, "Don Giovanni, you invited me to supper, and I am here." To which the Don replies, "I would not have believed it. But I'll do my best. Leporello, set another place." That seems to me a heroic reply, by a man who is not to be frightened out of his disbelief by a ghost, even a petrified one.

This opera about a man who makes love incessantly as part of his belief in the right of human beings to control their own lives was filmed by Losey in 1979. Compared with Bergman's audience contract for *The Magic Flute*, Losey's is disappointingly torpid, even though he had assistance in devising it. Rolf Liebermann, the former director of the Hamburg and Paris opera houses, is credited with the film's basic concept—a puzzling credit, because it is hard to see that there is a basic concept. The film was shot in and around several gorgeous Palladian villas near Vicenza in northeastern Italy, and no matter what else happens or fails to happen cinematically, a few architectural flowers of the Italian Renaissance are put at our disposal. But although Losey has some awareness of thematic depth in the work, he shows no firm, problem-solving filmic intent—this despite the fact that he is an experienced theater director and an even more experienced film director, the maker of such notable films as *Accident* and *The Servant*. So unhappily do opera and film collide in this *Giovanni* that we often ask ourselves why these actors are singing, a question that in itself points to the enterprise's lack of success.

Instead of aiding the film, the camera almost seems to be discomfiting it. The disguises in Act Two, when Leporello and his master exchange clothes, seem silly here. Losey has them use hand-held Venetian masks, but these masks only emphasize that the opera stage does not need them and that in film they do not much help. The

2. Bernard Shaw, *Shaw's Music*, ed. Dan H. Laurence (London: Max Reinhardt, Bodley Head, 1981), vol. 3, 708.

insistent camera is additionally cruel in a way that would not apply on the opera stage. It comes in close to the baritone and seriously questions his reputation for success with women. It also makes it hard for us to accept that this Zerlina is a young and innocent village maiden.

But aside from such matters—and there are many more—how does Losey try to deal with his elemental problem, the opera-film conflict? He knows that, in cinema terms, opera is relatively static; therefore, he takes primal measures, almost primitive measures, to avoid stasis. He moves. He moves everyone and the camera as much as he possibly can, hoping that continual shifts of angle and of background and brief tours down gorgeous corridors and majestic stairways will give the film a vital mobility. But since most of the movement seems a hasty addition to the scene rather than a part of it, we are so conscious of the fight against a conventional opera performance that we almost long for a conventional opera performance.

To help fulfill his desperate need for motion, Losey invents business for the performers. For example, after "Là ci darem la mano," it is impossible for the Don to take Zerlina to his castle because they are already there, courtesy of Losey's devisings. Instead, the Don takes her into a bedroom where, with open doors, they proceed to make love until they are interrupted by Donna Anna. But this added business makes it hard to understand why, a bit later, when the Don takes Zerlina into another bedroom, she screams, as the libretto requires. The two bedroom scenes just don't mesh. Furthermore, in the second act, an ensemble, singing away, moves into a large salon. Suddenly there is a group of people sitting in the room and watching them. The ensemble performs for these people. Who are they? Why were they seated there waiting? Only because Losey is feverishly trying to satisfy what he assumes is our appetite for constant visual variety.

Other instances could easily be added, but it is clear enough that Losey is caught in the crunch between opera and film. He is not the first film director, or the last, to have this problem. Like many directors before and since, he opted for the most obvious means of dealing, or trying to deal, with it; that is, he has chosen to pretend that his film is not an opera. But although he attempts to beguile our eyes, they will not allow us to accept his contract with the audience.

Le nozze di Figaro, directed by Peter Sellars

Peter Sellars's approach to Figaro is generally thought to be so anti-traditional that it may be as well to begin by noting how snugly it fits into a latter-day tradition, one that originated in the theater. His version of *Figaro* began production, in a direct historical sense, on May 1, 1874. That was the date when a company of actors from the provincial German city of Meiningen made their debut in Berlin. Their appearance was soon widely noted because it proclaimed to the world the arrival of an important new profession in the theater, that of the director.

Movement toward that profession had been visible earlier in Germany and England, but it was not until the duke of Saxe-Meiningen insisted on ensemble playing in his personal troupe in his small capital, insisted on one central vision to govern a production by that troupe, that the idea of directing as we know it became a permanent part, an expected part, of our theater. Since classical times, productions had been organized according to the traditions in a particular theater or according to the wishes of leading actors. After the duke sent his company to Berlin and then on a series of extensive tours, those circumstances began to change.

What the quality of the theater had been before and why the new profession arose where and when it did are fascinating subjects, but they are too complex to explore here. Let us note, however, that when the profession arrived, it quickly took hold throughout Europe and America. For the next twenty-five years or so, directors devoted themselves to reforming or initiating productions according to the expressed or implicit wishes of the author.

Most directors still practice their professions that way. But around 1900 some directors began to have a new sense of authority—in the literal sense of being authors themselves. The arts of performance, as distinct from the arts of playwriting and opera writing, had obviously always been present and essential; but now that their profession had become established, some directors began to feel that the performance arts should be exalted in order to make the production itself of supreme importance. They felt that the text of the play or the opera should be treated not as the production's reason for being but only as one of the contributory elements—like the acting and design and lighting—and that all these elements should now become components of a superseding art: the director's.

One of the most famous statements of this view came from Gordon Craig in 1905:

> The theater must in time perform pieces of its own art. . . . When [the director] interprets the plays of the dramatist . . . he is a crafts-man; . . . when he will have mastered the actions, words, line, colour, and rhythm, then he may become an artist. Then we shall no longer need the assistance of the playwright—for our art will be self-reliant.[3]

The history of directing in the twentieth century clearly is divided between those directors whose aim is "to interpret the plays of the dramatist" and those who, without absolutely discarding the dramatist, nonetheless use his work to serve their own purposes rather than his.

Peter Sellars, from the very beginning of his fulminant career, has been a fervent member of the Craig school. He began in the theater but lately has turned to opera because, he says, opera gives him more opportunity "to explore a secret world." Whether or not the theater really affords less opportunity, opera has certainly given Sellars plenty of chances to explore his own secret worlds.

I saw his production of *Le nozze di Figaro* on stage in the mid-1980s, and I went through my usual set of reactions to an unusual production of a familiar work. First, I asked why. Why had the setting been changed to the fifty-second floor of the Trump Tower in New York, with costumes to match? Second, I got pleasure out of the imaginative use of modern artifacts that Sellars chose to accommodate Mozart and da Ponte; for example, Cherubino's hockey stick and sweater mark him as a youngster full of physicality; even his much discussed solo sex miming seemed to fit up-to-the-minute, overbrimming youth. Third, I began to relish the whole transposition as a new plane on which to enjoy the opera. Fourth, I became conscious of matters that simply could not be transposed. For instance, at the end of the first act, to what army does a count residing in the Trump Tower send the

---

3. Edward Gordon Craig, *Craig on Theatre,* ed. J. Michael Walton (London: Methuen, 1983), 55, 56–57.

troublesome Cherubino? Fifth was the first reaction all over again: Why?

If I could not find a completely satisfactory answer, at least Sellars had one for himself. He told us that he was using an eighteenth-century work to comment on America today—class, power, corruption, and more. Well, those matters certainly need comment. But we might ask how the Mozart–da Ponte work managed to survive to our day, before Sellars came to its aid, if it had not been pertinent all along. Still, even if his argument had a touch of rationalization as well as reason, there was no denying—on the contrary, one could rejoice in—his vitality. And politics are hardly absent from *Le nozze di Figaro*, as Bernard Shaw observed:

> It is true that Mozart made no attempt to write political music in the sense of expressing not only wounded human feeling but the specific rancor of the class-conscious proletarian; but the wounded feeling is provided for very plentifully if only the conductor will allow the singer to put it in instead of treating him as if he were one of the second violins.[4]

Read "director" for "conductor," and we might agree that Sellars, consciously or not, followed Shaw's advice more vigorously than Shaw could have foretold.

At the least, and it is surely not a little, the Sellars approach energized his whole cast, who performed with great enjoyment of both the music and its novel presentation. This approach also helped that last scene, which is chockablock with masquerades and disguises—a notorious headache to opera directors. Sellars did not completely clarify the scene, but at least we could see what was originally intended.

Sellars later filmed his theater production of *Figaro* for television, and therefore had to make a contract with a film audience. The first point to be noted about this film of a radical production is that, as film, it is in no way radical. Bergman's *Magic Flute*, built around a relatively orthodox theater production that was conceived especially for the film, is much more adventurous cinematically. For example, during the *Figaro* overture, Sellars gives us a sequence of shots of people on Fifth Avenue in New York at Christmastime, a sequence that merely establishes place and season. During the *Magic Flute* over-

4. Shaw, *Shaw's Music*, vol. 3, 700.

ture, Bergman presents a collage telling us that this work grips all kinds of present-day people and that a little girl will figure prominently among them. Bergman's overture effectively *begins* his production. Sellars's overture is only a conventional preface *before* his production begins.

Bergman's contract with his audience, as we have seen, entails the amalgamation of five components virtually to compose a new form, unique and unrepeatable. Sellars's task is more limited: He is to record a particular theater production. Without referring to an actual theater—the audience, proscenium, and so forth—he preserves the lateral, mostly two-dimensional essence of a theater production. He does this without stultifying the performed opera but also without pretending that this is simply one more film. His frankness and his skill make his contract succeed.

His chief instrument is his vantage point. Sellars opts to work in close, as close as possible—a technique superbly suited to film and television. In a way, this choice justifies the film by amplifying the chief merits of his original production: its liveliness and its enlivening of the cast. His stage production (and consequently his film) had no trace of stiff opera singing accompanied by studied countenance and gesture; he evoked from his people the emotional verity of each moment. In this film those qualities are even more striking. The finespun, intricate interplay of the performers reflects the finespun music. When Stanislavski was working with opera singers, he said:

> How lucky you singers are. . . . The composer provides you with one most important element—the rhythm of your inner emotions. That is what we actors have to create for ourselves out of a vacuum. All you have to do is to listen to the rhythm of the music and make it your own. The written word is the theme of the author, but the melody is the emotional experience of that theme.[5]

In Sellars's theater production, it seemed as if he had overheard Stanislavski. In his film of that production, he seems to take this advice even more to heart. Even his editing is brisk and bright and underscores the rococo plot. Sellars cuts frequently from one character to another, not only to keep the plot's complications clear but to use the

---

5. Constantin Stanislavski and Pavel Rumyantsev, *Stanislavski on Opera*, trans. and ed. Elizabeth Reynolds Hapgood (New York: Theatre Arts, 1975), 22.

kinetics of the film to mirror the interweavings of intrigue. By the time we get to the last scene, the editing, like the performances, seems to have the pulse of the music.

Here, then, is an authentic twentieth-century production that derives fundamentally from the directorial explosion of 1874. Eighteenth-century opera, ultramodern theater, and film—to engage all three takes serene self-confidence and conviction, qualities that Sellars does not lack. His very daring in this engagement is part of his audience contract and helps to keep us involved even when we have reservations.

The three examples preceding, chosen to exemplify certain approaches to filming operas, of course do not begin to exhaust the possible approaches to this hybrid genre. Bergman's work can hardly even be called an approach, it is sui generis. Most films of operas, however, are simply records of actual performances or specially arranged performances for filming, with occasional arthritic attempts at cinematic limbering. They make Sellars's filming of a theater production seem all the more exceptional and all the more welcome. (The most successful attempt in what might be called the Losey vein—"This isn't really an opera at all, friends, it's just a film"—the most successful attempt that I know of is not with a Mozart opera; it is Francesco Rosi's 1984 film of *Carmen*. Rosi treats the opera as if it were a musical conceived for film, directs it under the influence of such excellent Hollywood musical directors as Stanley Donen and Vincente Minnelli, and manages to articulate *Carmen* in lithe and sinuous cinematic form.)

Mozart lives, films live, directors live, and the three will certainly continue to encounter one another. Few of those films can succeed aesthetically: the union is too strange. But if those few are exceptions, we can console ourselves by remembering that it is the exceptions that sustain any art or combination of arts. And when the usual kind of filmed opera is patently unsuccessful, we can at least amuse ourselves by imagining what Lord Chesterfield might have been thinking: possibly of his misspent half-guinea.

About the authors

WYE J. ALLANBROOK is on the faculty of St. John's College in Annapolis, Maryland. Her extensive writings on Mozart include the book *Rhythmic Gesture in Mozart: "Le nozze di Figaro" and "Don Giovanni"* (1983). She is the editor of the volume "The Classic Era" in the Norton revision of Oliver Strunk's *Source Readings in Music History*, which will appear in 1995. In 1994–95 she will be the Ernest Bloch Visiting Professor of Music at the University of California at Berkeley. She is currently engaged in a study of the nature of musical expression in Mozart's instrumental works.

WILLIAM J. BAUMOL is Professor of Economics and Director of the C. V. Starr Center for Applied Economics at New York University. Though well known for his work on welfare economics and its applications, he has also written studies of the economics of the performing arts, including *Performing Arts: The Economic Dilemma* (1966), coauthored with William G. Bowen. HILDA BAUMOL is President of Consultants in Industry Economics, Inc. With William J. Baumol, she has investigated the economic circumstances of artists and arts institutions. They have edited *Inflation and the Performing Arts* (1984) and written a number of articles on the economics of the arts.

LEON BOTSTEIN is President of Bard College and Professor of History and Music History there. He is also editor of *The Musical*

Quarterly and, since 1992, music director of the American Symphony Orchestra.

DENIS DONOGHUE holds the Henry James Chair of English and American Letters at New York University. He was for many years Professor of Modern English and American Literature at University College, Dublin, and briefly University Lecturer in English at Cambridge University and Fellow of King's College, Cambridge. His many books are mainly, but not entirely, about eighteenth-, nineteenth-, and twentieth-century English, Irish, and American literature. His experience of music is one of the themes of *Warrenpoint* (1990), a memoir of his growing up in a small town in Northern Ireland.

DAVID HENRY FELDMAN is Professor in the Eliot-Pearson Department of Child Study at Tufts University and Director of the Developmental Science Group. He is the author of two recent books, *Beyond Universals in Cognitive Development* (second edition, 1994) and (with Mihaly Csikszentmihalyi and Howard Gardner) *Changing the World: A Framework for the Study of Creativity* (1994). His book on child prodigies, *Nature's Gambit*, appeared in 1986.

HOWARD GARDNER is Professor of Education and Codirector of Project Zero in the Graduate School of Education at Harvard University, and Adjunct Professor of Neurology at the Boston University School of Medicine. He is the author of, among other works, *The Shattered Mind* (1975), *Artful Scribbles: The Significance of Children's Drawings* (1980), *Art, Mind, and Brain* (1982), *Frames of Mind* (1983), *The Mind's New Science* (1985), *To Open Minds* (1989), *The Unschooled Mind* (1991), and *Creating Minds* (1993).

STANLEY KAUFFMANN is Distinguished Visiting Professor of Theater and Film at Adelphi University of New York. He has been film critic for the *New Republic* almost continuously since 1958, has been theater critic for the *New York Times*, the *New Republic*, and *Saturday Review*, and was recipient of the George Jean Nathan Award for drama criticism in 1973. Among his many books are *A World on Film* (1966), *Figures of Light* (1971), *Living Images* (1975), *Persons of the Drama* (1976), *Theater Criticisms* (1983), *Field of View* (1986), and *Distinguishing Features* (1994).

JOSEPH KERMAN, Professor of Music at the University of California, Berkeley, is the author of *Opera as Drama* (1956, revised in 1989), *The Elizabethan Madrigal* (1962), *The Beethoven Quartets* (1967), *The Masses and Motets of William Byrd* (1981), *The New Grove Beethoven*, with Alan Tyson (1983), *Contemplating Music* (1985), and *Write All These Down* (1994), and editor of *Mozart, Piano Concerto in C, K. 503* (1970).

JAMES M. MORRIS is Director of the Division of Historical, Cultural, and Literary Studies at the Woodrow Wilson International Center for Scholars in Washington, D.C.

MAYNARD SOLOMON is the author of *Beethoven* (1977), *Beethoven Essays* (1988), and *Beethoven's Tagebuch* (1990). In addition to his work on Beethoven, he has written on Mozart, Schubert, and Ives. In 1992, he was Visiting Professor of Music at Harvard University.

MICHAEL P. STEINBERG is Associate Professor of Modern European History at Cornell University. He is the author of *The Meaning of the Salzburg Festival: Austria as Theater and Ideology, 1890–1938* (1990) and the translator of Hermann Broch's *Hugo von Hofmannsthal and His Time* (1984). He also serves as Associate Editor of *The Musical Quarterly*. His essays on Mozart, Mendelssohn, Wagner, Richard Strauss, and Theodor Adorno have appeared in *Opera News, The World of Opera*, and *New German Critique*. Among his current projects are a book on German Jewish thinkers from the Mendelssohn family to Walter Benjamin, and a study of music, culture, and knowledge from J. S. Bach to the present.

CHRISTOPH WOLFF is the William Powell Mason Professor of Music at Harvard University and Dean of Harvard's Graduate School of Arts and Sciences. He has published widely on the history of music from the fifteenth to the twentieth century, particularly on Bach and Mozart. His most recent books are *Bach: Essays on His Life and Music* (1991) and *Mozart's Requiem* (1994). He is a contributing member of the *Neue Mozart-Ausgabe* and chairman of the *Zentralinstitut für Mozart-Forschung* in Salzburg.

NEAL ZASLAW, Professor of Music at Cornell University, is a contributing member of the *Neue Mozart-Ausgabe* and the author of *Mozart's Symphonies: Context, Performance Practice, Reception* (1989),

The Classical Era from the 1740s to the End of the Eighteenth Century (1989), *The Compleat Mozart: A Guide to the Musical Works of Wolfgang Amadeus Mozart* (1990), *The Mozart Repertory: A Guide for Musicians, Programmers and Researchers* (1991), *W. A. Mozart: Portfolio of a Genius* (1991), and *Mozart's Piano Concertos: Text, Context, Performance* (1994). In 1991, the Austrian government knighted him for contributions to Mozart scholarship. He was recently named editor of a new version of the Koechel Catalogue.

Index

Page numbers in italics refer to illustrations.